MICROFINANCE AND ITS DISCONTENTS

MICROFINANCE AND ITS DISCONTENTS

Women in Debt in Bangladesh

Lamia Karim

University of Minnesota Press

Minneapolis

London

Chapter 5 was previously published as "Democratizing Bangladesh: State, NGOs, and Militant Islam," *Cultural Dynamics* 16, nos. 2 and 3 (October 2004): 291–318. Portions of the book were previously published as "Demystifying Micro-credit: Grameen Bank, NGOs, and Neoliberalism in Bangladesh," *Cultural Dynamics* 21, no. 1 (Spring 2008): 5–29.

All photographs are by the author.

Published by the University of Minnesota Press
111 Third Avenue South, Suite 290
Minneapolis, MN 55401-2520
http://www.upress.umn.edu

Library of Congress Cataloging-in-Publication Data
Karim, Lamia.
 Microfinance and its discontents : women in debt in Bangladesh / Lamia Karim.
   p. cm.
 Includes bibliographical references and index.
 ISBN 978-0-8166-7094-9 (hc : alk. paper) — ISBN 978-0-8166-7095-6 (pb : alk. paper)
 1. Microfinance—Bangladesh. 2. Women—Bangladesh—Economic conditions. 3. Non-governmental organizations—Bangladesh. I. Title.
 HG178.33.B3K37 2011
 332—dc22
                          2010032184

Printed in the United States of America on acid-free paper
The University of Minnesota is an equal-opportunity educator and employer.

20 19 18 17 16 15 14   10 9 8 7 6 5 4 3

Contents

Preface

I am a child of Western development discourses. Growing up, I would often respond to the question "tell me about your country" by saying that "Bangladesh is one of the poorest countries of the world." Western discourses of poverty defined how I had learned to apprehend myself, the "third world" and its realities, and human possibilities. I grew up and came of age against the backdrop of the Green Revolution, the Bangladeshi freedom war of 1971, the famine of 1974, and the global transformations of the 1970s, 1980s and 1990s that introduced neoliberal policies and market deregulations worldwide. My unlearning, which is an ongoing process, began in the 1980s as I encountered political literature about alternatives to the dominant development paradigm. My interest in development was triggered by Michel Foucault's work on power and knowledge and by Arturo Escobar's *Encountering Development: The Making and Unmaking of the Third World* (1995). I am not a development anthropologist; I am an anthropologist of development.

Bangladesh has one of the largest NGO sectors in the world, a situation that has been praised by the World Bank as a catalyst for change. It is home to the Grameen Bank and Building Resources Across Communities (BRAC), two of the largest microfinance institutions in the world. Hence, it makes sense to study the effects of microfinance from the paradigmatic site of the microfinance industry, Bangladesh. Microcredit is the extension of small loans, usually between $100 and $300, to poor people to start income-generating enterprises. This book is a study of the discourses, practices, and policies of the 2006 Nobel Peace Prize winner Grameen Bank and three of the leading nongovernmental organizations (NGOs) in Bangladesh: Building Resources Across Communities (formerly known as Bangladesh Rural Advancement Committee [BRAC]), Proshika Human Development Center (Proshika), and Association for Social Advancement (ASA). In particular,

I am interested in the social consequences on women's lives as a result of their involvement in microfinance programs.

My research interest in microcredit (which is now called microfinance), NGOs, and gender relations began in 1995 as a graduate student at Rice University. In 1996, I spent two months in Bangladesh conducting an initial field survey of my dissertation topic. During this time, I worked as a researcher for a local human rights NGO. This experience gave me some access to the internal workings of a small NGO, its connections to global funding operations and agenda-setting priorities, and to the playing out of those concerns at the local level. I had the opportunity to meet Nobel laureate Professor Muhammad Yunus of the Grameen Bank in Dhaka. The following year, I returned to Bangladesh to conduct research for this book over a period of eighteen months. It was my immersion in ethnography for an extended period that gave me the opportunity to critically apprehend how dominant development discourses and practices restructured certain forms of knowledge and actions as legitimate and acceptable, while delegitimizing and obscuring others.

What brought me to the study of microfinance and gender was a puzzle about rural women's entrepreneurship and economic empowerment. Bangladesh is one of the most economically depressed countries in the world, and yet the Grameen Bank and the other three NGOs I studied all boasted a 98 percent rate of loan recovery. Either rural Bangladeshi women were all becoming successful mini-entrepreneurs through these microfinance NGOs, or there was a hidden story behind these high recovery rates. I was provoked by the following questions: What gave one of the poorest countries in the world some of the most creditworthy clients? What does it take to empower women? Is money enough? Rejecting the moralistic discourse that the poor pay back because of a natural correlation between honesty and poverty, I felt instead that there was a complex picture behind these high repayment numbers. I chose Bangladesh for my research because I wanted to discover the story behind the rhetoric of these NGOs.

The initial research was conducted between 1998 and 1999, with follow-up research in 2007. During these years, I kept pace with the trends within the Bangladeshi microfinance industry. More important, I am from Bangladesh, I speak the language fluently, and I have social networks that connect me to the local research and activist communities. In my visits to Bangladesh, I noticed that microfinance had become one of the most regularized aspects of development programs. In order to update my earlier findings, in 2007 I conducted a small study of female borrowers of the

Grameen Bank who are known as Grameen phone ladies. These women had purchased Telenor cellular phones with their microfinance loans and were operating as village phone ladies. While on the ground, microfinance policies were being expanded to new areas, I found that the basic formulation of loans equal economic empowerment remained unchanged.

Given that so much euphoria has resulted over microfinance, why is it that we know so little about its consequences from alternative perspectives? Although recent research by independent scholars in Bangladesh documents that microfinance policies undertaken by Grameen Bank and the leading microfinance NGOs do not benefit the poor, such research remains relatively unknown outside Bangladesh. In fact, a robust critical discourse regarding microfinance is available in the vernacular literature in Bangladesh that is not accessible to Western readers. Hence, studies such as mine have an important role to play in exposing the consequences of microfinance in the lives of poor women. The present book fills this lacuna in the existing critical literature on microfinance. *Microfinance and Its Discontents* is an invitation to open up the debate on this practice, to entertain alternatives to the dominant discourses of knowledge, to push the boundaries, and to analyze the ways in which ordinary people make meaning of these policies and practices in their daily struggles with globalization.

There are numerous people to thank and remember. Most of all, I thank the countless women and men who shared their stories and allowed me into their homes and private lives. Without their help, this book would not have been possible. In Bangladesh, there are too many people to thank individually. But their help, criticism, and encouragement are folded into the narratives of which this book is composed. In most instances, I changed the names of people who participated in this research to protect their privacy unless they indicated otherwise and I was assured that revealing their identities would not compromise them. The place where I conducted my research has been given the fictitious name of Pirpur Thana.

Special thanks are due my research assistants, who were my fellow researchers, friends, and challenging interlocutors. My gratitude goes to my hosts in Pirpur, NGO workers, and friends who helped me through the difficult days of research. To Lipi, the girl in Pirpur who wanted to know if there is a place in this world where children do not have to work. Many, many thanks to the late poet Ahmed Sofa, who through his poetry and conversations made me see human possibilities in unanticipated places. To my mother, who passed away before I could finish this book. To Chenora and

Kanon, who kept me nourished with home-style cooking when the days were long.

I would like to thank the following people in Bangladesh for their assistance and friendship: Farida Akhter, Helaluddin Arefeen, Zakir Hossain, Syed Hashemi, Obaid Jaigardar, Enayetullah Khan, Thun and Ahmed Kamal, Manzurul Mannan, Farhad Mazhar, Anu Muhammad, and Babul D' Nokrek, among others. In the United States, special thanks go to the doctors at Baylor College of Medicine. At Rice University, my thanks go to Professors James Faubion, George Marcus, Julie Taylor, Lynn Huffer, Betty Joseph, Diane Strassmann, Stephen Klineberg, and to my friends Jae Chung, Kris Peterson, Shannon Leonard, Brian Riedel, Carole Speranza, among others. My appreciation to the reviewers of this manuscript, who helped me to clarify my ideas. Many thanks are also due Joan Acker, Ina Asim, Carol Silverman, Helen Fazio, Carol Stabile, and Lynn Stephen. And, finally, to the children of the Shilpi Sultan Pathshala, who showed me through their poetry and paintings that it is possible to dream a different world.

The research and writing for this book was funded with grants from the Wenner-Gren Foundation for Anthropological Research, William J. Fulbright Commission, Harry Frank Guggenheim Foundation, and the Humanities Center at the University of Oregon.

Abbreviations

ADAB	Association of Development Agencies in Bangladesh
AL	Awami League
AMWAB	Association of Muslim Welfare Agencies in Bangladesh
ASA	Association for Social Advancement
BIDS	Bangladesh Institute of Development Studies
BNP	Bangladesh Nationalist Party
BRAC	Building Resources Across Communities
CARITAS	Roman Catholic Relief, Development, and Social Service Organization
CCDB	Christian Commission for Development in Bangladesh
CDF	Credit Development Forum
CGAP	Consultative Group to Assist the Poorest
CIDA	Canadian International Development Assistance
DANIDA	Danish International Development Agency
DFID	Department for International Development
FFW	Food for Work
GB	Grameen Bank
GK	Gonoshastha Kendro
GO-NGO	Government-NGO
GSS	Gono Shahajya Sangstha
IMF	International Monetary Fund
NFPE	Non-Formal Primary Education
NGO	Nongovernmental Organization
NGOAB	Nongovernmental Organization Affairs Bureau
ODA	Overseas Development Assistance
PKSF	Polli Krishak Shahayak Forum
PROSHIKA	Proshika Human Development Center
SAP	Structural Adjustment Policy

SBE   Social Business Enterprise
SIDA   Swedish International Development Agency
USAID   United States Agency for International Development
VGD   Vulnerable Group Development
WB   World Bank
WFP   World Food Program
WID   Women-in-Development

Introduction   **Neoliberalism, Microfinance,
and Women's Empowerment**

> *Microcredit has proved to be an important liberating force
> in societies where women in particular have to struggle
> against repressive social and economic conditions.*
>
> —Nobel Peace Committee, *Norway, October 13, 2006*

NEOLIBERALISM RESTS ON the idea that human interest is best served through the withdrawal of the state from welfarist policies.[1] It is an economic order based on competition, efficiency, and entrepreneurship. This book is an ethnographic study of neoliberalism, microfinance nongovernmental organizations (NGOs), and gender in Bangladesh. It examines the effects of the discourses, policies, and practices of microfinance NGOs on the lives of rural women in Bangladesh. Microfinance NGOs promote the idea that the borrower knows best, and that the state should withdraw from the sphere of economic activities, leaving it to the unseen hand of the market. Microcredit is the extension of small loans to poor women to start income-generating businesses out of their homes.[2] In the 1990s, the term microcredit was replaced by microfinance. Microfinance refers to a broad range of financial services to the poor such as credit, savings, insurance, and pensions. However, these two terms are fundamentally equivalent. Both are instruments of finance capital, and both promote the idea of entrepreneurship over investments in the public sector.[3]

In development circles, the excitement over microfinance is exhilarating because "it promises to achieve what previous models of development could not attain" and "mark an important turning point in human history."[4] In fact, it can be argued that microfinance as a tool of poverty alleviation has taken on a religious fervor among its advocates. This excitement is akin to a "new wave of evangelists for microcredit."[5] In the 1990s, the Consultative Group to Assist the Poorest (C-GAP) and donor agencies made microfinance "a major donor plank for poverty alleviation and gender strategies."[6] In 1997, when the first Microcredit Summit was launched in Washington, D.C., research was presented in support of the notion that microfinance institutions are not only profitable and self-sustaining, but they are also capable of reaching and empowering large numbers of very poor women.[7]

In 1997, the Microcredit Summit initiative reached only 7.6 million poor families; by the end of 2006, it had reached 100 million poor households.[8] The goal of the summit is to reach 175 million poor households by 2015.[9] This growing euphoria resulted in 2005 being declared the International Year of Microcredit by the United Nations.[10] In 2006, when the Nobel Peace Committee conferred the Nobel Peace Prize on the Grameen Bank and its founder, Professor Yunus, it legitimized the microfinance model as key to women's economic and social empowerment. These endorsements have resulted in an unprecedented escalation in funds promoting microfinance in development.

At the core of this revolution is the Grameen Bank of Bangladesh, which claims an astonishing 98 percent rate of loan recovery from its female borrowers. It is striking to note that this microfinance revolution occurs in a country that is ranked 140th among all countries on the Human Development Report, with almost 36 percent of its population at or below the UN subsistence level of $2 a day. The fact that the poor women of Bangladesh have shown such remarkable entrepreneurship in the face of monumental odds and repaid their loans at an astonishing rate of 98 percent is what has galvanized world leaders, CEOs of multinational corporations, philanthropists, feminists, NGO leaders, and international development organizations to unite in support of microfinance that will give poor women the resources to invest in their communities, families, and children's lives.

Yet, despite the microfinance revolution, there continues to be a knowledge gap between what we know about these institutions from their sponsored research and publicity events, and their actual practices on the ground. My research fills this lacuna and analyzes the emerging period of microfinance in Bangladesh under neoliberalism, and as such it creates a record that is invaluable for understanding the forces that colluded to turn Bangladesh into the paradigmatic site of microfinance policies.

The four microfinance organizations that I studied were: the 2006 Nobel Peace Prize winner, Grameen Bank;[11] Building Resources Across Communities (BRAC), which was formerly known as Bangladesh Rural Advancement

BRAC Center, Dhaka.

Committee; Proshika Human Development Center (Proshika); and the Association for Social Advancement (ASA).[12] They were ranked as some of the top microfinance institutions (MFIs) in the world.[13] These institutions defined their client base as poor, a category that refers to families that live on less than ".5 acre of cultivable land or assets with a value equivalent to less than 1.0 acre of medium quality land."[14] They shared the microcredit model popularized by Grameen Bank, based on group formation, joint liability for individual loans, savings schemes, and strict fiscal discipline with minor variations. Moreover, they had close ties with international aid organizations and multinational corporations, and operated within neoliberal notions of privatization and profit maximization.[15]

Theoretical Frame

Soon after I began my research, I encountered the following paradox. An elderly widow told me that on the day she was returning home from the Grameen Bank with her loan, her nephew demanded that she hand it over to him. She added that he said, "Aunt, I know that you received a loan from the Grameen Bank today. I have need of money for my business, and as my aunt, it is your duty to give it to me." She explained that as a widow and as an aunt, it was her familial obligation to help her nephew. If she disagreed, the family would pressure her to relent. In another instance, I had asked the female assistant manager at a Grameen Bank office the selection criteria used to identify potential members. She mentioned that before they admitted a new member, they made a detailed list of all saleable possessions: the number of pots, pans, beds, chairs, trees, chickens, etc., they owned. She continued, "Before we give any loan, we make sure that we can recover our money. Why are you surprised to hear this? Grameen Bank is not a charity; it is a commercial enterprise."

These two ethnographic moments illustrate a fundamental irony of microfinance practices. On the one hand, we have the female borrower who is constrained by her kinship obligations and who has to transfer her loan to a male relative if he demands it. On the other, we have the bank manager who understands microfinance as a commercial venture and who imagines an autonomous and rational female subject who freely makes choices in the market. My research explores this contradiction between the rhetoric of microfinance organizations—that is, how these institutions produce "truth" about their programs—and the lived realities of the women who were situated in dense webs of social and kin obligations and reciprocities that constrained their economic activities.

Three authors have influenced my analysis in this book: Michel Foucault on governmentality, David Harvey on neoliberalism, and Arturo Escobar on development as discourse. In the book, I illustrate how microfinance NGOs manipulate existing kin and social relations to regulate the financial behavior of individual borrowers to create wealth for the NGOs. I term this NGO governmentality. According to Foucault, the role of modern governments is the management of populations.[16] Governmentality is the creation of a set of rules, conducts, and procedures that aim to achieve selected goals through the supervision of targeted populations. This concept articulates with the work of NGOs that govern rural populations, particularly women, through a range of tactics, instrumentalities, and programs; but most notable among these practices is the regularization of microfinance as an instrument of power between a resource-rich institution (NGO) and its poor clientele.

The capacity to manage the most personal sphere of rural life—the conduct of women—occurs because "the Grameen Bank and the organized NGO sector accounted for 86 percent of microfinance lending" in the rural economy.[17] It is this staggering power over resources that empowers NGOs to impose their will on their subject populations, such as requiring women to attend meetings and rallies; to take loans with product tie-ins; to become chicken breeders; and to act as the enforcers of NGO policies within the community of borrowers.

This concept of governmentality is closely linked to the politics of neoliberalism. Harvey's theorization of neoliberalism was instructive in comprehending the unfolding of microfinance policies in Bangladesh.[18] As noted earlier, neoliberalism is the withdrawal of the state from the economic and social lives of its citizens. In the aftermath of independence in 1971, the Bangladeshi state maintained a weak presence in the rural economy. In the void created by the absence of the state, the Western-aided NGOs stepped in to provide credit, education, healthcare, road reconstruction, and other essential services to rural populations. The goal of neoliberalism is to align people to a deregulated market as efficient producers and consumers. Within this economic arena, neoliberalism subjects citizens to act in accordance with the "market principles of discipline, efficiency and competitiveness," and microfinance NGOs have adopted these norms to shape the conduct of their borrowers as entrepreneurial subjects.[19] But people live in parallel social worlds where other forces, such as kinship norms, encroach on their behavior. It is at the intersection of these different worlds that my analysis of microfinance occurs.

The insights of Escobar (1995) on development as discourse are equally important to my analysis. In the discursive field of development, knowledge operates as a form of governmentality. Knowledge as governmentality regulates the subjects of development to act in accordance with those principles that promote particular ends and visions. For example, in Bangladesh the poverty discourse is conveyed by a plethora of studies, statistical surveys, conferences, and brochures with pictures of happy rural women—all held together by the discursive power of research aligned with the development industry. Thus, the discourse about NGOs designates them "allies of the poorest of the poor" who, because they are well-intentioned institutions, selflessly work toward the betterment of the most disadvantaged in the country. Escobar's theoretical illuminations helped me to navigate through the putative truths of development discourses that I encountered in my research.[20]

Given the theoretical framing, the book makes three new and significant contributions in the study of microfinance and women. Basing my analysis on earlier works that conceptualized the group as collateral in microfinance transactions, I develop this notion in a new direction. First, I analyze how NGOs have operationalized rural codes of honor and shame to manufacture a culturally specific governmentality.[21] Rural life is guided by the proper conduct of women, and women are the bearers of family honor. When loan defaults occur, and they do so regularly for poor people, the NGOs use the group of women to shame the defaulting woman and her family to recover the outstanding loan. In the face-to-face community of rural Bangladesh, public shaming results in heightened strife and dishonor for the women. This fear of shame by NGOs haunts rural men and women, and they regulate their fiscal behavior accordingly. I term this dynamic the economy of shame.

Second, I analyze a trend to which studies have paid little attention: how the NGO operates as a shadow state, and how this signals the privatization of state functions in many areas. Specifically, I show how the NGOs and their Western sponsors have privatized the Bangladeshi state by developing the NGO sector as an alternative provider of services to the poor. In rural economy, NGOs are the key providers of necessary services. They offer rural employment through their development programs. Moreover, NGOs are the primary institutions of rural credit. These relationships of dependencies between NGOs and their rural clients help to inaugurate the NGO as a quasi-sovereign shadow state. However, the language of neoliberal efficiency that is invoked by donors and NGOs alike obscures the withdrawal of the state from public life, a process that has enormous implications for the country.

Finally, I examine how development knowledge is produced within the cultural and hierarchical context of Bangladeshi society. There has been no study on microfinance that has examined the cultural production of NGO knowledge itself. In Bangladesh, NGOs, their Western sponsors, and a small coterie of NGO researchers circumscribe the discourse of development, and determine what can be made intelligible to the public. This small group of researchers determines the rules of NGO research, and they function as the gatekeepers of knowledge production. Hence, the construction of development knowledge itself has to be culturally examined. My book adds to the theorizations on NGOs and microfinance in these three specific areas and opens up new avenues for further research.

Globalization of Microfinance

Between the time of my research and the publication of this book, the expansion of the microfinance revolution has led to massive transformations in three areas. The first is the phenomenal rise in microfinance loans that has led to new institutional arrangements that link NGOs, development organizations, corporations, philanthropies, and individual investors as partners through microfinance institutions. Institutions such as the Teachers Insurance and Annuity Association–College Retirement Equities Fund (TIAA-CREF) now participate in microfinance through organizations such as Kiva. Thus, the new stakeholders of these NGOs are individual and institutional investors. This has entangled two contradictory impulses: the need to make profit and the need to help the poor. The effects of these contradictions on the everyday lives of the poor remain largely unexplored.

The second transformation is in the articulation of business arrangements between NGOs and multinational corporations that are known as social business enterprises (SBEs), a term coined by Nobel laureate Professor Muhammad Yunus.[22] Social businesses combine profits with social goals. These business arrangements are presented as a win-win situation for both corporations and poor consumers. It is assumed that through SBEs the poor will adopt bourgeois consumption norms, and consume goods and services similar to those consumed by richer clients. The adoption of such behaviors is considered beneficial for both the poor clients and the corporations.

The third, and final, transformation is the export of the Grameen model. Grameen Bank, BRAC, and ASA have become transnational microfinance institutions because they offer their financial services to the global poor. At a global level, these Bangladeshi NGOs have taken their microfinance expertise to other developing countries and to the poor in the West. Grameen recently opened a branch in Queens, New York, that targets Bangladeshi immigrants as loan recipients.[23] BRAC has opened branches in Afghanistan and East Africa. In Uganda, BRAC has partnered with the Mastercard Foundation to offer financial services to the poor.[24] ASA International Holdings, a subsidiary of ASA, has generated $150 million from investors to fund commercial microcredit lending outside of Bangladesh.[25]

While it is significant to have institutions from a developing country such as Bangladesh as leaders in addressing global poverty, the resulting practices do not necessarily represent the interests of the poor. That is to say, they are not grassroots organizations that the poor create and control for their welfare; rather, they are institutions that facilitate globalization at the grassroots level. All these territorial reconfigurations in the microfinance industry have resulted, among others things, in the redirection of funds that could have gone to national institutions for development projects.[26]

Perhaps the most significant change in microfinance policies is the acceptance of the idea that the interests of multinational corporations are compatible with the interests of the poor, and within the new economic order of neoliberalism, these partnerships are the way forward. In 1997, when the agricultural corporation Monsanto attempted to form a partnership with the Grameen Bank to sell environmentally friendly technologies to farmers, there was organized global resistance from grassroots activists, including the ecofeminist, Vandana Shiva, that prevented it.[27]

In contrast, by 2007, corporations had been facing few hindrances as they sought new markets in the global south through large NGOs. This was the case with the initiation of the Grameen Phone venture with the Norwegian telecommunications giant Telenor. Rural women were offered phone loans to operate as village phone ladies, a point I discuss in chapters 3 and 4. Similarly, the Grameen Bank and the French food giant Danone have started the production and distribution of yogurt by targeting poor children as its consumers. Grameen Healthcare and Veolia Corporation of France plan to sell arsenic-free bottled water to the poor in Bangladesh, which effectively creates a commodity from a public resource. BRAC has formed partnerships with multinational agribusinesses to distribute and promote hybrid and terminator seeds, breeder chickens, and maize cultivation methods in Bangladesh.[28]

It is important to note that NGOs in Bangladesh have also brought significant positive changes in the lives of their clients. NGOs have mainstreamed rural women as clients and workers. In addition to microfinance, BRAC has a successful primary school education that reaches millions of poor children in rural Bangladesh. BRAC has been at the forefront in privatizing healthcare. One of its most successful campaigns was the remarkable improvement in the child immunization rate, from 2 percent under the government to 82 percent under BRAC.[29] Similarly, BRAC has introduced rural *shasthya shebikas* (traveling health workers), who are also sales ladies for pharmaceutical companies.[30] It has also opened a private university called BRAC University that now trains a new generation of young people in Bangladesh, and a commercial bank, BRAC Bank.

Given their funding structure and organizational logic, I call these institutions corporate-like NGOs to distinguish them from smaller, grassroots NGOs that also work in development. In fact, these linkups with corporations are considered the economic road map for a disadvantaged state, and there is little critical discourse in the public fora about these issues. The provision of microfinance, healthcare, and other essential services has reconceptualized the NGO as "altruistic, autonomous, cooperative, efficient, empowering, participatory and transparent," all attributes that the postcolonial state does not possess.[31] After all, what could be more moral than NGOs that help the poor, particularly poor women, in a predominantly Muslim society to become disciplined, capitalist subjects working in the aid of a neoliberal global order?

Claims of Microcredit

The idea of the Grameen Bank was seeded in 1976, when Muhammad Yunus, a professor of economics at a local university, extended a personal loan of $27 to forty-two poor people in Bangladesh.[32] By 2006, that idea had transformed the twenty largest microfinance institutions (MFIs) in Bangladesh to reach "over 21 million clients, affecting 105 million family members in a country of 140 million."[33] While all the NGOs I studied followed the Grameen model of microfinance with some variations, I will restrict my analysis to the Grameen Bank here because it is the paradigmatic institution of microfinance.

The Grameen Bank has shown that neoliberal notions of self-help, individualism, and entrepreneurship for poor women are attainable, and has provided hard data to the global financial and development community that "poor women are bankable." That is, the poor have need for loans, and they pay back their loans. The work of the bank has brought together several important elements in a single financial instrument: microfinance, through which the eradication of poverty, the empowerment of women, and the spread of free enterprise would be achieved. The Grameen Bank has offered millions of poor women access to loans, lifted many of them out of poverty, and given others the resources with which to expand their small businesses. This is a powerful mantra in the world of development. The Grameen Bank has been termed bootstrap capitalism in one of the poorest countries of the world, where "shoeless women lift themselves up by the bootstraps."[34] For development organizations, the Grameen Bank functions as a powerful metonym of what works in development.[35] It is a compelling image to see women in a Muslim country handling money, participating in loan meetings, walking in public places, learning to write their names, and becoming small entrepreneurs. In the worldview of Western policy makers, if the "wretched of the earth"—Bangladeshi women—can make it in the abysmal conditions of that country, by extension anyone can.

The Grameen Bank achieved its global recognition through major accomplishments in four key areas. First, the Grameen Bank is celebrated because of its much-publicized 98 percent rate of recovery on its loans, a rate that rivaled that of Citibank Corporation. This has made microfinance into a financially viable option for developmental organizations that are increasingly withdrawing funds from non-self-sustaining economic enterprises in developing countries. However, the figure 98 percent does not make the important distinction between loans that are willingly repaid, and loans that are coercively recovered by these NGOs, a framing device crucial in understanding how these loan recovery techniques actually work on the ground.[36]

Second, Grameen has provided empirical data that the poor, particularly women, are good investment risks for the international financial community. That is to say, rural women are natural entrepreneurs who, if given capital, will act according to the norms of competition, hard work and thrift. In fact, conversations with Grameen Bank and NGO borrowers will reveal that while the women are the official borrowers of the loans, their husbands are the users. Professor Yunus himself has acknowledged this point when he stated, "Grameen Bank now lends to husbands, but only through their wives. The principal borrower still remains the wife."[37] Even within mainstream NGO research, this point has been acknowledged.[38] But these researchers have failed to analyze the distinction between the borrower (the loan recipient) and the user (the one who controls the use of the loan), and how being in the position of a loan recipient may have adverse consequences in the lives of women.

Third, the Grameen Bank claims that it does not require any collateral from the poor as a guarantee for loans, thereby eliminating financial bottlenecks for potential investors. In fact, research has shown that group formation acts as a collateral when loans become due, and group members act as enforcers for timely loan repayments.[39] I extend this analysis to show how loan recovery occurs through the instrumentalization of rural women's honor.

Finally, the celebrated claim of the Grameen Bank is that poor women are its shareholders.[40] During my research I found that between 1983 and 1999, the bank did not issue dividends to its shareholders.[41] None of the Grameen women I met had any notion of what it meant to be a shareholder, nor that as shareholders they could make claims on the bank for dividends. In 2007, the bank finally issued 20 percent dividends to its members, almost twenty-four years after its formalization as a bank.[42] While the bank claims that the women participate in shareholder meetings, to date there has been no media coverage of millions of rural women who cast their votes in shareholder meetings at Grameen centers across the country.[43] Moreover, Bangladeshi economist Anu Muhammad has noted that Grameen borrowers are not the owners of the new business ventures of Grameen Bank in telecommunications (Grameen Phone) and packaged food and water (Grameen Danone and Grameen Veolia).[44]

Grassroots Globalization, Neoliberalism, and Microfinance

The microfinance revolution became possible only when neoliberal structural transformations swept through nations in the 1980s and 1990s. Globalization has also been theorized by Appadurai as providing space for grassroots mobilization, and as a site for alternative paradigms to emerge.

> These social forms rely on strategies, visions, and horizons for globalization on behalf of the poor that can be characterized as "grassroots globalization" or . . . as "globalization from below." . . . [T]his kind of globalization . . . strives for a democratic and autonomous standing in respect to the various forms by which global power seeks to further its dominions.[45]

The grassroots globalization I studied in Bangladesh is contrary to Appadurai's model. It works through, not against, corporate capital, donors, the state, NGOs, and members of the civil society, and creates complex new maps of social interdependencies that are laden with the financial investments of multiple actors at the local, national, and global levels. Grassroots globalization weakens the sovereignty of the patriarchal home and family, and replaces it with the sovereignty of the market through NGOs, contracts, courts, and laws; and it also manufactures neoliberal subjects. The developmental NGO is the purveyor of this new economic sovereignty that is represented by capital interests (Western aid organizations and multinationals) and local institutional interests (NGOs).

In the 1970s, neoliberal economic policies, such as the dismantling of the welfare state and the removal of trade barriers, began in the United Kingdom under Margaret Thatcher, and in the 1980s in the United States under Reagan. This dynamic of globalization brought with it "an incipient de-nationalizing of specific types of power that used to be embedded in the national state and have now been relocated to global corporations, markets, NGO."[46] It was precisely at this juncture that Bangladesh entered the global economy as an independent state on December 16, 1971. By 1976, a country that was created on the principles of socialist ideals ceded ground to denationalization and privatization under a military dictatorship that remained in power until 1990.

The Grameen Bank is considered a pioneer in promoting ways for the neoliberal state to reduce costs of welfare.[47] The bank's founder, Professor Yunus, a strong advocate of neoliberal state policies, has reminded his audience many times that "[t]he world has forgotten the human tradition of self-employment . . . . When people lived in caves they went out to help themselves. There was no state to ask for help."[48] Harvey has argued that the "substantive achievement of neoliberalism" was in the redistribution of wealth from the poor to the rich, and credit was the instrument through which we saw "accumulation by dispossession."[49] His assessment of credit as an instrument of dispossession holds hauntingly true for Bangladesh.

> The neoliberal state should favor strong individual private property rights, the rule of law, and the institutions of freely functioning markets and free trade. . . . Private enterprise and entrepreneurial initiative are seen as the keys to innovation and wealth creation.[50]

Neoliberalism seeks to bring all human action into the domain of the market, and in order to function, this ideology "needs to store, transfer, analyse and create huge databases to guide decisions in the global marketplace."[51] Hence, the pursuit of information technologies has "compressed the rising density in market transactions in both time and space."[52] Along with the spread of information technology worldwide, Grameen borrowers have become the purveyors of information technologies as the owners of cell phones in rural areas. Known as Grameen phone ladies, they rent their Telenor cell phones to rural people so that they can make local and international calls. In this network of globalization, the Grameen woman represents an idea and an ideology, the untapped capabilities of poor women as viable entrepreneurial models for capitalist expansion.

Neoliberalism has introduced notions of efficiency into development discourse, and with it the increasing bureaucratization of development. Ferguson has argued that development has transformed from an organic process in the 1960s to "a project" in the 1970s. "[T]he second meaning, much more in vogue from the 1970s onward, defines itself in terms of 'quality of life' and 'standard of living,' and refers to the reduction or amelioration of poverty and material want. . . . 'Development' is no longer a movement in history, but an activity, a social program, a war on poverty on a global scale."[53] This shift in conceptualizing development from a process to a project has created the need to evaluate development as a quantifiable process, such as the decline in fertility rates, number of loans distributed, students enrolled in primary schools, or number of children immunized.

Development takes place not only at the mundane level of improvements in nutrition, health, and literacy, but also at the level of ideology through the enactment of treaties, policies, and programs that generate new social meanings and identities. These strategies of governance have profound implications for the way postcolonial subjects think of themselves as actors in this world, and of the possible kinds of selves they believe they can be and of the actions they believe they can perform.[54] In Bangladesh, NGO leaders are transnational actors who have created new routes of circulation with global activists, world leaders, corporations, and wealthy investors. Similarly, women who are hired by NGOs to run small enterprises speak of themselves as "entrepreneurs," although careful analysis will show that these women are often contract workers. Thus, "Neoliberalism as a technology of governing relies on calculative choices and techniques in the domains of citizenship and of governing."[55]

Discourses of governmentality entered development through the management of the "third world" woman's reproductive body, and in countries such as Bangladesh, women's and men's fertility became the first site of governance.[56] In the 1980s, the microcredit policies of NGOs became the second instrument of governmentality in development discourse. Microcredit promoted the ideal of a citizen both as an entrepreneur and a consumer; and poor women as good managers of resources came to the forefront of development discourse. In the 1990s, the third site of governmentality was through good governance, which ideally included the management of people's aspirations toward political goals identified by NGOs and their sponsors.

Over time, I would argue, the aim of microfinance programs is to constitute a subject who is increasingly globalized, and whose loyalty is not to a national ideology but to the market. In this scenario, the sovereignty of the nation-state is gradually replaced by the sovereignty of the individual and the market as the arena of individually directed rational action. Thus, it is the individual as the entrepreneur/consumer who becomes the sovereign actor in the new global arena. In its ideal sense, credit enables locally situated actors connect to new avenues of capital circulation that invent them as agents acting out "rational" decisions in remote corners of the world. Yet, as this ethnographic study shows, these processes are not linear; instead, they are fraught with market uncertainties, environmental disasters, constraints imposed by kinship bonds, changing rural dynamics, and social obligations.

Research on Microfinance

The research on microfinance NGOs in the 1990s was pivotal in establishing the transformative power of microfinance, but it is important to examine what constitutes this research. Yet, much of the research that supports microfinance as the tool of economic empowerment is based on studies conducted on a few select institutions, such as the Grameen Bank, Bolivia's BancoSol, Foundation for International Community Assistance (FINCA), and Bank Rakyat Indonesia (RBI). This research is quantitative, survey based, and policy oriented, and as Fernando notes below, these methods are not the best tools for analyzing social transformations and power relations.

> The methodological and conceptual issues in current studies on microcredit cast serious doubts on the claims about its impact on social transformation. . . . Most of the positive claims about microcredit are based on quantitative indicators, such as number of borrowers and lending institutions and loan repayment rates. Outcomes measured by these indicators do not reveal the institutional processes through which such outcomes are achieved. . . . While microcredit is touted as a global movement, current studies have failed to explore beyond its immediate project environments.[57]

Among the mainstream microfinance advocates belonging to multilateral and bilateral donor agencies and the NGO establishment, there is agreement that microfinance helps to reduce poverty and improves women's socioeconomic status.[58] The proponents claim that microfinance programs have made significant contributions in two areas: (1) poverty reduction at household, village, and national levels; and (2) improvements in social indicators such as health, schooling, fertility, income generation, increased women's status within households, women's mobility, and decreased violence against women. I discuss the literature on these two areas below.

Shahidur Khandker, a World Bank economist, conducted the seminal and most comprehensive study cited by the World Bank and the Microcredit Summit Campaign Office, the two leading institutions promoting microfinance, as evidence of the positive economic effects of microcredit.[59] Comparing data from 1991–1992 to 1998–1999, Khandker found that "5 percent of borrowers may lift themselves out of poverty every year by borrowing from a microfinance program."[60] He estimated that this 5 percent of borrowers corresponded to 1 percent of households in rural areas in each year. Basing his analysis on these figures, he concluded that microfinance could account for "some 40 percent overall reductions in moderate poverty in rural Bangladesh."[61] According to a Grameen Bank's internal survey, 58 percent of all its 7 million borrowers have crossed the poverty line.[62] That is, over 4 million have passed the poverty benchmark through microfinance activities. These studies have helped to establish the importance of microfinance in combating poverty.

Yet, the conclusions about poverty reduction through microfinance are not uniform. Morduch examined Khandker's data and found "small or nonexistent program effects." He also found that income from grants was included under Grameen's "profit" margin, which falsified the actual profit.[63] He also stressed that the role of subsidies had exaggerated the profit margins of the Grameen Bank during its formative years. For example, the Bangladesh Bank had purchased Grameen Bank's bonds at a rate lower than that offered by the national banks.[64] David Hulme and Paul Mosley (1996) in a study of twelve lending institutions in seven countries concluded that microcredit had a negligible effect on the poor.[65] In a review of microfinance studies from the 1990s to the early 2000s, Rahman concluded that although microcredit had the ability to help those above the poverty line, the poorest households are better served by other strategies.[66]

More recent studies have also questioned the reliability of the poverty reduction claims of microcredit advocates (see, for example, *What's Wrong with Microfinance* 2007 and *Livelihood and Microfinance* 2004). Bateman's study on deindustrialization in Bosnia has shown that the longer-term effects of microcredit policies have a negative impact on social capital and in generating sustainable development.[67] In 2005, Catholic Relief Services (CRS) went so far as to issue a paper called *Microfinance 2010*, which mandated the divestiture of all microcredit holdings within five years.[68] CRS leadership recognized that microfinance had turned them into moneylenders and had distanced them from their original mission of charity focused on girls' education, maternal health, and emergency relief.[69] Haque and Yamao studied three hundred microcredit borrowers of Grameen, BRAC, ASA, and Tenjamara Mohila Sabuj Sangstha (TMSS) and found that these microfinance institutions did not help the hardcore poor to escape poverty.[70] In 2007, Abul Barkat, an economist who has researched the Grameen Bank for fifteen years, found in his study that 80 percent of women borrowers were caught in a spiraling debt trap.[71]

On another front, studies have also concluded that involvement in microfinance programs results in salutary effects on women's income potential, mobility, improvements in fertility rates, per capita food consumption, housing, education, and sanitation. Mayoux noted that microfinance creates "virtuous spirals" of economic benefits to women and their families in wider social and political environments.[72] In an oft-cited study, Hashemi and Schuler claimed that microfinance "increases women's mobility, their ability to make purchases and major household decisions, their ownership of productive assets, their legal and political awareness and participation in public campaigns and protests.[73] Pitt and Khandker (1998) found that microfinance programs promote investment in schooling and raise awareness of reproductive health issues.[74]

However, Morduch's 1999 study contradicted Pitt and Khandker's findings on school enrollment, and instead found "that children of borrowers were not substantially more likely to be in school."[75] Caldwell et al. noted that multiple factors—such as availability of family planning, education of girls, and urban and off-farm activities—had all contributed to a decline in fertility rates, and no one cause (microfinance) could be isolated.[76] Several studies have found that intra-household dynamics could even disempower women within households because their husbands and male relatives controlled the loans.[77] Some feminist scholars have found that women's integration into informal economy through microcredit NGOs has increased the work burden on women, which has led to the exploitation of their own children, particularly daughters, and has done little to help these families out of poverty.[78]

Kabeer mediated these conflicting claims over microcredit by analyzing some of the oft-cited studies in microfinance.[79] She found that "the negative evaluations focused on the processes of loan use, while the positive focused on outcomes associated with, and attributed to, access to loans."[80] She concluded that these studies varied "considerably in the significance and meaning attached to cooperation and conflict between men and women within the household and consequently to autonomy, dependence and interdependence within the household."[81]

Given the above discussion, I locate my study within a small but critical scholarship that is emerging on microfinance policies and their social effects.[82] Both Aminur Rahman (1999) and Jude Fernando (2006) conducted ethnographic research in Bangladesh as doctoral students from Canada and the United States, respectively. Rahman's study was the first scholarly ethnographic study on the Grameen Bank. Moreover, as a Bangladeshi, Rahman was able to conduct his ethnography by weaving himself into rural social dynamics.

Rahman's ethnographic study *Women and Microcredit in Rural Bangladesh* (1999) revealed some stunning data that have been verified by my ethnographic research. Rahman found that "women become the primary target of the microcredit program because of their positional vulnerability." He analyzed the escalation of violence against women due to current practices of grassroots lending to the poor.[83] He also found that that village-level factions were often reproduced within microcredit groups that the Grameen Bank promoted as a form of solidarity and a trust-building network. In order to marshal resources and power, he found that "more than 90 percent of borrowers have relatives in the Grameen loan centers who build and maintain their own small factional groups within a larger solidarity group," which leads to discord and division.[84]

In his study of Grameen Bank and ASA, Fernando found that local traders and moneylenders were the beneficiaries of microcredit loans. In his area, which was close to the commercial center of Tangail, in Bangladesh, he discovered that families deposited their entire loans with local traders and moneylenders in exchange for a supply of daily rations.[85] Moreover, "women borrowers consistently pointed out that they would be better off with state subsidies on education, healthcare and agricultural subsidies."[86] Yet, as Fernando notes, field officers had no incentive to communicate these facts in their reports because the mandate from their head office was to maintain a high recovery rate.

In a ten-year longitudinal study conducted in fifteen villages, Muhammad (2007) found that only 5 percent of women could use loan money productively.[87] In his research, he found that 50 percent of borrowers could not improve their economic situation, and they could pay their loans only by borrowing from multiple sources. He noted that in 45 percent of cases, the situation of women had deteriorated.

In a survey study entitled *Socio-Economic and Indebtedness-Related Impact of Microcredit in Bangladesh*, Ahmad concluded that "some of the microcredit borrowers have benefited in terms of reasonable increases but in the majority of cases there has not been a significant increase in income."[88] The study also found that only 10 percent of women controlled the use of the loans; 72 percent of women said that after enrollment they were "occasionally given more importance in family decision-making"; 28 percent of the women faced physical violence from another member of the family, usually the husband, and 60 percent of these female respondents noted an increase in physical torture. Instead of a decline in dowry payments as claimed by the Grameen Bank and other microcredit NGOs, this study found that 82 percent of microcredit households have accepted dowries.[89]

Overview of the Book

My initial research was conducted in Bangladesh between 1998 and 1999, with additional visits to Bangladesh in 2004, 2005, and 2007. In each of these trips, I met with women and men in villages. In December 2007, I conducted a small study of female cell phone owners, known as Grameen phone ladies, which I discuss in chapters 3 and 4. The original research had two sites, one rural, the other urban. I hired research assistants in both locations to aid me with data collection. The name of the place in which I conducted the research was changed to Pirpur Thana (fictitious name), and the names of local people have also been changed to protect their privacy. I have indicated these changes in the endnotes. Although I live in the United States, I am from Bangladesh. I speak the language fluently, I understand the cultural codes, and I am familiar with verbal and nonverbal modes of communication. While I did have research assistants who facilitated my work, I could easily communicate with people and follow the local dialect. Unlike most foreign researchers, I did not have to rely on NGOs to access local people. I used my personal connections to go to the villages and to enter the discursive domains of NGOs—that is, the uneven spaces between their rhetoric and practice. Most importantly, academic research foundations in the United States funded my research. Thus, I was not constrained by the policy dictates of developmental organizations faced by consultants and local researchers.

In chapter 1, I analyze the political and economic foundations that led to the creation of the NGO as a shadow state. NGOs in Bangladesh grew in the crucible of a war-ravaged postcolonial state that lacked economic sovereignty, and the donors that implemented a dedicated NGO sector to reach rural communities. I also examine the transition of the NGO sector from the 1970s conscientization model to the market model in the 1990s, which led to a series of conflicts between the NGOs, state, left political parties, and the clergy. These conflicts have modified the roles of each of these critical actors in a postcolonial society, and have aided in the inauguration of the NGO as a quasi-sovereign actor in the rural economy.

Chapter 2 is an overview of the research terrain. It sets the frame of my research, the questions, my positionality, the cultural constructions of the researcher, and my relationship with my interlocutors in the field. In this chapter I analyze how my first visit to a Grameen Bank office exposed me to the "syndrome of the missing borrower," and how NGOs organize their power to recover any impending default. These initial ethnographic moments yielded a different route with which to develop my inquiry. In this chapter, I have replaced the concept of credit with debt. I analyze microfinance as mediations of debt relations between NGOs and borrowers, and that opened a new window toward analyzing rural social relations.

Chapter 3 begins with a discussion of the emergence of social business enterprises (SBEs) in two areas, Grameen Danone and Polli Phone. In the twenty-first century, NGO linkups with multinational corporations are considered beneficial to both consumers and the rich corporations. In this chapter, I develop the concept of NGO governmentality. I analyze how increased indebtedness has created heightened forms of strife and subordination in the lives of the female borrowers. In particular, I examine how kin obligations have become enmeshed with indebtedness, creating toxic effects that lead to strife and competition among women borrowers.

Chapter 4 explores the everyday practices of NGOs through eight case studies that are mired in the uncertainties that the onrush of globalization and neoliberalism has triggered in the rural economy. These case studies cover a wide range of women and men as "entrepreneurs" and as failed market subjects, from the phone ladies to the female moneylender to the BRAC chicken breeders. These narratives that show that individual women borrowers are usually positioned extremely vulnerably vis-à-vis the NGO, their kin, group members, and others who are often stakeholders in their debt.

Chapter 5 is a case study of a confrontation between the NGO Proshika and the clergy of a prominent madrassah in Bangladesh. The conflict in question was over the constitutional right of rural women to participate in a public rally, an act that was banned by the clergy. While the NGO Proshika interpreted the actions of the clergy as antidevelopment and antinationalist, the analysis in this chapter shows that the NGO was equally complicit against the women. Instead, what I discovered was a complex weave of status and power games between two institutions, the clergy and the NGO Proshika, both struggling for sovereignty over their rural subscribers, the poor women.

Chapter 6 analyzes how the rhetoric of NGOs is held together by the power of discourse. This poverty discourse is produced by NGOs and those affiliated with the NGO industry, from World Bank officials to NGO practitioners to scholar consultants. I examine how different categories of people have become inducted into the NGO establishment, which makes it difficult for alternatives to the NGOs' way of doing things to be heard, or to be validated as a legitimate discourse and practice in NGO-dominated spaces. But I also show that there is a space in the vernacular where there exists a critical and lively debate about the actions of Western-aided NGOs.

In the Conclusion, I offer a summary of my findings and recommendations for oversight and regulation of current NGO activities. Instead of supporting the development NGO, I suggest that we invigorate citizens' groups as sites of collective action so that Bangladeshis can become the makers of their own destiny.

Since social relations are variable across space and time, the point of this ethnography is not to generalize its findings statistically. The importance in research is to navigate the differences in truth claims. Writing about the conflicting conclusions on the benefits of microfinance in women's lives, Kabeer noted that the problem lies in the use by some of "statistical data and significance tests for their findings, while others relied on more qualitative, sometimes anecdotal, evidence."[90] I would argue that insightful answers lie in the interstices of these different approaches that take into account the power relations and the cultural environment within which these separate knowledges are produced.

Beyond its hagiographic transcripts, microfinance is fundamentally a relationship of inequality between the creditor and the debtor. While credit is theorized as "trust" by microfinance proponents, analyzing it as debt shows us how debt functions at the confluence of two powerful forces: the financial responsibility to return debts and the social consequences of breaking the "trust" between the borrower and her community. Once debt relations begin to link people together inside modern institutions that require different constructions of self, the system implodes from within, creating in its place market subjects who become disconnected from the original rules of reciprocity, and who ground themselves instead in an emergent market ethos. Thus, there is a fundamental paradox here. Perhaps what allows for the effectiveness of microfinance programs locally—the instrumentalization of kinship codes of honor and shame—contains within it the "seeds of its own destruction" and self-transformation, to echo the words of Leo Strauss on liberalism.

This book is about a range of micropractices that are constituted, legitimized, and enacted by men and women who are caught in the multiple webs of economic globalization. These micropractices create new pathways and opportunities for those who are market savvy and can take advantage of the processes of globalization. Simultaneously, they foreclose options for those who are less able to take advantage of the market and its uncertainties. As Herzfeld has noted, "Freedom of choice—the right to self-determination—is now largely accepted as the antithesis of repression. It is in questioning the degree to which the rhetoric of choice corresponds to local perceptions and desires that we can begin to get some purchase on the implications of various development schemes."[91] To analyze these implications—the explicit and the not-so-explicit narratives—I examined how ordinary women and men who are caught in the multiple webs of NGO-lending schemes make meaning of their everyday struggles with globalization.

I invite the reader to move beyond the hagiographic transcripts that inform current practices of microfinance policies. Instead, I ask the reader to carefully examine the consequences on poor women, the implications for the postcolonial state when essential services are outsourced to the NGO sector, and the state of knowledge formation when NGOs dominate the production of development knowledge through hegemonic practices. Tsing has described global connections as friction, suggesting that "roads create pathways that make motion easier and more efficient, but in doing so they limit where we can go. . . . Friction inflects historical trajectories, enabling, excluding and particularizing."[92] Let us then begin with the question of what is being enabled, excluded and particularized through microfinance policies in Bangladesh.

Chapter 1 **The Structural Transformation of the NGO Sphere**

THIS CHAPTER RECOUNTS how Bangladesh, labeled as a failed state, became the paradigmatic site for one of the most sophisticated NGO sectors in the world, and the heartland of the microfinance revolution. Here I analyze the processes that were set in place in the 1970s, 1980s, and the 1990s that aided in the creation of an independent and Western-funded NGO sector in Bangladesh. In each of these decades, programs and policies were implemented that introduced rules, procedures, tensions, and alliances among the state, international development agencies, the clergy, and the NGOs. I examine how these alliances and accommodations led to the creation of the NGO as a shadow state in the rural economy. By a shadow state, I refer to the quasi-sovereign status of the NGO as a provider of essential services and employment in the rural economy.

In the contemporary era, a new actor called the NGO has emerged as an important stakeholder in development at the local, national, and international levels. While the term NGO was officially used in 1949 by the United Nations, it is in the 1990s that it has become a popular term.[1] For its advocates, NGOs are said to combine the best of "businesses, governments and charities" and to act in accordance with humanitarian interests.[2] This has led to their characterization as "magic bullets" and as "something of a panacea for the problems of development."[3] Their size and abilities have turned some NGOs into significant players "in social welfare and employment markets at the national level" with important consequences in the lives of local populations.[4] For its detractors on the left, such reliance on NGOs is considered a flawed model of development.[5]

Silliman has noted that the institution of the NGO is not "monolithic." It covers a wide gamut of organizations, from small groups espousing a social cause or left-wing political persuasions "to elaborate organization entities with broad membership bases, large budgets, professional staff, and

1

considerable political clout."[6] On one level, an NGO is a not-for-profit institution that operates as a means for organizing resources and people. Such organizations claim to be independent from the government. They are often conceptualized as humanitarian organizations. On another level, NGOs, through their work in service provision, operate as instruments for pacifism. In exchange for credit and other services, NGOs regulate their clients' habits and behaviors through complicity in their programs rather than through coercion. Yet, on another level, NGOs represent morality in development because of their work with the disenfranchised of society— poor people, women, marginal farmers, and indigenous people. And finally, NGOs help to privatize the state by taking over many of the services and functions reserved for the state and public-sector institutions.[7]

The above statements are strikingly true of Bangladesh. In Bangladesh, the state and NGOs have developed in parallel and parasitic structures of dependence on Western-aid organizations. By supporting the NGOs in their work in rural reconstruction, the government was assured of some level of rural development and of closer ties with donor countries that contributed the aid. Within a short time, though, this pragmatic partnership between the aid-delivery needs of the donor community and the NGO as its grassroots representative evolved into a complex relationship. Increasingly, donors resorted to the NGO sector as the preferred channel to funnel development dollars to the country. NGOs in rural Bangladesh are the primary providers of services such as microfinance, primary education, reproductive healthcare, cell and solar technology, rural road reconstruction, potable water, pisciculture, forestry, ecological protection, and democracy training, to name a few. These services led to the creation of the NGO not only as the dedicated source of resource distribution but also as the pathway through which Eurocentric developmental agendas entered rural communities.

Bangladesh is one of the most transnational sites for the study of NGOs and microfinance. In the early 1990s, when markets became deregulated globally, the World Bank heralded Bangladeshi NGOs as some of the most effective agents of change in the twenty-first century.[8] There are over 23,000 registered NGOs in the country, and nearly 20 million rural women are associated with NGOs as clients.[9] Ninety-five percent of NGO borrowers are women.[10] For example, in 1990, there were fifty-nine NGOs that worked with microfinance; by 2006, that number had risen to 2,000.[11] This effective network of NGOs has led to a profusion of dollars coming into microfinance institutions to empower rural women.

Grameen Bank Head Office, Dhaka.

In order to manage the inflow of foreign funds to this sector, the government established the NGO Affairs Bureau (NGOAB) in 1990. The following chart illustrates the phenomenal growth in this sector in Bangladesh. At its inception in 1990, the NGOAB approved eight projects for a total of

TABLE 1. Flow of foreign grant fund through NGO Affairs Bureau. At a glance, since inception and up to August 2009. NGO Affairs Bureau, Chief Advisor's Office, Computer Section

Period (July–June)	Approved Projects (Number)	Released in USD Each year	Local NGOs	Foreign NGOs	Total NGOs	Cumulative Amount Approved in USD	Cumulative Amount Released in USD	Cumulative Approved Projects
Brought Forward	8	5,429,242.13	267	80	347	372,306.98	5,429,242.13	8
1990–1991	464	106,602,013.05	368	93	461	158,914,312.71	112,031,255.18	472
1991–1992	549	121,638,071.12	485	105	590	446,023,797.83	233,669,326.30	1,021
1992–1993	626	195,705,767.02	571	121	692	845,908,000.74	429,375,093.32	1,647
1993–1994	581	171,009,063.26	679	128	807	1,160,932,020.41	600,384,156.58	2,228
1994–1995	579	209,504,743.72	788	134	922	1,601,619,427.39	809,888,900.30	2,807
1995–1996	702	259,301,939.71	880	137	1,017	1,968,429,369.88	1,069,190,840.01	3,509
1996–1997	746	250,142,747.04	995	143	1,138	2,138,307,604.04	1,277,716,836.43	4,255
1997–1998	705	206,866,718.65	1,093	151	1,244	2,155,160,722.85	1,382,083,839.81	4,960
1998–1999	1,045	273,500,513.35	1,215	154	1,369	2,411,849,205.75	1,576,402,466.51	6,005
1999–2000	776	182,350,040.46	1,347	167	1,514	2,401,228,958.28	1,583,596,677.36	6,781
2000–2001	868	250,896,727.78	1,448	173	1,621	2,760,753,809.07	1,834,493,405.14	7,649
2001–2002	746	208,282,010.05	1,506	173	1,679	2,914,090,119.79	1,946,223,130.71	8,395
2002–2003	794	279,644,085.69	1,621	179	1,800	3,189,404,327.11	2,225,867,216.40	9,189
2003–2004	939	313,073,381.60	1,705	184	1,889	3,684,487,133.98	2,538,940,598.00	10,128
2004–2005	1,193	274,017,716.57	1,802	186	1,988	4,003,860,307.81	2,812,958,314.56	11,321
2005–2006	930	347,527,379.61	1,870	190	2,060	4,460,653,208.20	3,160,485,694.17	12,251
2006–2007	908	322,612,586.11	2,000	198	2,198	4,139,533,569.57	2,896,150,937.08	13,159
2007–2008	1,462	523,114,188.81	2,115	206	2,321	4,581,685,688.05	3,419,265,125.88	14,621
2008–2009	1,042	486,188,205.78	2,192	221	2,413	4,995,708,970.62	3,905,453,331.66	15,663

$372,306, and the number of registered NGOs stood at 347. At the time of my research in 1998–1999, the foreign grants approved through the NGO Affairs Bureau (NGOAB) stood at $2,411,849,205 for 1,045 projects. In the fiscal year 2008–2009, the NGOAB had approved $4,995,708,970 for 1,042 projects.[12]

This growth has helped to entrench the leading NGOs as key players with the state. For example, a study conducted in 1992 revealed that only thirty of the nation's largest NGOs get 80 percent of the total foreign funds given to NGOs. Of that figure, 60 percent of funds was controlled by the eight largest NGOs: BRAC, Proshika, CARITAS, CCDB, ASA, Gono Shahajya Sangstha,[13] Nijera Kori, and Gonoshastha Kendro.[14] By 2006 that number shrank to only three microfinance institutions—Grameen Bank, BRAC, and ASA—that were very large, covering 90 percent of the country.[15] This pyramid structure of funding has left the bulk of the smaller NGOs dependent on the largesse and growth of the ten or so larger NGOs.

Strong donor support for the NGOs has enabled these organizations "to supplant the state as the primary source of services and credit for tens of millions of Bangladeshis."[16] In the early 1990s, two-thirds of the total rural credit was provisioned through the NGO sector;[17] by 2001, almost 86 percent was provided through the Grameen Bank and the organized NGO sector.[18] For example, food rations are distributed to very poor rural women through a program known as Vulnerable Group Development (VGD), which is a working relationship between the Union Council Chairman (the institution that comprises the lowest rung of elected state officials) and BRAC. NGOs form the everyday face of the state in rural society. In taking note of these changes, Muhammad commented that the investment in NGOs as an alternative to the state came out of the "privatization strategy of the World Bank and most donors."[19] He cautions us not to misrecognize the developmental NGO as a non-state actor that works solely in providing assistance to the poor. In developing this point he adds, "The history of NGOs in Bangladesh reflects the constant struggle and adjustment between Bangladeshi government and NGOs. Both represent the state. And both operate under the hegemony of international capital."[20] Given this background, let us examine the political history of Bangladesh that led to the creation of this vast NGO apparatus.

Political History of Bangladesh

In 1947, when the British left India, East Bengal became part of Pakistan and was renamed East Pakistan. As East Pakistan (1947–1971),

Bangladesh had the status of an internal colony of Pakistan. The seat of the government was in West Pakistan. The military and high civilian officials were drawn from the province of Punjab in West Pakistan. Raw goods from East Pakistan—jute and tea—were exported to West Pakistan to develop West Pakistani industrial growth. Under Pakistani rule, Bangladesh was economically exploited, politically suppressed, and culturally dominated.

From the very onset of Pakistan's creation in 1947, Bengalis (later known as Bangladeshis) resisted Pakistani cultural and political colonization. The founder of Pakistan, Muhammad Ali Jinnah, had initially declared Urdu the national language of Pakistan in March 1948, a decision that was met with widespread protests in East Pakistan. Ninety-five percent of East Pakistanis spoke Bengali, and they formed 60 percent of the population of Pakistan. Jinnah's call was withdrawn with his death in 1948. In 1952, President Liaqat Ali Khan attempted to reinstate Urdu as Pakistan's state language. Khan's declaration instigated massive civilian protests in East Pakistan that became known as the Language Movement. It was this nationalism that instigated the independence of Bangladesh from Pakistan in 1971.[21]

In 1956, President Liaqat Ali Khan was assassinated. This was followed by a brief period of political turmoil until the Pakistani military ascended to power in 1958. The country remained under military dictatorship until 1971. In the mid-1960s, popular unrest began to rise in both East and West Pakistan for a return to democracy. Facing increased popular opposition, the military dictator Ayub Khan finally held parliamentary elections in 1970. The Awami League Party of East Pakistan won 60 percent of the popular vote in a landslide victory. The Pakistani military was reluctant to hand over the reins of government to Bengalis, an ethnic group they had dominated since 1947. On the midnight of March 25, 1971, the Pakistani army launched an attack on its own citizens in East Pakistan. Official figures state that during the nine-month war an estimated 300,000 were killed, and over 10 million refugees fled to neighboring India. India, with its own political interests in bifurcating Pakistan, actively supported and participated in the war. On December 16, 1971, the Pakistani forces surrendered to the Indian army, and Bangladesh gained its independence, only to find itself under the shadow of Indian hegemony.[22]

Civilian Rule (1972–1975)

The first democratically elected prime minister of Bangladesh was Sheikh Mujibur Rahman of the Awami League (AL). In the aftermath of the war in 1971, the AL government of Prime Minister Sheikh Mujib (as he was known) faced the formidable task of resettling at least 10 million refugees with the infrastructure of the country in shambles and a bankrupt treasury. The AL government introduced a four-point platform of nationalism, secularism, socialism, and democracy. In keeping with their socialist model, banks and industries were nationalized, and private sector investment was restricted. The policies had disastrous effects on the economy. Most political writers on Bangladesh are in agreement that while "Sheikh Mujib was able to rouse mass sentiment for a nationalist revolution, he proved unequal to the more challenging task of running the problem-ridden new state."[23] His tenure (1972–1975) was characterized by lawlessness, endemic corruption, and nepotism.

Bangladesh for the first four years of its existence was a secular state. Sheikh Mujib focused on the consolidation of his power rather than on repairing the war-ravaged economy. He clamped down on communists who challenged his authority.[24] Perhaps the greatest threat to him came from his own actions. He changed the parliamentary form of government to the presidential form through a constitutional amendment that introduced a one-party political system that was called Bangladesh Krishak Sramik Awami League, and appointed himself president for another five years. This usurpation of government and power generated fear in the public that he would soon announce himself dictator for life.

The military that had participated in the liberation war expected to have a prominent role in governing the country. Instead, during "Mujib's regime, the importance of the military was reduced by limiting its interaction with the political system; officers were circumvented in the defense decision-making process by the development of a para-military force (Rakhi Bahini); and the budget was sharply reduced."[25] In 1974, a famine broke out in the northern districts that was poorly handled by Sheikh Mujib's government, leading to the deaths of thousands of people.

In this atmosphere of impending totalitarianism, economic stagnation, famine, and one-party dictatorship, Sheikh Mujib and members of his family were gunned down in a midnight coup on August 15, 1975, that was received with public apathy. For the next fifteen years, Bangladesh was under military rule. The growth of the NGO sector and the military regime was parallel and dependent. They both ushered the country into globalization, neoliberalism, and privatization.

Military State: Privatization and Islamization (1975–1990)

Between 1975 and 1990, the military state tilted Bangladesh toward privatization, which was promoted by the World Bank and Western donors on the one hand, and toward policies of Islamization that were adopted by the military dictators to form closer alliance with the Middle East on the other hand. The first military dictator of Bangladesh was General Ziaur Rahman (1975–1982). He was the person who first declared the independence of Bangladesh on March 26, 1971, a proclamation that granted him national status. Zia, as he was called, was charismatic and was considered a leader who had played a decisive role in nation building. He ascended to power in November 1976 as the chief martial law administrator.[26]

Zia was able to turn around the economic debacle of the Sheik Mujib era and redirect Bangladesh toward economic stability and some growth.[27] In a country that is 80 percent agrarian, he understood that his base had to be the rural population. He substantially solidified rural support through elections of the Union Councils in 1977. Officials elected to these bodies are responsible for the allocation of resources within their administrative units, and Zia's approach brought rural elites into resource sharing at the local level. He introduced a nineteen-point socioeconomic program on "self-reliance, people's participation in administration, a strengthened rural economy, incentives for the private sector, decentralization, and the safeguarding of the rights of all citizens."[28]

While Zia is known for his rural development programs, his regime also introduced privatization through the denationalization of industry and increasing investment in the private sector. During Zia's rule, industrial investment peaked in 1977–1978, and then it stabilized.[29] The U.S. government was instrumental in facilitating the process of privatization in agriculture. Zia's government received USAID grants of $293 million for the Fertilizer Development and Improvement Program, to be implemented in two phases to "privatize the procurement, distribution and marketing of fertilizers in order to increase food production."[30]

During this time, the 1982 New Industrialization Policy, later revised in 1986, replaced the national planning model of the Awami League toward the creation of the private sector and export processing enclaves.[31] Under this policy, support for large-scale investments in the agricultural sector and village cooperatives declined sharply. Instead, governmental rural credit was available through the Bangladesh Small Cottage Industries Corporation and the Bangladesh Rural Development Bank. Both of these state organizations promoted "individualized credit, self-reliance, and poverty alleviation."[32]

Notably, Zia's coming to power coincided with the 1975 UN Decade for Women, which had made gender a central category in aid policy. In order to gain international acceptability and donor funds, Zia made women an important aspect of his development program. Zia capitalized on the "discovery of women in development" by Western donor agencies that had tied aid to the UN mandate that improvement in the status of women was an indispensable part of aid programs. Zia appropriated women-in-development (WID) issues to raise Western support for his government. He established the Ministry of Women's Affairs and formed the National Organization for Women.[33] He recruited women into the police force, which was a first for Bangladesh. He also reserved fifteen seats in parliament for women. This number was later raised to thirty by General Ershad, the second military dictator. Despite these measures, the ability of women to be elected to parliament still lags behind. In 2001, only seven women were directly elected to parliament.

The military leadership appropriated Islamic precepts as part of its state policies to legitimize its rule and to appease different constituent groups, such as the domestic Islamic parties and Arab countries.[34] The Ja'maat-e-Islami, which was outlawed by the Awami League government for its collaboration with the Pakistani army in 1971, was reinstated after the military took control, and their exiled leader, Golam Azam, returned to Bangladesh from Pakistan. Zia removed secularism from the constitution and replaced it with the phrase "bismillah ir rahman ir rahim" (in the name of Allah, the all Merciful and Beneficent) in 1977.[35]

Thereafter, all state functions and radio and TV programs began with this Quranic invocation. Women on the state-owned TV station had to cover their hair. Zia also wrote into the constitution that Bangladesh was part of the Islamic Ummah, the brotherhood of Muslim nations. On a symbolic level, Zia introduced the hanging of framed sayings from the Quran and the Prophet Muhammad in government buildings. State symbols and authority were manipulated to privilege Islam as the religion of the country. The state flag flew on Muslim holidays, and special prayers and messages from Zia as the head of the state were broadcast to the people. Quotations from the Quran, Hadith (the sayings of the Prophet), and Sunnah (the life of the Prophet) were daily features, and the Muslim call to prayer was broadcast five times a day on state-owned radio and TV stations. Zia adopted Islamization not because of his piety but because of politically motivated ends.[36]

On the administrative level, Zia opened a new Ministry of Religion, whose role was to promote and protect the religious life of Bangladeshi citizens. The Islamic Academy, which was formerly a small institution, was transformed into the Islamic Foundation, the largest umbrella organization of research on Islam in the country. He also opened an Islamic University that had a research center for students from Bangladesh and overseas Muslim countries.[37] Zia also allowed Islamic political parties that were banned after the independence of Bangladesh to again participate in electoral politics, thereby establishing a religious foundation for his constituency. These changes enabled him to appease local Islamic groups in the country, and helped him gain legitimacy as a Muslim leader among Islamic countries.

Zia also changed the national identity of the people from the ethnolinguistic category *Bengali* to the territorial signifier *Bangladeshi*. Although the category *Bangladeshi* was supposedly a more inclusive category that embraced all citizens, whether Bengali speaking or not, it effectively narrowed the definition of what it meant to be a Bangladeshi, and introduced an Islamic wedge into the national consciousness.[38] Through these policies, he introduced a new discourse of religion-inflected nationalism, one that broke with the earlier secularist nationalism upon which the country was inaugurated, and brought in a new identity of being a "modern" Muslim the Bangladeshi way. The definition of this new identity marker remained ambiguous.

Moreover, in order to consolidate his power base, he started his own political party, the Bangladesh Nationalist Party (BNP), which took as its founding principle Bangladeshi nationalism. The party ideology was the commingling of religion with ethnic identity. The creation of BNP also bifurcated electoral politics in Bangladesh along religious lines; BNP supporters are overwhelmingly Muslim with few Hindu and ethnic minority supporters, whereas Hindus and other religious and ethnic minorities overwhelmingly support the Awami League. (After his assassination, his widow Khaleda Zia became the leader of the party, perpetuating politics based on religious identity.) Politically, Zia distanced the country from India and the Soviet Union and tilted it toward the United States and the Middle Eastern countries. Zia was also able to garner petrodollars for his development plans from Middle Eastern countries that saw him as friendly toward Islam. Aid from Saudi Arabia increased enormously during Zia's regime.[39] In fact, Saudi Arabia, a key ally in this transition to Islamization, recognized Bangladesh as an independent state only after the military coup in 1975.

The result of these calculated moves was paradoxical. One side of the official face of Bangladesh took on an Islamic appearance, while the other side brought women into the public sphere as police officers, members of parliament, laborers in public works programs, and NGO beneficiaries. White identifies these strategies as more political than religious in orientation and writes: "These moves are congruent with one another: both are calculated to appeal to donors (the United States and Saudi Arabia, respectively) and both were used in Bangladesh in an attempt to create a constituency for the party in power."[40]

Second Military Dictator (1982–1991)

The second military dictator, General Hussain Muhammed Ershad (1982–1991) came to power after the assassination of Ziaur Rahman in 1981. General Ershad (popularly known as Ershad) was a repatriated military man from Pakistan who had played no role in the independence struggle of Bangladesh. Moreover, he lacked the charisma and the national following of either Sheikh Mujib or Zia. On assuming power, his sole base was the military. Similarly to Zia, Ershad adopted a two-pronged policy. He promoted Islamic ideology to attract Islamic political parties on the one hand, and he sponsored the growth of the NGO sector to garner Western-donor support on the other. Unprecedented levels of corruption characterized his rule. By the late 1990s, Ershad had become increasingly alienated, with public demonstrations against his rule occurring daily. However, what led to his eventual downfall in December 1990 was the withdrawal of support of Western donors who had propped him up to begin with.[41]

Following in the footsteps of Zia, Ershad attempted to recast himself as a pious religious leader of a Muslim nation, a ploy aimed at bolstering his political base at home and his public image abroad.[42] He made a number of calculated moves to appease Islamic groups and clergy. He exempted mosques from paying utility bills; he regularly patronized mosques and madrassahs; and he attended Friday prayers. He established the Zaqat Board to administer the mandatory tax incumbent upon all financially able Muslims. He also set up the Department of Religious Affairs to facilitate pilgrimage to Mecca by Bangladeshis.[43]

In order to strengthen his political base, he fostered Islamic parties and madrassah education. Islamic political parties mushroomed during his regime. There was also a growth in Islamic political party newspapers (*The Dainik Inquilab, Jago Mijahid, Dainik Millat, Shaptahik Muslim Jahan*, etc.) that gave these parties their own propaganda machinery.[44] In an effort to Arabize the Bengali culture, Ershad introduced Arabic as a mandatory language requirement in schools, a move that was violently protested by university students, which forced him to withdraw its implementation.

Ershad's boldest act to Islamize Bangladeshi society was the adoption of Islam as the state religion by a constitutional amendment in 1988. While feminist groups, intellectuals, and the leading nationalist parties rallied against Ershad, and the feminist NGO Nari Pokkho brought a case against the government in the highest court (a case that has not been heard to date), in the end it was Ershad who won. By making Islam the state religion while granting the religious freedoms of all groups, he changed the political climate in Bangladesh, and polarized the nationalists/secularists and the Islamists in the country.

These policies of Islamization sharply impacted the secular education system in the country. The military state supported two parallel forms of education: the national public school system, which was quasi secular (although all students had to take religious education in any one of the four major religions in Bangladesh: Islam, Hinduism, Buddhism, and Christianity), and a government-sponsored madrassah system called the Alia Moderesin Madrassah. Funds allocated for secular education were thus diverted to madrassah education, thereby weakening an already under-funded national education system. Alongside the government madrassah system, the independent madrassah system, known as Quomi madrassah, also grew during General Ershad's regime. The Quomi madrassahs received their funds from the Middle East and followed an outdated syllabus patterned on the Deoband School of India.[45]

In more recent years, the government-sponsored madrassah system has introduced some science teaching into the curriculum, and its graduates are more competitively placed than Quomi madrassah graduates. In contrast, the Quomi madrassahs primarily teach students how to read the Quran, Hadith, and Sunnah, and teach an ultraorthodox interpretation of the sharia, the body of Islamic jurisprudence. But growth has also brought reform to the government madrassah curricula, with the introduction of science subjects along with an increase in the enrollment of female students and female teachers. In 2005, there were 3,450,083 students enrolled in government madrassahs, of which 47.8 percent were female.[46] This rise was partially due to the female stipend program provided by the government to retain young girls in secondary education, but it also reflects the recognition by rural families of the importance of female education in a globalized world.[47]

Similarly, under the military, Islamic NGOs grew through government patronage. The role of Islamic charitable organizations was to collect and distribute *zaqat*, and run schools and orphanages for the poor. During natural calamities, Islamic NGOs had played a role in distributing aid to the poor and needy. Under Ershad, Muslim charities began to receive funds from Middle Eastern countries. As the Islamic NGO sector expanded, they too formed the Association of Muslim Welfare Agencies in Bangladesh (AMWAB), similar to the secular NGO organization called Association of Development Agencies in Bangladesh (ADAB). In 2008, AMWAB had around 320 registered Islamic NGOs that worked with rural clients within an Islamic framework.[48] These policies undertaken by the two military dictators introduced competing notions about the roles of women, education, and NGOs in rural economy.

The Transformation of the NGO Sphere

This brief history of privatization and Western government patronage sets the stage for the transformation of the NGO sphere. Between 1947 and 1971, primarily Christian missionaries operated in rural East Pakistan. CARITAS began work in 1967. Other missionaries were CARE, World Vision, Red Cross, and OXFAM. The East Pakistani government facilitated the work of these NGOs in rural development because it eased the "government's responsibility in investing in social welfare activities."[49] Although their work was in rural development, these NGOs largely targeted the indigenous populations that had converted to Christianity. During the early phase of NGO development, the Christian missionaries maintained a low profile because they were working in a Muslim country.[50]

For this handful of NGOs, the opportunity to change from service providers to relief operators came in November 1970, when Bangladesh (East Pakistan) suffered a devastating cyclone that killed over 50,000 people. Given the lack of investment in East Pakistan, rural infrastructure was poorly developed and graft was common among government officials. The NGOs with their grassroots ties had a service-delivery network in place to provide relief to the victims far more efficiently than through the existing state channels. This was the first time that the fledgling NGO sector came into the view of international aid organizations. Soon after the independence of the country, when aid flowed into the country for war reconstruction and rehabilitation of the refugees, the NGOs were able to step in as rural service providers.

Access to foreign aid and rural development responsibilities led to the consolidation of this amateur sector. On December 10, 1973, the Association of Voluntary Agencies in Bangladesh (AVAB) was formed, with nine voluntary agencies as members.[51] In 1976, the name of the organization was changed to Agricultural Development Agencies in Bangladesh (ADAB) to reflect this new direction in policy.[52] Meetings were held at ADAB to determine whether it would be "a representative body dedicated to policy negotiations with the government."[53] But this approach was rejected because several of the NGOs involved already had "direct contacts with the government" that they wanted to maintain.[54] As the work of NGOs expanded in the nonagricultural sector, the name was changed to Association of Development Agencies in Bangladesh (ADAB).[55]

Although Christian NGOs spearheaded the NGO movement, the movement soon became indigenized. By the mid-1970s, indigenous NGOs such as Bangladesh Rural Advancement Committee (now known as Building Resources Across Communities [BRAC]), Proshika Human Development Center (Proshika), Gonoshastha Kendro (GK), Gono Shahajya Sangstha (GSS, now defunct), Nijera Kori, Association for Social Advancement (ASA), and the Grameen Bank—which is not registered as an NGO and does not belong to ADAB—began to grow. In the 1970s, the local NGO movement was characterized by a sense of patriotism and communitarian ideals. Their ethos came from a missionary sense of altruism for the poor— landless and marginal farmers, women, and children—combined with a sense of patriotism for the newly independent country. Many NGO workers were former freedom fighters who had fought to liberate the country from Pakistani domination. For some of them, working for an NGO meant working for the poor, which was seen as a noble sacrifice for their country. Many were also members of leftist political parties who had turned to the NGO sector for employment. For these men and women, working for an NGO was reconceptualized as a radical transformation of agrarian social relations from below.

The majority of the large NGOs had a people-oriented focus in their formative years. Professor Yunus, a U.S.-trained economist who taught at Chittagong University, began to work with the poor after the famine of 1974. Fazle Abed of BRAC was a former Shell Oil accountant who was inspired by the work of Paulo Freire. Dr. Zafarullah of Gonoshastha Kendro ran a Maoist healthcare NGO. ASA's founders had "worked with radical elements and used guerilla tactics to achieve their aims" but abandoned that position to work through an NGO.[56] Hasan of GSS had tried "to create a powerful network of committees and activists to eventually compete in national elections."[57] Leaders of Nijera Kori and Proshika were secular nationalists who had organized their rural clients to fight against the landed elites in the 1970s and 1980s.

The early NGO movement was distinguished by the deliverance of much-needed social services—such as literacy, reproductive healthcare, potable water, and child immunizations—to the poor.[58] In its early days, the NGO movement was inspired by the work of the Comilla Project (now known as Bangladesh Academy for Rural Development). It was a government project started by a former colonial Indian Civil Service officer, Akhter Hamid Khan, during Pakistani rule.[59] The Comilla Project started farmers' cooperatives to spread the use of the Green Revolution technology in the 1960s. The model was based on group formation, weekly meetings, awareness creation, and member savings plans. Although NGO leaders saw rural development as the organization of the poor and landless farmers, they were aware that "the main problem of the rural poor is the power of the rural economic elite, allied with the urban and political elite, to maintain the existing agrarian structure and even enhance it in their favor."[60]

Two schools of thought defined the NGO model of development in the 1970s. The first school (BRAC) advocated a mainstream theory of scarcity whose explanatory framework was that the poor were poor because they lacked access to resources. The role of the NGO was to become an effective service provider in the areas of education, health and sanitation, family planning, and credit to alleviate poverty. This was known as the integrated rural development model. The competing school of thought (Proshika, Nijera Kori, and GSS) claimed that the problem of poverty was structural. According to this perspective, poverty was not caused by a lack of resources, but by the existence of a hierarchical power structure that sustained and reproduced inequities in the system. In the late 1970s, Proshika, Nijera Kori, and GSS took the lead in the "conscientization of the poor"—organizing and teaching poor people to fight against the rural elites who controlled land and water rights.

This approach resulted in conflicts with local elites and caused disruptions in the work of NGOs.[61] Facing potential disruption in its rural work, BRAC adopted a market approach to service provision. Instead of fighting the rural elites, it concentrated on delivering nonformal primary education to children and social services to the poor.[62] Although BRAC followed Paulo Freire's model of "conscientization," its strategy was more pedagogical (learning about strategies of dealing with oppression through group lessons) than organizational (organizing of the poor to challenge the entrenched rural power structure).[63] These ideological cleavages within the nascent NGO movement split them into competing groups, and although they worked side by side in the villages, they had conflicting messages for the rural poor and diverging ways of solving rural poverty. The fact that BRAC has distanced itself from its original doctrine was humorously apparent to me when the manager at their Mymensingh Training Center (TARC) told me that in their meetings they sit in a horseshoe shape "to keep an eye on everyone"!

State, NGOs, and Left Politics

In the 1970s and early 1980s, there was a rise of leftist political groups and secret societies in Bangladesh. These underground political parties posed a threat to the military, and hence it cultivated the NGO as an instrument of rural pacifism. By supporting the growth of the NGO establishment, the military state effectively bifurcated the left by introducing a resource-rich organization to work with the poor. The left and the NGO sector both fought for the allegiance of the same clientele: the rural poor. High unemployment and party ineptitude in gaining political power had forced many former cadres of the communist parties to join NGOs. Remarking on the mood in those days, a former activist communicated the following to me:

> We had constant fights with the NGOs. NGOs saw the landless as an economic unit, we saw them as a relational unit. We would go to the villages and find out that the NGO workers had urged villagers not to come to our meetings. NGOs did anti-left propaganda. They would tell villagers, "Why go to them? What can they give you?" Thus instead of fighting the military state, we fought the NGOs, whom we saw as depoliticizing our work. After the 1990s, the communist parties have realized we do not live in a bipolar world.[64]

In an interview, Professor Badruddin Umar, who was the party leader of Bangladesh Krishak O Kheth Majoor Federation (Bangladesh Farmers and Agricultural Workers Federation), mentioned that NGOs have depoliticized politics in Bangladesh by creating an environment of opportunity that is restrictive.

> NGOs provide employment; they do not generate employment. It is not that kind of process. . . . It exploits the situation of unemployed youths in our country and creates conditions that do not allow for other forms of recruitment, political recruitment for example, to occur. To rural people, they [NGOs] preach a kind of economism instead of a political progressive consciousness. Their goal is the extension of credit instead of industrial development. In this way, political outlook is hijacked.[65]

Much of the NGO pro-poor lobby was rhetorical in nature and had gained few real benefits for the poor. Despite the work of the conscientization NGOs, Hashemi noted that the distribution of government lands has been negligible. According to him, NGOs, because of their patronage by the state and donors, were unwilling to extend their critique of rural society beyond that of the minor figure of the village elder. He pointed out that NGOs failed to advocate for raising the minimum wage, government distribution of land, or debt settlement boards to grant reprieve to peasants from high-interest rates.[66]

In my research area, where Proshika had worked for twenty years, local people laughed when I asked them about land distribution under Proshika. They told me that the public land redistribution movement was largely ceremonial, with very little real benefits accruing to the poor. As one local activist who had worked in the area said, after some time rural elites ignored Proshika because they could easily repossess the land/pond once the ceremonial performances were over.

> Let me tell you how these things happened. Proshika officers would organize its members and occupy some land under a government order. Proshika would organize a poor people's rally at a local school ground. Proshika leaders would give speeches, which would be followed by some patriotic songs. The ceremony would end with a meal of kitchri [rice and lentils] for Proshika members. The whole event was set up as a media event. It would be reported in the press as a triumph of Proshika and the poor over the rural elites. The donors, especially Scandinavian donors, would be pleased with Proshika for fighting for social justice. A few days later, however, the local elites with their hired goons would reoccupy the pond or land that was ostensibly under the control of the poor members. Things would revert back to the old way.[67]

The late 1980s had brought the microcredit model to the forefront of the NGO movement. The Grameen Bank's phenomenal success in collecting loans from poor customers demonstrated a market model that the donor community endorsed strongly as sustainable. Many NGOs, because they were donor dependent, had to abandon their earlier conscientization efforts and adapt to the microcredit model. Microcredit programs emphasized fiscal responsibility and loan collections over the social organization of farmers for land and water rights, and constructed poor women as natural entrepreneurs who were financially viable. This shift in NGO programs from political to financial work resulted in a reordering in NGO corporate culture. NGOs now sought rural women who were creditworthy as well as workers who kept track of financial statements and budgets and who could recruit and maintain fiscally responsible clients. Commenting on this new model, Hashemi noted an important transformation in NGO corporate culture.

Staff recruitment, which used to favor political activists, now inducts staff with higher university degrees and greater professional competency. . . . Management too has changed from being decentralized, where local political issues determined actions to be undertaken, to a situation of centralization where specific programs (such as education, legal aid, etc.) are pursued by the local staff with directives from the center rather than being based on collective decision made at the local level.[68]

The NGO worker now occupied a subject position far from the eager field-worker whose job was to rouse and organize the rural people against the entrenched power structure. Hashemi has termed this a "paradigm shift" in NGO culture, which now emphasized professionalism over idealistic values of social transformation.[69]

Military State and NGOs (1980s)

During the 1980s and 1990s, the structural adjustment programs of the World Bank and IMF emphasized the NGO sector, foreign direct investment in the energy sector, and the export of the country's gas reserves to help grow the other sectors of the economy. Huge reserves of natural gas and coal were discovered in the northern districts, which brought many multinational corporations to bid for exploration tenders to Bangladesh.[70]

The second dictator, General Ershad, ruled in an environment of privatization promoted by multilateral aid organizations and Western governments that strongly supported the NGO sector. By establishing a good working relationship with the NGO sector, Ershad attempted to legitimize his rule as a benevolent dictator. He developed the NGO sector as a countervailing force to the major political parties, BNP and Awami League, that opposed his rule. By doing so, he also satisfied the demands of the donors, in that he allowed the NGOs to carry on relief and rehabilitation efforts unhampered. This alliance between NGOs and the state created new structures of dependencies that became entrenched in the 1990s.

Ershad facilitated the routinization of NGOs by simplifying the registration process for NGOs. In Bangladesh, NGOs are registered as voluntary organizations under both the Social Welfare Agencies Ordinance (1961) and the colonial-era Societies Registration Act (1860), which prohibit political work by civic organizations. In 1989 the government proposed a single regulatory law for the NGOs, called the Social Welfare Agencies Registration and Control Act of 1989, to replace two former laws: the Foreign Donations (Voluntary Activities) Regulation Ordinance of 1978 and the Voluntary Social Welfare Agencies (Regulation Control) Ordinance of 1961.[71]

The flood of 1987 was a watershed year for catapulting the NGO lobby into national prominence. In 1987 Bangladesh faced a devastating flood that brought three-fourths of the country under water. When Ershad requested aid assistance from Western donors, they notified him that they would release aid through the NGO sector. Ershad's government was notorious for corruption, whereas the NGO sector was considered less corrupt and more efficient. The donors also pointed out that the state did not have an infrastructure in place to deliver aid to the affected people. The NGOs did. NGOs needed the services of the state to carry out their development mandates, and the military state needed donor patronage and relief operations.

The partnership created an opportunity for the pro-activist NGO groups (Proshika, Nijera Kori, and GSS) to advocate the government for the redistribution of government land (khas) to the poor. In exchange for their help, these NGOs also pressured Ershad to sign the United Nations Declaration on the Protection of the Child. Finally, Ershad worked with NGOs on a project called Street Blossoms (*Pother Koli* in Bengali), which aimed at improving the living conditions of street children. The emerging alliance between the NGOs and the state became visible in a 1987 reception for Ershad by ADAB that heralded him as a "friend of the poor." At the reception, Ershad said, "For a developing country like Bangladesh it is not possible for the government to do the work of development alone. Everyone has to be unified. NGOs can play an important role in this respect. . . . We are trying to redistribute lands to the landless. NGOs can make our programs effective by organizing the poor and landless."[72] Ershad already had a history of collaborating with some NGO leaders. He had worked closely with Zafarullah (GK) and ratified the controversial Essential Drugs Bill in 1982 that helped to indigenize the drug industry.[73]

Ershad's golden handshake with the NGOs led to resentment among the state bureaucrats. The common perception grew that funds that should have been traditionally earmarked for the government now found their way into NGO accounts. Sobhan notes that these funds were not intended for the government in the first place. "The apprehension on the part of the government that NGOs are rivals in a zero-sum game is unfounded because donors have been very clear that if funds are not channeled to NGOs they would be spent elsewhere and would not revert back to the government."[74]

For government bureaucrats, the independent management styles of NGOs further exacerbated the relationship: on the one hand, NGOs were reluctant to be brought into the jurisdiction of the state bureaucracy; on the other, state bureaucrats felt that NGO leaders should be subordinated to their authority. In turn, NGO leaders accused the state machinery of being inefficient and bureaucratic, and of holding up project approval and fund disbursements, thereby making it very cumbersome for NGOs to operate.

In addition, government authorities noted that the NGOs should hire local personnel over their preference for foreign nationals, and the pay scale of NGO executives and their foreign "experts" (anywhere between 30,000 to 160,000 taka a month) should be brought closer to government pay scales.[75] Given that a transparent NGO accountability system was not in place, there were widespread allegations of graft within the NGO sector after the floods. While graft in these circumstances—the unregulated growth of a sector flush with donor money—is neither surprising nor very illuminating, it worsened the ongoing tensions between these two sectors of the economy: government and NGO officials. These tensions came to a head-on collision in 1992.

State and NGO Relations (1990s)

By 1990 the NGO lobby had shifted allegiance away from Ershad and formed an alliance with the national political parties—the Awami League and the Bangladesh Nationalist Party—that were trying to oust him from power. This shift in alliance coincided with the new policy agenda of donors that now favored trade liberalization and democratic governance. The emphasis on "good governance" opened up a vacuum in the political space that the NGOs could occupy as the "allies of the poor." The political implications of such policies—good governance for whom and to what effects—are muted in policy debates, and the dialogue is often delivered in a techno-corporate language of poverty alleviation and women's empowerment.[76]

Given the turn to democratization, activist NGOs such as Proshika, Nijera Kori, and GSS could depend on support from two powerful groups: donors interested in good governance issues (such as USAID, CIDA, and EU) and national parties that now patronized NGOs as huge vote banks. But the politicization of the NGO landscape brought forth new alliances and fractures within NGOs. Proshika and Nijera Kori supported the Awami League (AL), and BRAC and the Grameen Bank the Bangladesh Nationalist Party (BNP).[77]

In the 1990s, three significant conflicts concerning the NGO sector emerged in the public domain. First were the internal disputes and ideological disagreements among the NGO leaders over the role of NGOs under democracy. Second were the rifts that emerged between the state bureaucracy that sought to bring NGOs within its jurisdiction and a recalcitrant NGO sector that had developed its own independent management style. Third were the struggles that erupted between the militant Islamic groups and the NGO sector. These three conflicts reshaped the NGO–state dynamics in Bangladesh, leading to accommodations and collaborations that have blurred the distinctions between these institutions.

Conflicts within NGO Leadership

By 1996, the apex organization of development agencies in Bangladesh—Association of Development Agencies in Bangladesh (ADAB)—had openly developed into a fully politicized body. Leaders of Proshika, Nijera Kori, and GSS saw their work as political and wanted to use the institutional power of ADAB to make political gains. Yet, BRAC leadership was careful to eschew an openly political role and become closely identified with a national political party. Elaborating on this point, Abed mentioned, "Any organization that works for change is doing politics but NGOs are not in the business of becoming identified with a political party. It will harm their work in the long run."[78]

The first conflict was a power struggle over the leadership of ADAB. It pitted Zafarullah against the alliance of Nijera Kori, Proshika, and BRAC. In 1989 Zafarullah was elected chair of ADAB. Zafarullah had opposed the 1990 pro-democracy movement against Ershad because he was working with his government to pass a pro-poor national health bill. In 1991 he was ousted from ADAB. Some of the NGO leaders saw him as too closely aligned with the military government to promote the national health bill, and hence against their democracy movement.[79]

The second power struggle took place at the annual meeting of the Association of Developmental Agencies in Bangladesh (ADAB), in November 1997. This time there was a disagreement between BRAC and Proshika leadership. The director of BRAC, Fazle Abed, disagreed with Qazi Faruque's (Proshika) open politicization of ADAB. The group led by Abed (BRAC), Father Timm (CARITAS), and Mahmudul Hasan (GSS) accused Qazi Faruque and Khushi Kabir (Nijera Kori) of representing the political interests of the Awami League. However, the Proshika–Nijera Kori lobby won the ADAB elections in 1997. Qazi Faruque of Proshika became the new director of ADAB. The 1997 Annual Report of ADAB had accused Abed and his allies of refusing to "sign a memorandum of understanding with regard to the overlapping of target areas among NGOs," which was creating loan recovery problems for certain NGOs.[80] These forms of political struggles, while internal to these organizations and their leaders, also signal the transformations at work within the NGO establishment. By 1998, ADAB was a fully politicized body aligned with the national party in power at that time, the Awami League. Control of ADAB lent legal weight and credibility to Proshika to sponsor its own programs under the rubric of democratization, as chapter 5 shows.

Conflicts with the State

The second conflict was of a longer duration and redefined relations between state and NGOs. The most significant act of politicization of NGOs occurred when sixteen NGOs signed the Gono Adalat (People's Court) verdict in 1992.[81] Gono Adalat is a symbolic People's Court that leading Bangladeshi civilians had formed to try those who supported the Pakistani military in 1971 for war crimes. The Gono Adalat is made up of people who aspire to a secular Bangladesh. One of the key persons accused in Gono Adalat was Professor Golam Azam, the chief of the Ja'maat-e-Islami (the largest mainstream Islamic party), who had returned to Bangladesh after the military takeover in 1975 from self-exile in Pakistan, where he had lived since 1971. Golam Azam and his Ja'maat party were closely affiliated with the Bangladesh Nationalist Party (BNP) government and their pro-Islamic policies. Thus, by becoming part of the Gono Adalat, these NGO leaders identified themselves as anti-BNP government that was elected to power in 1990.

Democratization also opened the space for more activist NGOs to make a frontal attack on rural elites through aggressive participation in local elections. In 1992, GSS put up members in five constituencies in the Nilphamari district. In the first day of voting, the majority of GSS members won their seats. Government officials and members of political parties had generally ignored the activities of GSS members. Yet, when the results came in, it was evident to them that GSS had the organizational capabilities to defeat them. This galvanized local elites to unite against GSS members. Armed goons were hired to prevent GSS members from casting their votes in the remaining elections. In addition, GSS offices were burned, their books confiscated, their members' houses torched, and GSS female members beaten.[82]

The government of Prime Minister Khaleda Zia (BNP) ordered an investigation into GSS activities. The report, entitled "A Survey of NGO GSS's Nilphamari Activities," stated that GSS was engaged in teaching an antistate philosophy to its organizational groups. Furthermore, the report concluded that GSS was misinforming the poor and creating an antigovernment attitude in them. The NGO Affairs Bureau chief also submitted a report titled "NGO Activities in Bangladesh" to the prime minister that alleged that these "NGOs had received around 1,800 crore taka (1 crore = 10 million) in the last two years, of which 60 percent was used for staff salaries and administrative costs."[83] This report targeted BRAC, GSS, Proshika, and CARITAS. In the report, an investigation into the remaining 40 percent of the money that was unaccounted for was suggested.

> NGOs show unconditional loyalty and subjugation to the donor agencies which is a threat to the state and the present government. . . . They give political statements from time to time, participate in local elections, publish newsmagazines with political propaganda, carry on religious activities and proselytization by taking advantage of illiterate and poor people. Besides they are involved in embezzlement, irregularities, corruption and anti-state activities.[84]

The same report stated that forty-six NGOs had taken 13.8 million taka from Western donors between 1988 and1991 without informing the government. Among these NGOs were BRAC, Proshika, GSS, and CARITAS. The NGO Affairs Bureau (NGOAB) then published a report on fifty-two NGOs that were breaking NGO registration laws and were engaged in proselytization work among the poor members.[85] Following these allegations, the prime minister's office cancelled the foreign funds registration of ADAB, the apex organization of NGOs. The NGOAB had also lodged formal police complaints against several foreign nationals and certain NGOs for financial irregularities. Facing pressure from U.S. and Scandinavian ambassadors, the prime minister's office was forced to rescind the arrest warrants within forty-eight hours and reinstitute the registration of ADAB.[86] This incident is cited by Bangladeshis as an example of the power of the leading NGOs to coerce the government to their will.

The result of this confrontation was a clarification of the importance of NGOs in national development and planning from the perspective of donor agencies. The confrontation was followed by actions by donors against the state through the withholding of funds, which made it apparent to the new BNP government that they needed the support of donors to keep their development projects running. The conflict resulted in a series of high-level talks between NGO leaders and government officials, with ambassadors from the United States and several other European countries acting as mediators. In these negotiations, the NGO sector and the donors demanded a streamlined and efficient system of operations. They complained about red tape, slow processing of project approvals, and funds disbursements.

The BNP government of Khaleda Zia took several steps to improve the operational conditions of NGOs. The government removed the existing NGOAB chief, who had brought these allegations in the first place. The official powers of the NGOAB were curtailed. The NGOAB would have to get clearance from the prime minister's office before filing any formal charges against any NGO. The government also agreed to review existing laws governing the operations of NGOs in the country, making it easier for NGO projects to be approved and foreign funds to be released. Immediately following the talks, funds for thirty-five projects pending approval were released.[87]

All these changes led to the creation of an institutional environment that was hospitable toward NGOs. The role of the NGOAB thus became one of facilitator of NGO projects, and not that of a watchdog.[88] The primary function of the NGO Affairs Bureau became one of record keeping and disbursements of funds, not one of monitoring NGO activities. Although on paper the NGOAB is still supposed to monitor projects to ensure strict adherence to rules, it does not have the personnel or the incentive to carry out its supervisory function. The NGOAB instead depends on the local district commissioner's offices to report on project illegalities. The district commissioner's offices are notorious for their corruption, and there is no incentive on their part to monitor NGO-funded rural projects.[89]

Following these conflicts, the World Bank, Asian Development Bank, and several Western donor agencies stepped in to foster better government–NGO (GO–NGO) relations in all sectors of the economy. The government of Bangladesh also encouraged NGO participation by stating that projects within the National Development Plan were to be carried out by NGOs. The NGOAB was placed directly under the prime minister's secretariat—and housed in a separate building outside the secretariat—to allow ease of access between the two offices. The language used to describe this reconstituted relationship between state and NGO (GO–NGO) is worth noting. Officials now use terms such as *governance, collaboration, partnership, brokerage, facilitation,* and *dialogue* to describe the evolving relationship between the state and the NGO sectors.

Another donor–NGO collaboration was the creation of the Palli Krishi Shahayak Foundation (PKSF). The role of PKSF is to grant microloans to medium-sized regional NGOs. Through the establishment of PKSF, the government, the NGO sector, and the World Bank are brought into closer cooperation. The government received loans from the World Bank, which it disbursed to regional NGOs through PKSF. Thus, all these institutions became dependent and linked through the structure of microlending. Similarly, donor–NGO collaboration also resulted in a new partnership called the GO–NGO Consultative Council (GNCC). GNCC is a group that facilitates better understanding and complementarity between the government and the NGO sector. Through GNCC, large NGOs (such as BRAC, Proshika, and others) have set up liaisons with the government by rotating government officials every two to three years at the various NGO headquarters. This liaison person resolves conflicts that arise between the NGO and the state.

NGOs also demanded the inclusion of poverty issues and microfinance in the national budget. In 1996, NGOs organized a poor people's rally of 100,000 in front of the national parliament to demand the implementation of policies aimed at eradicating poverty. In this, the NGO Proshika played a pivotal role. Although it was largely a symbolic rally, it demonstrated to the government the power of NGOs to gather thousands of their clients in one place—in other words, an enormous vote bank for the party that supported NGO policies. In 1996, the AL government for the first time invited NGOs to participate in pre-budget consultations. Poverty eradication was made a goal of the 1997–2002 Five Year Plan. In the 1996–1997 budget, 100 million taka was allocated for poverty reduction projects, and another 100 million taka was assigned to PKSF for the expansion of microfinance. In the budget it was noted that the "poorest of the poor are deprived of institutional credit." Hence, credit, and not employment, was conceived as the key bottleneck in rural development. Not surprisingly, the focus of the NGO/Proshika-sponsored pro-poor budget was on increasing microfinance to the poor, an area they were heavily invested in.[90]

Conflicts with the Clergy

The third conflict that rose was between the NGOs and the clergy. While NGOs and the state became partners in governance in the 1990s, the relationship between the clergy and Islamic parties on the one hand, and NGOs on the other remained unstable. The development policies of NGOs had begun to encroach on the traditional constituencies of the rural clergy—the poor, women, and children. Islamic charitable organizations, schools, and orphanages run by the clergy faced increased competition from these Western-aided NGOs in terms of resources and programs. The enormous funding abilities of NGOs granted them tremendous power to negotiate the terms of the most intimate sphere of a Muslim society: the conduct of its women. This incursion of NGO and donor ideas about the conduct of Muslim women led to tensions within the rural clergy and Islamic political parties that aspire to an Islamic state. Like the NGOs that occupied the political space as allies of the poor after democratization, Islamic groups inside Bangladesh were searching for social triggers that would catapult them into partnership with the state.

The democracy movement in Bangladesh coincided with global Islamist movements in Egypt, Algeria, and Afghanistan, and with the demand for the creation of Islamic states in many Muslim countries. Some of the Islamists from the Quomi madrassahs in Bangladesh had gone to Afghanistan to fight against the Soviets in the 1980s. These men had returned to Bangladesh with a renewed energy to establish an Islamic state. Not surprisingly, the removal of military rule created a space for Islamic political parties to demand the inclusion of Islamic teachings in matters relating to the state.

In this political climate of uncertainty in Bangladesh, Hindu right-wing militants destroyed the sixteenth-century Babri Masjid in Ayodhya, India, in 1992 because it was allegedly built on the mythical birthplace of the Hindu god Ram. Following the destruction of the Babri Masjid, there were religious riots in both India and Bangladesh. In India, Muslims were under heightened attacks, with over 2,000 killed in the aftermath of the Ayodhya riots.

In response to the riots in Bangladesh, Taslima Nasrin, a little-known Bangladeshi author, wrote a novella entitled *Lajja* (*Shame*, 1992), which chronicled the fictional story of the persecution of a Hindu family by Muslims in Bangladesh. Taslima's book gave the Islamists a weapon with which to fight Bangladesh's fragile democracy.[91] The Islamic militants took to the streets with a vengeance, demanding her death as an "apostate." For the clergy, Taslima symbolized Western liberal female decadence and an affront to Islam for suggesting that the Quran should be thoroughly revised. Caving in to the demands of Islamists, the BNP government filed a case against Taslima under the Penal Code for offending religious sentiments. Finally, under pressure from Western governments and the International

Writers Association (PEN), the Bangladeshi state exiled Taslima to Sweden on August 10, 1994. She has been living in exile ever since.

Surprisingly, a novel written by a middle-class feminist writer, whose novels are not read by the majority of Bangladeshis, became the catalyst of attacks against rural women and NGOs by Islamic political parties, madrassah students, and rural clergy. The clergy and rural elites accused several young women of committing adultery, and they were publicly stoned, flogged, and in once instance, burned to death.[92] Alongside these sporadic attacks on women, the militant Islamic press began to spread fabricated stories about anti-NGO activities in the country. In June 1993, a pro-Islamic weekly called *Shaptahik Muslim Jahan* reported that BRAC had wrapped the corpse of a child of one its members in black cloth and buried him. Muslims are wrapped in white cloth. The color black is associated with black magic and satanic rites.

In October 1993, another Islamic daily called *Dainik Inquilab* printed a report that is popularly known as "Allah or Apa."[93] In the report it was alleged that a BRAC teacher had asked the students to close their eyes and ask Allah for candy. Then she was supposed to have said, "Ask Apa [BRAC teacher] for candy." She then put candy in their hands and said, "Who gave you candy, Allah or Apa?" The students replied, "Apa gave us candy." By citing this story, the clergy alleged that atheism was taught to the students in BRAC schools. Apa as the personification of BRAC represented NGO power in rural society. This story circulated widely through the weekly prayer sermons of the clergy. It was also alleged by some that the owner of the Daily Inquilab Group of Industries, which is a pro-Islamic publication, purposely planted this story in his newspaper because his group had lost several printing tenders to BRAC printers.[94]

Following these stories, Muslim clerics began to make inflammatory attacks on NGO activities during their weekly Friday prayers at the mosques. According to them, NGOs were converting the poor to Christianity and dishonoring Muslim men by making their women "shameless" by bringing them out in public. In their weekly sermons, the clergy talked about the hypocrisy of Western countries that kill Muslims in Bosnia, Iraq, and Palestine, and then offer help to Muslims in Bangladesh. The Western donors were described as "indigo merchants of colonial Bengal," and their activities compared to the East India Company, which brought India under British rule. A popular ditty that the clergy have popularized among rural people is, "Why have imperialist NGOs come to Bangladesh?

Yunus [Grameen] and Abed [BRAC] have invited them in" (neel kor NGO ken achchey deshe, Yunus Abed anchey deke).

In their sermons, the clergy alleged that at the time of independence there were only 250,000 Christians in the country, but in 1993 the figure stood at 2.5 million.[95] The NGOs were responsible for this mass conversion of Muslims into Christianity, clergy members claimed. In a country with a very high unemployment rate, the clergy were able to exploit the fears of unemployed Muslim men who saw the Christian NGOs in Bangladesh (CARITAS; Christian Commission for Development in Bangladesh [CCDB]; and Health, Education, and Economic Development [HEED]) as hiring Christians and indigenous people. The clergy also claimed that at BRAC schools, students were taught to "sing and dance," which is not acceptable according to Islamic dictates. Another circulating rumor was of the supremacy of "shaheb [NGO field-worker] over shami [husband]."[96] NGO offices rotate their field-workers so that they do not develop any long-term relationship with local people. The clergy interpreted this "coming in contact" with multiple non-kin men by the women as "NGO-sponsored prostitution."

The clergy and their followers targeted NGOs by burning their offices, harassing NGO officers, and issuing fatwas against women who participated in NGO activities. The clergy ostracized five thousand families of women who worked in NGOs. Fifty cases of clergy-enforced divorces were reported. In many villages, women were forbidden to leave their homes. Women were made to wear the burqa when they went outdoors, and were told to disassociate from NGO-sponsored economic activities. BRAC schools were burned and mulberry trees used in sericulture production were hewed down. According to a former BRAC researcher who had investigated these allegations, 1,547 BRAC schools were affected through reduced attendance, and its Rural Development Program (RDP) was also severely affected.[97]

But the clergy were not alone in these attacks against BRAC. Alongside the clergy, government primary school teachers, rural men, and former BRAC employees joined in the violence against NGOs. With its highly successful NFPE programs, BRAC, with donor backing, had been advocating for the privatization of primary education at the national level. If primary education became privatized, it would lead to the loss of employment for many government primary school teachers. Thus, government employees took to the streets and torched BRAC and NGO schools.

Another point that came out from conversations with informed people was that BRAC's NFPE program had exploded in the 1990s due to expanded donor funding.[98] While on paper BRAC had opened many NFPE schools, in reality a lower number of schools had been established. In many instances, local BRAC officials had stolen the money allocated for the schools. These attacks gave corrupt BRAC officials an opportunity to cover up their graft by alleging that the "schools were torched."

In order to comprehend the sources of this simmering malcontentedness among rural people, one has to go beyond the NGO script of the clergy as antidevelopment. Through its income-generating commercial policies, such as sericulture, BRAC had begun to commercialize common properties. BRAC had leased thousands of acres of government land along rural highways for planting mulberry trees for sericulture production. Rural people had previously used these lands to graze their cattle. In leasing the land, BRAC had effectively closed off land for those farmers who relied on them for grazing. BRAC hired female employees to guard this land from cattle grazing, a step that caused friction between the local farmers and BRAC. The farmers had initially gone to the local BRAC offices to ask for their grazing rights, but they were told that the land now belonged to BRAC. Faced with the unwillingness of BRAC to recognize their traditional grazing rights, the farmers turned to the only other group in the village, the clergy. Given this opportunity, the clergy were able to reinvent themselves as protectors of the poor. As one Imam of a mosque said, "The mulberry trees yield benefits to only one percent of the poor. But it is causing trouble to most of the villagers. Now poor people cannot graze their cattle."[99]

Another group that participated in these attacks included former BRAC employees from the sericulture sector who had lost their jobs with BRAC. In the first year of planting of mulberry trees for silk production, BRAC employed two female NGO members as guards for each kilometer of road. From the second year onwards, only one guard was hired. Thus, 50 percent of women employed by BRAC Rural Development Program lost their livelihood after one year of employment. Many of them joined in hewing down the trees out of their anger at BRAC.[100]

The clergy also concocted a Doomsday myth that confounded female labor with sexual promiscuity. According to the clergy, one of the first symbols of the advent of Doomsday is when seven women will chase a man for sexual gratification. Escaping them, the man will climb up a tree, and from above urinate (male urine here refers to semen) in the mouths of these sexually willing women. During the attacks against NGOs, the clergy reminded their worshippers of this story. The clergy alleged that the involvement of women in sericulture cultivation, which is part of a global trade in silk goods, made rural women "promiscuous." In the patron–client social relations of Bangladesh, rich men exercised control over the labor and sexuality of poor women. The wages paid to women were kept very low due to a lack of competition and women's lack of negotiating power. Not surprisingly, rural women preferred to work with NGOs for better wages. Rural men and clergy were thus brought into competition with the NGOs over the labor of poor women. Women's employment outside the home loosened male control over their bodies and income, and these NGO activities caused deep disturbances among rural elites.

New Modes of Governance

Following this crisis, NGO leaders recognized the importance of developing mutually beneficial relations with vested groups of rural people. As a result, the earlier brash approach of young NGO men flush with foreign money to start their operations in villages independently of local outreach was revisited. In an effort to create good relations with the clergy, BRAC took a series of measures. In its primary education, BRAC adopted religious instruction, a policy they had eschewed in the past, and hired clergy as teachers in its schools.[101] In their training sessions, BRAC managers were trained to show respect to the clergy and to cultivate cordial relations. BRAC officials also began to attend the daily Friday prayers at the local mosques. At these social gatherings, BRAC officers would interact with the clergy and local elites and invite them to visit their offices. As a former BRAC employee explained, "We realized the need to be known in the community. In the past we were seen as outsiders, and it was easy to attack us. Once we established personal relationships, it would be harder for the clergy to attack us."

The use of motorized vehicles by BRAC (and other NGOs) was an underlying cause of the clergy's anger toward NGOs. Although there is an increase in motorized vehicles in Bangladesh, they still remain a symbol of technology and modernity in rural society. The clergy found it offensive that men who did not belong to their villages would drive past them in motorcycles, often with a female NGO field-worker sitting behind them, while they walked to town. These questions were about local conceptions of honor and status that BRAC leadership recognized they had to respect. While BRAC did not stop its female field-workers from driving motorcycles or riding bicycles, it accommodated the concerns of the clergy.

BRAC officials were instructed to show respect to the clergy when they saw them on the streets. They would voluntarily offer the local cleric rides or let him borrow their motorcycles for important occasions. Most importantly, BRAC introduced monthly meetings called liaison meetings between

BRAC, the clergy, and the local administration so that grievances could be addressed before they escalated into violence. At these meetings, the clergy were shown their due respect, feasted, and given honoraria at the conclusion of the meetings. Packets containing money (about 100 taka) were given to the clergy as a thank-you at the conclusion of the meetings. NGOs also began to give loans and jobs to relatives of, and people nominated by, the local clergy. The NGO, as the newest elite in rural society, recognized the social power and influence of the local clergy. This led to mutual understanding between these two groups of their relative social importance and jurisdiction with regard to rural society.

During my research, in 1998, heavy floods occurred. The waters stayed for six weeks, from early August to mid-September. Standing waters had destroyed the crops, prevented agricultural labor from earning money, and forced many to sell their livestock at below-market prices. Apart from the destruction of people's livelihoods, there was another issue that profoundly disturbed me. As a child growing up in Pakistan and Bangladesh, I recalled the public's participation in flood relief efforts. In 1998, public participation was relatively absent. I mentioned my feelings of unease to a friend who worked for an NGO. Listening to my questions, the friend mentioned:

> What is surprising is the change in public response between the floods of 1988 and the floods of 1998. In 1988 there was a spontaneous response from the people. Everyone, including students, housewives, laborers, government officials, and day laborers all donated something (money, bread, clothes) toward the flood relief effort. In local neighborhoods, youths went around with a harmonium singing songs and collecting donations of rice, lentils, clothes, and small sums of money from people. Housewives volunteered their time to make rotis [flattened bread]. In every neighborhood, thousands of rotis were rolled and distributed among the flood victims. Everyone participated. In 1988 people felt that their participation counted. What they did for their fellow citizens made a difference in their lives. Now we have become indifferent.[102]

During the 1998 floods, BRAC received funds from donors to reconstruct rural roads. During my research, I found out that they had completed the work within a month. As part of rural road construction, BRAC paved the road leading to the local mosque, which was not a public road. This was done as a gesture of goodwill by BRAC. As the local BRAC manager explained,

> The local cleric came to me with the request. I spoke with my divisional manager, and we decided that it would be in our interest to do so. Now all the

villagers can go to the mosque and pray. The clergy recognize that BRAC can be of use to them. If the cleric now says something against us, someone from the congregation can remind him, "Did you not also take help from BRAC?" In the village, all these relationships are interlinked. The purpose is to create systems of mutually reinforcing benefits with local elites.

One day my research assistant Rina and I stopped by the tea shop of Ramzan in one of the villages in which I was conducting my research. We would often stop by Ramzan's shop and exchange news and gossip. I asked Ramzan what he thought of the rapid work of road reconstruction by BRAC in the area. Ramzan replied with a wide grin, "If the money for road construction had gone to government officials, it would have just filled their coffers. Now NGOs build roads for us. Do you know why? So their officers can travel to the interiors to recover loans they have distributed. They cannot steal all the money like government officers; they need to maintain their communication with the villages. But we benefit as well. We can travel to the markets, sell our produce, and find work."

In contrast, 2007 showed a different aspect of this evolution of Bangladeshi NGO governance. On January 11, 2007, Bangladesh came under a caretaker government backed by the military. In November of that year, cyclone Sidr hit the southern coast of Bangladesh at 220 miles per hour, causing utter devastation in its wake. In December 2007, when I visited Dhaka, I found a lively engagement from ordinary citizens in helping the victims of the cyclone. The older days of community participation with neighborhood collection boxes; groups of women rolling out rotis; and young men singing nationalist songs and collecting money and clothes were replaced by a well-orchestrated campaign run by NGOs skilled in the art of fund-raising.

BRAC was well positioned to receive donations from individuals at home and abroad. BRAC Bank ran a global relief campaign. Local relief drop-off centers were also set up by BRAC. This streamlined process of collecting donations was efficiently run, and it made more urban people donate because they did not incur additional expenses in time and effort. Yet, the production of professional relief operations by NGOs also distances ordinary people from a personal stake in nation building. It renders the state increasingly irrelevant to the vast majority of its citizens, the rural poor, as the NGO steps in as the patron.[103]

By 2007, relief operations had become a privatized NGO enterprise. The NGO, following the rationalities of a bureaucratic institution, has emerged as an able relief operator, both from a state and donor perspective. Flood relief has moved from being a national campaign to a private campaign run by NGOs and paid professionals. In a country that is prone to annual floods, it is the NGO, and not the state, that emerges as the guarantor of the security of rural people.

Most importantly, though, the devastation of cyclone Sidr occurred at a time when microfinance programs had become deeply entrenched in rural society, with several thousand NGOs working in this field. When the media reported that the NGOs were using coercion against their borrowers to recover their loans, the caretaker government finally issued a statement that NGOs must forgive all outstanding debts for six months to the people affected by Sidr. The large NGOs (BRAC, ASA, and Grameen) were asked to partially write off these loans. Many of the medium- and small-sized NGOs are dependent on the profitability of microfinance programs (which have high interest rates) for their institutional sustainability, and they continued to collect outstanding loans from cyclone victims. A report conducted by Action Aid found that the NGOs continued to harass the borrowers to repay the loans.[104] Such behavior indicates the power of the NGOs to act in accordance with their internal mandates, and the failure of the state to bring these non-state actors within its jurisdiction.

This chapter has analyzed how global ideological trends in neoliberal policies, donor mandates in privatization, and local conditions coincided to invent the NGO as a powerful institution. The relations between the state and the NGO are in a constant mode of adjustments and negotiations. In the context of Bangladesh, the categorical distinction between the government and the nongovernmental organization (NGO) has become blurred in many areas, leading to the creation of the NGO as a shadow state in the rural economy.

Chapter 2   The Research Terrain

THIS CHAPTER IS an overview of the research terrain that informed my ethnographic study of NGOs, microfinance, and women. Through their work in microfinance, the leading NGOs have a dual effect on social lives: they bring economic opportunities to rural people and, simultaneously, introduce them to NGO-sponsored programs. The power of these NGOs as service and loan providers to financially strapped poor women creates what I term "NGO governmentality," a mode of governance through which NGOs modulate the behaviors of their rural clients toward NGO objectives. I found that NGOs achieved their goals primarily through compliance rather than through coercion, although coercion was used when adherents were unwilling to act according to enforced rules. Through NGO loans, rural women were constituted as both the subjects and objects of development. In development discourse, rural women played scripted roles as "entrepreneurs." Rural women were constructed as autonomous subjects who were thrifty, hardworking, and good husbanders of resources. In reality, their lives were intersected by multiple levels of obligations and reciprocities that circumscribed their social roles. In order to understand how the knowledge of microfinance and women was organized at the local level, we begin with a discussion of how the ethnography was conceived and conducted.

Ethnographic Frame

This ethnography is not a descriptive study of rural women and their everyday lives. It is a study of the discourses, practices, and policies of the Grameen Bank, BRAC, ASA, and Proshika. It is also an analysis of social and gender relations in rural Bangladesh that are mediated by microfinance.

Foucault has called governmentality the instruments, rationalities, and tactics of governing populations in modern societies. To govern, he notes, is to govern entities and relations toward certain objectives.[1] He suggested that we conceptualize this relationship of power as a triangulated relationship of sovereignty, discipline, and government that work in collusion with each other.[2]

> To govern a state will mean . . . to set up an economy at the level of the entire state, which means exercising toward its inhabitants, and the wealth and behavior of each and all, a form of surveillance and control as attentive as that of the head of family over his households and goods.[3]

When we apply Foucault's definition of governmentality to the context of postcolonial countries—where the state does not have a pastoral relationship of care toward its citizens, being instead characterized by endemic corruption, violence, nepotism, and inefficiency—governmentality emerges as a set of culturally coded instrumentalities. Bringing Foucault's insights to bear on microfinance, we find that credit is made up of relationships of power, that is, relationships of domination and subordination between the creditor (NGO) and debtor (borrower). Microfinance as an instrument of power offers the creditor the leverage to manipulate the actions of the debtor toward NGO-specified goals. But, as my research shows, membership with NGOs and their services also produces new relations of antagonism, dependence, meaning, and identity that construct new ways of behaving and acting. While an NGO may apply coercion to guide and shape the behavior of its clients, it does not infinitely manage the behavior of its subjects. NGO female subjects also exist in parallel social worlds that have other rules that constrain and regulate their behavior. Thus, while the NGO is a dominant actor in rural society, it is not always hegemonic over its subject populations.

As noted in the Introduction, Bangladeshi NGOs have tremendous power in their ability to provide services and resources to rural populations. Given the lack of credit opportunities for rural people, microfinance NGOs were able to instrumentalize their governance over rural subjects by extending or withholding loans. Thus, it is necessary to theorize the relationship between NGO governmentality and microfinance. I have theorized microfinance as a structure of debt, that is, a relationship of power and inequality. Envisioning microfinance as debt opened a different way of examining how women's roles were mediated by money. Credit is conceptualized as trust in modern financial institutions. These financial institutions "trust" their borrowers based on indicators such as education level and future income potential. Yet, the extension of credit in rural Bangladesh, where discourse is carried on through face-to-face encounters, has to be measured by a different set of social indicators.

Credit and debt are two sides of the same financial instrument. While credit is theorized as a positive attribute, to be in debt is a social embarrassment. Debt is a regulator of social behavior. In theoretical terms, debt ties the present and the future together: once in debt, the debtor's present behavior determines future payoffs. Debt creates a state of domination and subordination between creditor and debtor, and it has both a financial and a social component. In face-to-face communities, this relationship becomes more intensified because the debtor and the borrower know each other, and failure to fulfill one's debt obligations causes the debtor to lose face, which is in excess of losing one's material assets to a bank.

More importantly, these borrowers are not isolated and autonomous subjects; rather, they are relational subjects who live in extended families in villages. Within these living arrangements, kinship ties control subordinated individuals, particularly women within the family. Thus, when a woman has access to a loan, she is obligated to transfer it to her husband, kin, or social superiors. The woman as the loan-taking subject is now accountable to two forms of authority, her husband/family and the NGO/group of borrowers who are jointly responsible for the timely repayment of her loan. Thus, if she fails to meet her debt obligations, it results in a breach of trust that extends to the kin group and the wider community. This is a very significant point in understanding how microfinance adversely affects the lives of women borrowers, a point that is developed in the following ethnographic chapters.

A variety of sources were considered in this research. These include ethnographic data; case studies; newspaper reports; and interviews with a cross-section of women, their husbands, NGO field-workers, NGO managers, members of rural elites, activists, researchers, and scholars. I investigated how different communities made up of NGO beneficiaries and workers, government officials, researchers, donors, clergy, and activists participated in NGO development discourses and practices. Sometimes the participants were knowledgeable about these discourses and willingly participated in NGO programs and scripts. These people were usually NGO researchers and activists. There were others—NGO field-workers and women beneficiaries and their families—who were critical of NGO discourses but participated in NGO programs because of their economic dependence on these institutions. But whether rural or urban, rich or poor, male or female, everyone had a public and a private script of NGO-sponsored development and modern roles for women. My role as an ethnographer was to access these scripts from various sources, to gain the trust of the community, to analyze the ethnographic material, to give it shape, and then to interpret the narrative.

The research was conducted over a period of eighteen months. It had two research sites, one urban and one rural. In both sites, I was helped by research assistants who were members drawn from the local communities. The rural part of the research was conducted in a cluster of villages in a region that I have named Pirpur Thana. As an ethnographer, my methodology was to have a flexible conversation format with the women. I met with the women in multiple gathering places: in the NGO meeting centers and offices, in their homes, in their neighbors' homes, and in public places. The one criterion I used for selecting the women subjects was that their membership with an NGO had to be longer than a year. The bulk of them were long-term NGO members. There was no control group—that is, non-NGO members—because all the women I met belonged to more than one NGO. In fact, on average, they belonged to six or seven NGOs. The majority of the women were married, but some were also widowed or abandoned. Their ages ranged from 18 to 65 years.

In my methodology, I adopted Marcus's notion of "follow the thing."[4] Marcus notes, "This mode of constructing the multi-sited space for research involves the tracing of circulation through different contexts of a manifestly material object of study . . . such as commodities, gifts, money, works of art, and intellectual property . . . ."[5] He goes on to add that the purpose is to allow "the sense of system to emerge ethnographically and speculatively by following paths of circulation."[6] I tracked the circulation of credit through the stories of these women that led me to new narratives of microfinance. Over the course of the research, I had spoken to over 300 women, and collected about forty life stories. I also talked to rural men and NGO officers. As these stories formed patterns, I developed a more focused form of contact with specific women and men.

In writing this book, I have refrained from inserting my voice visibly in the text because I wanted to retain the focus on the women and their stories. As the ethnographer, I was one among several people with whom the women and men were interacting at any given time. The women who shared their stories, the NGO field-workers, the activists, and the researchers were all my collaborators, whether knowingly or not. Hence, there is no one particular knower in this book. Keeping that in mind, I have refrained from an extended discussion about my relationship with rural women as an insider/outsider ethnographer. I have written about the lessons learned from my encounters with the women and men in a methodology paper to be published separately.

"Insider" and "outsider" categories are not static relations; they are constituted through different relationships with the communities in which we work.[7] Naples offers three insights that I found useful in my research: (1) we are never fully inside/outside the "community"; (2) our relationship with the community is constantly negotiated; and (3) these interactions are themselves located in shifting relationships among the community residents.[8] During my research I was constituted variously as female, single, researcher, daughter of X, one who lives in the United States but is not a white American woman, etc., and my interactions were filtered through these constructions with different groups. As people got to know me better, these initial constructions were also renegotiated and replaced with new ones.

In my research, I followed Marcus's notion of a multi-sited ethnography,[9] which is an exploration of "chains, paths, threads, connections, juxtapositions" that link the disparate sites within an ethnographic environment. Situating my research in a multi-sited frame offered a flexible mode of inquiry and freed me from the fixity of place to examine the different sites of knowledge production and their manifestations in rural, urban, and global locations that were all connected sites through the circulation of microfinance loans and its global discourses. I tracked how NGO loans traveled in rural society, and what were their effects on social lives, gender relations, and knowledge production. Following the idea of loans soon led me to other chains, as the incident of the missing borrower shows in this chapter, and eventually helped me to arrive at a more nuanced understanding of how rural social relations are mediated by debt relations.

NGO meeting places are pedagogical environments where poor borrowers are taught capitalist norms of discipline and investment, and the cultural properties, such as "trust, norms, and networks, that can improve the efficiency of society by facilitating coordinated actions."[10] In NGO group meetings, for example, globalization was scaled and compressed as women borrowers collectively raised money to send a male kin to Malaysia to work as a migrant laborer. The migrant Bangladeshi man in Malaysia was now dependent on the contractor who had hired him and on the Malaysian government in his ability to return the money loaned to him by the women, who, in turn, had to pay installments on that loan every week to a microfinance institution. These multiple constellations get condensed inside loan centers, homes of individual women, markets, and other sites, as borrowers try to harness the uncertainties associated with global movements of capital and people.

I consider ethnography a process that one inhabits as a critical interlocutor. While it is a process that involves fieldwork and the actual process of writing the fieldwork into a bounded narrative, ethnography is not reducible to an either/or proposition, although fieldwork and writing remain integral conventions of the methodological tradition of anthropology. Ethnography lingers with the ethnographer long after the actual process of "doing it" formally ends. It is a mode of constant critique and the reading of, and intervening on, the *silent* discursive power relations that are written onto bodies, structures, and languages within which we operate. Critical ethnography shifts beyond the native's point of view, beyond "thick description," beyond advocacy, beyond collaboration, and toward new modalities of thinking and acting, of being-in-the world, of dialogue and engagement with other actors who are also engaged in research and activism to find innovative answers toward understanding the human condition. This process of being in the world through ethnography brought me to citizens' groups as an alternative to microfinance NGOs, a point I discuss in the Conclusion.

The Beginning

The Case of Proshika Violence

When I arrived in Dhaka in late October 1997, rumors were circulating in development circles about the police excesses of Proshika, one of the largest NGOs in the country. Friends in Dhaka advised me to investigate the incident concerning Proshika members at Matikata village in Kuliachar Thana, in the Bhairab district. Thana is a unit of rural government that falls below the district level. According to newspaper reports, on July 5, 1997, three Proshika women borrowers along with a child were killed in a highway accident when they were being transported to the local police station.[11] The women were members of Proshika Bhumiheen Samity No. 1 (Landless Society No.1), which was established in 1991. This group had fourteen members. On February 27, 1995, the group borrowed 25,000 taka ($543) from Proshika to recover mortgaged land.[12] The loan was to be repaid in twenty-four installments within two years, but the group members fell behind on payments. Unable to recover the outstanding loan, Proshika lodged a case on December 18, 1994, against the fourteen defaulting members. When the women did not show up in court, the judge wrote in favor of Proshika and issued a warrant for the arrest of the loan defaulter women. At the time of the arrest, according to the leader of the group, Pandit Banu, the group was only 2,400 taka (approximately $52) in arrears. In an interview with the newspaper *Bhorer Kagoj*, Syeda Nasima, the manager for Proshika in Kuliachar Thana, said that there were twenty groups in her area that had taken loans of over 2 million taka ($43,478) for 848 projects. Of these, there were cases pending against ten of the groups, a 50 percent rate of default.[13]

Following the court decision, a fourteen-member police force was dispatched to arrest the fourteen defaulting women. When the police arrived at the village, most of the women hid in the nearby fields and could not be located. The police found three of the women, Rahela, Ayesha, and Roshena. Roshena was pregnant and had her one-and-a-half-year-old son with her. The Union Council chairman, who is the highest-ranking elected local official, requested the police to wait until their husbands had returned from work in the evening so a settlement could be brokered. When the police refused, the chairman requested that the pregnant woman and her child be left behind.[14] The women also pleaded with the police to be allowed to walk to the police station, instead of being loaded into the police car like criminals. Ignoring the pleas of the chairman and the women, the police forcibly loaded them into their car. On the way to the jail, an oncoming bus smashed into the police car, killing all three women, the child, the driver, and one constable. In the aftermath of the accident, angry villagers burned the local Proshika office. They had threatened NGO officers with dire consequences if they showed their faces in their village. NGO officers could not go into Matikata or surrounding areas to collect loan installments for several months.

A number of themes emerged from this case that were important considerations in my research. In particular, this case indicated the vulnerability of poor rural women who were indebted to the NGO Proshika. Moreover, while the rhetoric of Proshika was about helping the poorest of the poor, it had begun to resort to the use of state power, the police in this case, against rural borrowers to recover its investment. Although it was an incident that concerned a single NGO (Proshika), it was disturbing to realize that an NGO that had a public image of being pro-poor was engaged in coercive actions against the very people—poor women—that it aimed to protect and empower.

The Missing Borrower of Grameen Bank

In the initial days of my research, I, like so many other overseas researchers in Bangladesh, spent considerable time at the Grameen Poverty Research unit, which is the research arm of the Grameen Bank. A high-ranking officer at the research institute facilitated my first visit to a Grameen Bank office. He provided me with a young male guide to assist me in my travel. This young man was occasionally employed to do research at this institution.

We took an early morning bus from the terminal and headed toward Tangail, located sixty kilometers from Dhaka. Tangail is one of the areas most frequented by foreign researchers and aid officials who come to study or evaluate aid programs because of its proximity to the city. Most researchers, especially foreign ones, work in areas close to the city, primarily in Tangail, Manikganj, and Matlab. These regions, located within sixty kilometers of the city and easily accessible by road, have emerged as key research sites in Bangladesh, and many of the monographs on development are conducted there.

I arrived at the branch of Grameen Bank in Tangail in mid-morning to see the operations of that institution. In the first two days of my stay, we visited several Grameen Bank centers with the branch manager always present. These centers, located at the houses of members, are where the groups gather for weekly payments on outstanding loans. Upon my arrival, the Grameen Bank manager took on a brotherly attitude of taking care of me, which translated into monitoring my movements very closely. I was not allowed to go anywhere without him. Every time I mentioned that I wanted to walk around the village by myself, he said that because I was considered a female guest of the Grameen Bank, it was his duty to ensure my safety. He added that he would "lose face" if I wandered unescorted in the village. Visibly annoyed by my request to be left alone, he mentioned that people from the headquarters sent foreign visitors without vetting him, and that these visits interfered with his work.

When I arrived at the first center meeting, the manager told the gathered women, "You have a guest here today. Tell her what improvements have occurred in your lives by becoming Grameen Bank members." I tried to tell him that I was interested in hearing what the women had to say, but my comments were ignored. At the center meetings, I heard several women tell their Grameen "sir" (the field-worker is also addressed with *sir* by Grameen members), "Sir, take our money quickly. Do you not know that today is also BRAC collection day?"

After I had attended several Grameen group meetings, a young woman asked me to visit her home. The Grameen manager urged me to go to her house, adding, "You will be able to see how she has benefited from Grameen loans." Upon arriving at her house, I saw that it was large and tin roofed. She told me that she had bought a sewing machine with her loan, and that she made clothes for children. Now her business had expanded for her to hire another person to help out. In her house, she had some furniture: a table, several chairs, a bed, a table fan, and a steel cabinet in which she kept the clothes. She appeared to be a perfect example of Grameen success. When I asked her what her husband did, she replied that he was a soldier in the army, and with his salary she was able to pay her weekly installments while she slowly built her tailoring business. The first successful Grameen candidate I had met was a member of the rural middle-class whose husband had a regular salary from the Bangladesh military. Her ability to pay back the loan depended on his source of income.

The Grameen Bank required its borrowers to begin repayment of the loan the week after it was taken, making it almost impossible for the borrower to repay the money from an investment of the loan itself. For example, it takes six months for a cow to give milk and for the borrower to make money by selling that milk. In rural societies milk cows are not sold unless the family has fallen on hard times. Yet, Grameen Bank borrowers who took cow loans were expected to begin repayment on the loan the following week. A payment schedule such as this is only possible when the borrowers have some other source of income either as day laborers or through fixed employment, as it was the case with this woman's husband. This woman did not belong in the category of "poor" households, not even prior to joining the bank. Yet, this middle-class rural woman was showcased as a successful Grameen story.[15] In the following months, I came across many such women who were members of the rural middle class and who had joined the NGOs to start small businesses, to buy luxury items, or to help their husbands expand their businesses.

On the second evening of my stay at the branch, I was sitting in the office when one of the field-workers came and spoke to the manager, "We cannot find Badal Shah. Proshika has called a *shalish* tomorrow and Badal Shah's wife will come and petition." Shalish is a village adjudicating board formally made up of rural elites who deliberate cases brought by villages and who dispense justice.[16] Their judgments are socially binding on the members of the community. My ears pricked up when I heard the name Badal Shah. I had heard this name mentioned several times during the course of the day. Whenever the name came up, the manager and the accountant would go off into a corner and whisper urgently. I could ascertain that they were uncomfortable discussing Badal Shah in front of me.

After overhearing this exchange, I asked the manager to explain the situation. Badal Shah, a Hindu man, was a borrower of Grameen Bank who had missed two consecutive weekly payments. Borrowers confided in the field-worker that Badal Shah had fled to neighboring India with money from Grameen and several other NGOs. Many of the borrowers in Tangail were Hindus. They would often cross to neighboring West Bengal, India, to attend festivals and visit family, and sometimes to engage in trading and smuggling.

With Grameen, Shah had an outstanding loan of 10,780 taka ($234). As the manager explained, "Poor people have so many wants. If we don't keep them on a tight leash, fiscal discipline will break down." According to him, Proshika had called a shalish the next morning to "divide up his belongings." Interestingly, NGOs have begun to conduct their own shalishes in villages, and to use the power of the community to enforce their decisions as morally binding on the group.

The manager said that he would attend the meeting to claim Grameen Bank's rightful share to Shah's property. I asked the manager to take me to the shalish the following morning, but he hedged with many excuses—too far, no place for a woman, you have to travel on my motorcycle, internal affair of Grameen, your presence will only complicate matters. He repeatedly asked me, "What does this have to do with your research?" Finally, he told me to meet him at 8:00 a.m. the following morning at his office. When I arrived at the office at 7:30 a.m., I was informed that the manager had left an hour earlier.

Left alone for the first time, I visited the homes of several women and spoke to them privately. The young man who had accompanied me from Dhaka toured with me. After some initial conversation, several of them revealed that they were members of several NGOs. When I asked the women who used the money, they unanimously said, "We give it to our husbands." The women looked upon these loans as household money. According to them it was a man's job to use money in the external world. The husbands of these women worked as day laborers, making it easier for them to repay the installments on loans every week. Grameen Bank had very few members whose husbands had seasonal employment because these households did not have the disposable income to pay the loan installments on a weekly basis. Talking to the women, I learned that the interest paid was a flat amount. The women paid the same interest whether the capital was 10,000 taka or had been paid down to 100 taka.[17]

When the exhausted manager returned in the evening, I heard the story of Badal Shah's shalish. Badal Shah was a cobbler (muchi). His monthly income varied from 3,000 to 5,000 taka ($65–$108). When the manager reached the village, Shah's wife and other villagers had already gathered there. The branch manager from Proshika was delivering "a threatening speech" on what would happen to the villagers if they became loan defaulters. Present at the meeting were branch managers of several other NGOs from the area, such as BURO-Tangail and the Social Development Society (SDS). The assembled managers concluded that Badal Shah had borrowed the following amounts (in taka) from all these NGOs:

Grameen Bank	10,780
Proshika	30,000
BURO-Tangail	18,000
Social Development Society	15,000
Total Debt:	73,780 ($1,603)

Badal Shah's total debt, 73,780 taka, was more than fourteen times his monthly income!

The manager said that the outstanding number could be much higher because Shah may have borrowed from other sources that were not known. He added, "Proshika had already confiscated his cow. They were going to sell off his cow to recover some of their losses. When I arrived, the Proshika manager was making a list of Badal Shah's saleable assets. Shah's wife wept and asked for a few days' reprieve. She said that he would return in ten days." The manager argued that Grameen and all the other NGOs had a right to Shah's assets and Proshika alone could not lay a claim to the assets. Instead, the Grameen manager suggested that NGOs needed to carve out their credit territories and share member lists to prevent membership overlapping. The meeting was inconclusive, and Shah's wife was given an extension to pay back the money.

Facing similar situations in many villages, Grameen Bank officials had sat down with BRAC (which started its credit program in 1986) for a high-level meeting in Deldoar Thana, in Tangail, a few months earlier.[18] Fazle Abed, managing director of BRAC, and Dipal Barua, the third in command at Grameen Bank, had attended the meeting in which the decision was made that BRAC would not recruit from Grameen-dominated territories. However, BRAC later reneged on its promise and started to recruit members from Grameen's area. BRAC and ASA, who were late entrants to the microfinance program, were unwilling to concede financial territories to Grameen.

The Badal Shah case gave me the following sketch with which to think about my research. Fearing repercussions, Shah's peers had notified the Grameen officials about his disappearance; this information was immediately reacted to by the bank officials; his wife was left to cope with the consequences and with the anger of the NGO officers; one could borrow from multiple sources with no oversight; multiple NGOs had descended on a single woman to make claims on her assets; and all these NGOs were fighting turf battles over creditworthy clients. Most interestingly, neither Grameen Bank nor Proshika officials were concerned about the effect of their coercive actions against Badal Shah's wife, although both of these NGOs spoke of empowering poor women. What I learned from my first visit was that Grameen Bank maintained strict fiscal discipline. These disciplinary rituals were instrumentalized through meetings, group formations, and the surveillance of borrowers by borrowers. Because of an increase in lending by NGOs, there were multiple stakeholders who now made claims on the assets of this one man. Yet, it was the wife who was held accountable by all the NGOs and was publicly humiliated, as was noted by the Grameen manager ("she was weeping and asking for a reprieve").

I made several more trips to Tangail and Mymensingh[19] using my own connections.[20] Both places were close to the capital, Dhaka, and had an influx of researchers and foreign guests. This made the local population research-aware, and they saw the information they could provide to researchers as a commodity. When I asked them questions, many of them would respond by asking, "What is it that you want to know?"

As I met more people working with NGOs and established closer relations, some interesting facts emerged. I learned that BRAC had a model village in Mymensingh, where their training center (TARC) was located. They said that BRAC also had a traveling group of villagers who would go to different places to perform for foreign guests. Foreign dignitaries and Western donors were taken to these specific locations for their official visits to witness these scripted shows of development.

A former NGO manager told me that prior to a visit by donors for project appraisals, they would go and buy fish from the local markets and throw them into a selected pond. When the donors came the following day, the NGO officials would cast a net into the pond and show the abundant fish caught as evidence of the success of their pisciculture project.[21] Such incidents never occurred in front of me; but that such a theater of development existed was corroborated by the report of Transparency International of Bangladesh (2006), which found that "NGOs have some well-trained beneficiaries who always speak of the positive aspects of the NGOs every time the donors go for field visits."[22] In the eyes of local people, these NGOs are powerful institutions that can manipulate donors through these scripted performances. Given some of the encounters I had in this region, I decided to relocate my research to an area at a distance from Dhaka, the capital—a place that was not so contaminated by researchers and the wariness of NGO managers.

Rural Setting

After several months, I asked a friend to help me set up residence in his natal village. I have changed the name of the place I worked in as well as the names of my hosts, NGO field-workers, and my research assistants to protect their privacy. The rural segment of the research was conducted in a cluster of villages I will call Pirpur Thana, a fictional name. Pirpur Thana was in southwestern Bangladesh, approximately 120 kilometers away from Dhaka.

Pirpur Thana was a midlevel center of business activities. It covered an area of 279.98 kilometers, with 46,138 families registered at the Thana office. Grameen Bank, BRAC, Proshika, ASA, and six other NGOs all had their main offices in the center of the thana. Thana is a subdistrict level of rural administration. Five commercial banks were located in the area. Functional literacy was 40 percent, which was the national average. There were 115 primary schools. In addition to that, there were thirteen middle schools and thirty-nine high schools, along with four bachelor-level colleges. There were also twenty-six Islamic schools. There were twenty-eight markets spread over the thana area that did brisk business on designated market days. Pirpur had eighteen registered clubs for social activities.[23]

Cycle-van drivers waiting for passengers. They had purchased these transportation vans with loads from NGOs.

Bamboo bridge for crossing streams. Streams and narrow rivers crisscross all over Pirpur, making some of the remote villages quite inaccessible.

My friend had started a regional microfinance NGO in Pirpur in 1996 to create employment for his relatives. His rural relatives would often come to him seeking jobs. Frustrated with their continuous demand for jobs, he decided to open an NGO in his village to "take care of the unemployment problems in his extended family" and "at the same time to help the poor." I have given the NGO the fictional name of Empowering the Poor (ETP).

He hired his nephew Tareque to run ETP. Tareque had been a BRAC manager for ten years. He had the management skills to build a new organization. In Pirpur, I stayed at the house of Tareque and his wife, Anowara. Tareque's paternal cousin, Rina, became my research assistant.[24] Tareque and his wife were high-status people in Pirpur Thana. Anowara was a primary school teacher. They had two small children, a son and a daughter. They lived in a brick house with electricity, running water, and many of the accoutrements of modern life—a television set, a refrigerator, and furniture.

The trip to Pirpur Thana from the capital city Dhaka was onerous, which prevented many researchers from visiting this area. One had to take a bus, then a ferry, and then another bus to get there. The wait at the ferry station was often between two to three hours. On a good day, the trip would take between eight to eleven hours. In Pirpur, Rina was my research partner. She was new to research but sharp and enthusiastic. She quickly picked up the details of her work. She was the primary breadwinner in her family. At the time of my research, Rina was a third-year college student. She lived with her widowed mother, one sister, and two brothers. She moved to her paternal cousin Tareque's house in Pirpur once we started the research.

Rina was from East Baligram, one of the villages I covered. The daughter of a well-respected schoolmaster, Rina came from Chowdhury Bari (a high-status kin group) in East Baligram. Her father had opened the first primary school there and was respected in their village. Following his death, the family moved to town. Her family was in financially straitened circumstances. After my departure from Pirpur, Rina joined the family NGO, ETP. My relationship with Rina was one of professional friendship and cordiality, but neither of us cultivated a personal friendship. I did ask Rina a few times about her personal life, but she did not want to divulge much, and although I mentioned several times that I would like to visit her mother and siblings, she never followed through on that.

In Pirpur, the category of the researcher was missing from the local vocabulary, but I encountered a different problem. When I said that I was writing a book on village life, the people would look at me curiously and ask, "Why?" The more market-savvy people asked me, "What is your benefit [they used the English term *benefit*] in finding out all this information? Who will pay you?" Even in Pirpur, local people saw information about rural society as a commodity. Most of the villagers thought that I was an NGO worker who had come to scope out the terrain in the hopes of opening a new NGO branch office. Moreover, I lived in the house of local NGO people, which also meant to them that I must be associated with an NGO in Dhaka.

In his ethnography of Grameen Bank, Aminur Rahman established a kin-like relationship as a new brother (natun bhai) in the village.[25] My approach was different. I entered rural social networks through honored members of rural society. Rina's and Tareque's families were prestigious families in Pirpur. Rina's family status and connections enabled her to gain the trust of rural people. Women would share information with Rina because they identified with her as one of their own. They would often call her "our daughter." Rina as a college student signified upward mobility. Many of the women who shared their stories wanted to help one of their own do better in life. Rina's family's status was the key to unlocking the life stories of the women. This was aided by the fact that ETP as a new microfinance institution was becoming known in the areas we traveled to. Many people had met Tareque and they had a positive reaction to him. The majority of the managers hired by the NGOs BRAC, Proshika, Grameen, and ASA were not linked by kin ties to the villages they worked in. This is a policy of the leading NGOs to prevent nepotism within their ranks. Because outsider male NGO officers work primarily with rural women, there is an uneasy relationship between them and men in these communities. To rural people, Tareque represented a local man who had returned to his village to help his own. There was goodwill toward him and his new organization during this time.

Rina would go to someone's home, begin the conversation with them, and later introduce me. We both took notes. On the way back to our house, we would share the subtler points of the conversation with the women, discussing who told the truth, who did not, why they would not talk to us, etc. Sometimes I would get dismayed and say to Rina, "They are not telling us the truth." Rina would laugh and say, "Don't worry, everything will come out." Without access to Rina's social networks and family status, it would have taken me much longer to uncover the stories that unfolded. Rina helped to facilitate an understanding with the women that I would come only if they desired to share their stories, and if it would not create tension between them and their families. While Rina's presence often helped to mute some of the embarrassment, it was still an acutely difficult process for me to participate in the conversations. Many times Rina and I left because it was not appropriate to ask further questions of a woman who had suffered humiliation because of her inability to repay.

The other person in Pirpur who provided me with a host of insider information was Tareque. Sometimes in the evenings, Tareque and I would discuss his experiences as a former manager of BRAC. Tareque's experience and his arbitration skills were sought by several junior NGO officials in his area. After their day's work, these NGO field-workers would drop by his house for advice. After my research began, Anowara, Rina, and Tareque often had heated discussions about women's empowerment. As the miracle stories of microfinance began to show their fractures (a point discussed in the following chapters), Anowara and Rina asked pointed questions of Tareque, who advocated microfinance policies. As these two women said, "We do not see how women are being empowered through loans."

Several young NGO field-workers would come to their house on a regular basis. These young men were amused by my attempts to discover what was going on. The relationship with these NGO field-workers was difficult to nurture because they often saw me as a thorn in their side. My comments to villagers often contradicted what they were doing in the villages. However, over time they came to trust me, or they became accustomed to my face suddenly appearing at a loan meeting. I think they finally realized that I was not intent on "sabotaging them" in front of the borrowers. At a certain point in our relationship, trust began to build up, and they shared some of their experiences with me.

Rural Women

My relationship with the women and the NGO field-workers was complicated. During the earlier phase of research, when I heard of NGO excesses in loan recovery tactics, I had asked villagers to organize to resist the oppressive behavior of NGOs. Some of the families facing the pressures of NGO loan recovery tactics reported to the field officers that "someone from the city" was going to take action against the NGOs. Some of the NGO officers became quite incensed with me and told their members, "Who is she? What can she do to us?" In the bazaar, I would come across NGO officers who would say that I was asking their clients questions without their approval or that I was working in their village. Following some of these exchanges, some of the women said to us, "Sir/Apa has told us not to talk to you." There were others who said, "We will talk to you if we want to. NGOs have not bought us with their money." When women did not want to talk to us, we would leave them alone. I did not visit the NGO offices of BRAC, ASA, Proshika, and Grameen until the end of my research, when I had gathered sufficient information about their work to ask them more pointed questions.

The social distinction between the women and myself was one of class and education. The women saw me as an urban and privileged woman who had come to their village. My class and cultural codes (mannerisms and language) set me apart, but I was a Bengali woman, like them. I spoke Bengali fluently. I could communicate with them, although there were those occasional moments when we failed to communicate because of differences in spoken dialects. I speak literary Bangla, which is the norm in my mother's family, and not Bangal, which is the dialect of East Bengal.[26] It made some of the women laugh and ask, "What did she say?" Rina would intervene by adding that I talked funny because I had lived abroad for so long. My hair was cut short, which looked strange to rural women. Rina helped resolve this awkwardness by telling the women that I had been sick, so my head had to be shaved. My body language and the way I looked, walked, and talked,

Women husking paddy.

was outside the acceptable conduct of rural comportment. Even in the traditional female attire of shalwar-kameez, Rina and Anowara remarked that I walked "like a man," and that I made direct eye contact with all men, including older men, which was socially unacceptable. I would talk to the men as easily as I would talk to the women. I was not aware of the negative impact of some of my behaviors until Rina pointed them out to me.

In rural Bangladesh, newcomers are introduced to the community through their natal or affinal links. The first question Bangladeshis ask upon meeting a stranger is, "Where is your village home?" This address helps to establish association by kin ties, even if many times removed. Since I was not a local woman who could be identified by her familial associations (daughter of the house of X), my credibility with the women was dubious. Did I have a husband? Where was he? What about my children? Moreover, being a single woman who had no children posed problems for me. Once, when I had decided to tell some women that I had a husband in America hoping that it would dispel some of the concerns they had about me, the women caught me off guard by asking, "Where is your nose ring?" The nose ring is the symbol of married female status in rural Bangladesh. When I told them that I was an urban woman and I did not wear a nose ring, they laughed and said, "That is what you say." After that incident, I decided to be honest and tell them that I was single, but this was not a satisfactory answer for many women. I depended on Rina to interject and guide the conversation toward the questions that we were trying to ask. Ultimately, it was my guest status with Tareque's family, a socially respected local family, that helped to ease the difficulties I faced as a single female and as an outsider to their community.

On another occasion, a young man who was traveling with me from Pirpur observed that I was an enigma (odbut) because I did not take the accepted steps of a Bengali woman's life—birth, marriage, and children. This resulted in a lively conversation between us, with me berating him for his narrow understanding of women's lives, and with him saying that "this is all that I have been exposed to." It was with middle-class people that I engaged in *adda*, a form of leisure and orality that Bengalis love, and a concept that I explain later. This informality created a space, especially for men, to ask me about my life in the United States, a place many of them were curious about and hoped to visit someday.

My not having a husband was a cause of friction with rural women, but I think that this and my not having children helped to level some of the class differences with rural middle-class women such as Anowara. One day Anowara came into my room and mentioned that she sometimes wanted to talk to me about "female matters." Then she said in an embarrassed tone, "How can I talk to you about these things? Alas, apa, you are unmarried." Anowara could identify with me through this expression of lack on my part. Despite our material and social differences, I lacked more than she did. Sitting across from each other on the bed, Anowara, a primary school teacher in Pirpur, had more symbolic capital than I did, a woman who was doing her doctoral studies in America. She had a husband and a son while I had neither. These were momentary occasions when our material and social distance was partially bridged.

However, my relationship with Anowara soured for a number of reasons. Anowara saw access to English education as the way to upward mobility for her children. She would often mention that her son's prospects were nil because he attended a village school. She wanted me to use my influence with her relative who had started ETP to find a job for her in the capital, so she could then enroll her daughter in an English-instruction school. While I did mention this to my friend in Dhaka, he disagreed because the point of opening ETP was to create rural employment. My failure to reciprocate and to successfully advocate for her child understandably caused her some annoyance. In Anowara's household, Rina had the status of a poor relative because of her family's lack of wealth. Rina did most of the housework. I once mentioned this to Anowara and that created a rift in our relationship.

Often after that, Anowara would complain in a high-pitched voice within my earshot that Rina was "becoming dark from walking in the sun doing work for Lamia Apa."

In another instance, I had communicated to my friend in Dhaka that ETP had engaged in oppressive behavior toward their borrowers by breaking the houses of defaulting members to recover money (I discuss this concept in the next chapter). This incensed my friend in Dhaka because he had given strict instructions to Tareque not to "break" houses of defaulting members. By exposing some hidden truths about ETP to its founder, I had breached Tareque's family trust, and Anowara was rightfully annoyed with me.

Ethnography and Survey

In the rural part of the research, I examined how microfinance loans circulated in the local economy and how different communities became connected in interdependent relationships through the circulation of money. I found that women members borrowed on average from between five to six NGOs (a pattern seen earlier with Shah), and that they borrowed from NGO A to pay NGO B, and so on. The women were becoming heavily indebted, but it was difficult to track how these continuous transactions took place. These circulations were complicated networks of loans being recycled through multiple groups. Although the women were becoming heavily indebted, many of them could forestall their bankruptcy in the interim by lending to traders, richer farmers, and to members of the rural middle class. This is because the need for capital far exceeded what these NGOs provided through their loan programs.

Toward the end of my research, I added a survey to make some of these circulations clearer. In the survey, I asked the following questions: total number of memberships in NGOs; years of NGO membership; what was the intended purpose of the loan money and what was it used for; who controlled the money (woman, husband, or other male relatives); the total amount borrowed from all NGOs; the total amount outstanding; whether they had to buy product tie-ins such as hybrid seeds or breeder chickens; whether there were any fees paid to the NGOs; and what categories was the money used in (agriculture, petty trade, repayment of prior debts, personal consumption, moneylending, dowry, health, and education). Since the expenses of these families were very little, the majority of the women could recall in what categories they had spent their money.

Rina conducted the survey over a period of one and a half months. She surveyed 158 households, which were all members of the four NGOs included in my research. The households were randomly chosen, and we covered women from seven villages (East and West Baligram, North and South Rajdi, Minajdi, Shikarmongol, and Gopalpur) spread over a ten-kilometer radius. Some of these villages were located in the countryside and were difficult to access; some were close to the town of Pirpur and its bazaar. On average, each survey took two hours to complete. Sometimes Rina had to go back two or three times to get some of the missing data. The survey information was collected while the women did their household chores. These women did not have the leisure to sit for two hours while someone filled out a questionnaire. I was present during some of the survey gathering, but for the most part I was absent. Following the completion of the survey, Rina and I went to the homes of the individual borrowers to ask more in-depth questions.

The survey was an addition to my ethnographic research, and it corroborated my ethnographic findings and offered data in the following areas: (1) primarily, men controlled the use of the loans, although their wives remained responsible for the loans; (2) the majority of the loans were not invested in productive activities, with most going into personal consumption; (3) new loans were used to pay back old debts; (4) women were members of multiple NGOs and borrowed at a ratio much higher than their income. Out of the 158 women surveyed, 96 said that they had used NGO loans to pay off old loans. Out of 158 households surveyed, only five women controlled the use of the money. In 142 cases, the husbands used the money. In ten cases the money was used jointly. In one case, a male relative used the money. And 110 women admitted to memberships in multiple NGOs.

Loan Amount (Taka)	Number of Borrowers
3000–5000	16
5000–10,000	20
10,000–20,000	21
20,000–50,000	37
50,000–75,000	25
75,000–100,000	36
>100,000	3
Total Borrowers	158

Loan amounts of the borrowers surveyed.

With the availability of increased microfinance, social relations were becoming monetarized, and most of the borrowers engaged in some form of moneylending. An interesting subject formation that resulted from extensive moneylending was that of the female moneylender, known as *chhoto mahajan*, that I discuss in the following chapter. I found that the women who lived closer to the market used the money themselves or were intensively engaged in moneylending. Anthropologist Fernando, who did his research in Tangail, found that petty traders were the beneficiaries of the loans through moneylending and proxy membership.[27]

When I conducted the survey among the women in the village, I found that many did not say that they were moneylenders. Yet, I knew that the majority of these women were engaged in moneylending. For these Muslim women there was embarrassment associated with openly confessing to usury, a Quranic prohibition. When I pointed out that a neighbor or trader had told me that they had lent them money, the women termed it help (shahajya). In their worldview, they saw moneylending as acts of goodwill. They did not self-identify as moneylenders, and hence they did not break any Islamic injunction against usury. Had I looked at the survey as "scientific" data, I would have noted that there was no moneylending among the women borrowers, but as an ethnographer, I came to different conclusions about the hermeneutics of moneylending within a community of Muslim women.

Urban Setting

The urban component of my research was conducted in NGO offices, seminars, conferences, and conversations with activists, scholars, and researchers. In Bangladesh, social reputation is critical, and one's access to knowledge is built through status-based connections. If one is introduced to members of a community as the honored guest or as the relative of a well-regarded person, access to the hidden transcripts becomes a less formidable task. My access to rural communities became possible through honored members in these communities who introduced me and facilitated conversations. In the capital, Dhaka, I was able to use my family's connections to access many people.

My reception by the local intellectual/researcher was typically expressed as goodwill tinged with ambivalence. My late father was a well-known sociologist at Dhaka University, but his prestige had also brought him a fair share of detractors. He was the professor of many of the people I encountered in the field. So, I took on the identity of the daughter of their former professor in the eyes of some of these people. My relationship with them was negotiated through their memory of my father. While my father's name opened many doors, it also closed others. But overall, I received a cordial reception by most people.

Initially I sought Western norms of research, an established form of documented evidence, whereas the local norms of research were based on the status of the interlocutor. In a face-to-face community, oral discourse is an important form of interlocution. In order to be accepted as "one of us," the researcher must have time to participate in endless *adda* sessions. Adda is a male-dominated discourse. It is an art of speaking that is cultivated by the Bengali bourgeois class.[28] Addas usually happen in the evening over tea and fritters in someone's house or in a clubhouse. The ability to participate in addas is essential in conducting cultural analysis of Bengalis. In this male-dominated adda space, I was spoken to rather than asked for my opinions. As a silent listener, I became privy to fragments of conversation, which became an important mode of investigating what counted as "valid knowledge" in this culture.

I examined opinion pieces and unpublished papers presented at conferences as part of the local archive of development knowledge. The vernacular press is a rich source of the critiques of NGOs and development, a site that is often overlooked by foreign researchers, many of whom do not read or write in Bengali. Bangladeshi intellectuals assume roles as public intellectuals. They regularly write opinion pieces in newspapers and journals for a wider audience, and many of them speak at public events. Moreover, Bangladeshi intellectuals often present papers at local NGO conferences that they do not publish because intellectual recognition is not necessarily authorized through the Western route of the publishing industry. This is a different way of producing knowledge. Encyclopedic knowledge is what is valued in Bangladeshi society, and the status of the interlocutor is very important. In keeping with this model of the public intellectual, knowledge is not based on citation and scholarly publication, but on one's ability to hold forth on a topic for a sustained period of time in a public forum.[29] These public events are remembered, discussed, and debated by the gathered people in their discourses on knowledge.

Discursive Notions of Gender

Now that the reader has an introduction to the process of my fieldwork, let me turn the discussion to a consideration of rural society and some of the social relations, norms, and concepts that were important in guiding my investigation. Bangladeshi social life is based on patron–client relations. The rural economy is agrarian with medium-sized landlords, small holdings, and a large number of sharecroppers. The latter are dependent on a reciprocal relationship with the richer farmers. The manners of social life in rural Bangladesh conform to Scott's observation that "virtually every instance of personal domination is intimately connected with a process of appropriation. Dominant elites extract material taxes in the form of labor, grain, cash, and service in addition to extracting symbolic taxes in the form of deference, demeanor, posture, verbal formulas, and acts of humility . . . figuratively, a ritual subordination."[30]

The traditional patron–client relationship has been challenged by the incursion of developmental NGOs into the rural economy. In fact, NGOs are the modern landlords in rural society. These existing clientelist relations have been appropriated by NGOs in their practices to create social demarcations. NGOs have the power to grant loans, goods, services to millions, and jobs to the rural middle class. NGO offices have the symbols of power and influence. While NGOs seek to bring capitalist modernity to rural society, analyzing their patterns will show that they invoke hierarchical relations with their rural clients. NGO officers often tell rural people that they eat NGO rice by taking loans, and hence they are morally obligated to repay the money. Rice is the staple of the Bengali diet. They also say that one should respect the NGO as much as one's parents. Not only does the invocation of a discourse of filial duties infantilize poor people, but it also contains within it the notion of sacrifice, which the borrower must show toward its new fatherlike benefactor, the NGO. There were many stories of NGO officers who had told their borrowers that NGO loan payments had to be paid before they buried a dead child, statements that are not only unethical but violate all Islamic norms concerning burial.[31]

Rural social life is made up of the patrilineage (gusti), homestead (bari), and neighborhood (para).[32] Gusti is the anthropological term for patrilineage of groups of men who are agnatically related and who live in physical proximity. The neighborhood in a village is usually made of several patrilines. The eldest male relative takes on the role of the elder of the patriline. He conducts all legal matters, dispute settlements, marriages, divorces, and other exchanges on behalf of the patriline. In social discourse, people first name their village as a place of identification and kinship, followed by neighborhood and lineage. Hence, a person will introduce himself in public by the following: "I am X, son of so and so, from Gopalpur (village) and belong to Chowdhury Bari (the Chowdhury lineage)."

Gender roles, while undergoing gradual shifts, are specialized in rural Bangladesh. Within the homestead, women are barred from areas where non-kin men may have congregated. Men work in primary agricultural activities, while women participate in secondary agricultural activities, mostly within the home. Men have the responsibility of "attending to activities relating to the market or those that occur outside of the home."[33] Women care for the children and manage the daily running of the household. Major decisions with regard to the education of children, investment in business, and health expenses are usually the domain of men.[34]

The notion of *purdah* as a metaphor for the proper conduct of women in public places organizes rural discourse. Purdah refers to the seclusion of women within the household, and this usually happens in higher-income families, or in public places through the observation of female bodily comportment. Although Bangladeshi rural women seldom wear the burqa (the head-to-toe covering) in public, they conduct themselves with propriety: they keep their eyes downcast, voices low, hair tied, heads covered with the edge of their saris, and they avoid eye contact with non-kin men.[35] There are two types of women who do not wear the burqa when traveling outside the home, the poor and the modern. Poor women cannot afford the expense of a burqa. It would also constrain them from the physical work they have to do to earn a living. As for the modern woman in rural society, she may have "a preference to participate in activities outside the home," and she has been influenced by the norms of urban female behavior.[36]

The concept of purdah, or the seclusion of women, in Bangladesh is complicated by regional variations. If there is a prominent *madrassah* or a charismatic religious Islamic leader in the area, the women practice the more visible forms of purdah, such as veiling themselves in public and avoiding public spaces. The women of sharecropper households cannot afford to observe purdah. Purdah for lower-income women is a mode of physical and moral conduct. The physical aspect of purdah is the proper comportment of their bodies in public. Spiritual purdah is the purity in thought and actions. It is the spiritual aspect that structures the notion of purdah for poor women who do not have the material means to observe the seclusion practices of the upper classes. The notions of honor and shame are further complicated by the fact that in a face-to-face society, one's private conduct is public knowledge. Although the private and public spheres are separated through physical boundaries, and the women are segregated in upper-class families, it is the women who are the guardians of private life. Older women strictly enforce the rules of sexual and social contact among younger women. Women are privy to the complicated intimacies of private lives, forms of knowledge they use toward the improvement of their own lives within the extended family.

Maneuvering within the rigidity of the patriarchal family structure, older women maintain their authority and power within the household by ensuring that younger women comply with the rules of female behavior. In rural society, women's physical mobility is restricted, and their conduct is carefully monitored.[37] Older female members act as the guards who closely monitor the goings-on of younger women, and women who breach the rules are immediately punished. Despite these stiff regulations, women in rural Bangladesh create their own avenues of "freedoms" by breaking, challenging, and mutating these restrictions. Some of them stay out late, are seen in and around town, and speak to non-kin men. Such trespassing women were referred to as *mukh chalu* (forward or outspoken), that is, women whose mouths are loose; they speak too much, and they are forward in their behavior.

Cultural Meanings of Credit

Although Bangladesh is the heartland of microfinance, there is no linguistic equivalent for the word *credit* in Bengali. Rural people use the term *reen* (loan) to speak of credit. In colloquial Bengali, the word that comes closest in meaning to credit is the word *baki*, that is, the purchase of goods based on social knowledge and familiarity. The closest English translation of baki is due. These transactions take place in situations in which the borrower and the lender know each other, and usually involve small sums of money. The lender knows when the borrower will receive money, and he extends goods based on social knowledge.

One common term for purchase in advance is *agam*. Another term used to describe a credit relationship is *dhaar*, which means to loan or to borrow. To loan or borrow is based on the concept of trust and on a social relationship between lender and borrower. Traditionally, it did not involve any interest on the amount lent. Another related phrase that is no longer in common usage is *korjo hashana*, which means good work. It refers to the extension of loans without interest. In Muslim societies, korjo hashana was considered an act of piety. It is not surprising, thus, that this concept has fallen into disuse both linguistically and practically.[38]

Bangladeshi anthropologist Mannan distinguishes between two uses of money in rural Bangladesh—moral and immoral—that borrow their meanings from the Quran.[39] Immoral money is the money that circulates in the public domain and is used to lend, mortgage, buy, and sell products, and it is the money that has become contaminated by charging interest (riba). Interest payment on trade or a loan is forbidden in the Quran. Moral money is money that is donated (daan) to benefit public works, mosques, and the poor. It is the proper use of money toward improving the lives of poorer Muslims and keeping with the notion of *zaqat*, one of the pillars of Islam.[40]

Mannan goes on to note that there are two common sayings among rural people: "If you donate money, your money will grow from divine blessings" (Taka daan korle bhu-gone borkot hoi), and "One must donate to the poor because they have a religious right to the money of the rich" (Goribder daan korte hoi, dhonir Takar upor oder hoq ache).[41]

Poor women are unable to donate. So, the loans these women extended to other needy women were conceptualized as a form of donation by them. When one lends to another in times of distress, there is not only an obligation to pay back at some point in the future, but also an obligation of moral indebtedness to the person for the help one received. It is in this sense that the women moneylenders made sense of their practice of usury as a form of help or shahajya. By helping fellow human beings, they remained faithful Muslims.

The Discourse of Shame

In rural Bangladesh, men and women use the terms honor/faith (maan/imaan) and shame (lajja/sharm) in their daily discourse. The notion of maan is linked to the notion of imaan for Muslims, which means faith and piety. A Muslim has imaan (faith) and is a keeper of the word of Allah, and the faithful does not break her or his word of honor. To do so would mean that a Muslim breaks the covenant with Allah. The notion of faith for Muslims is suffused with the idea of upholding the honor of one's religion, Islam. This becomes more urgent in a landscape saturated by loans, because in Islam it is mandatory to pay back all of one's worldly debts prior to death.[42]

The notions of honor/shame are gender specific and denote subtle social hierarchies in the community. Women have shame (lajja/sharm) and men possess honor/respect (maan/shamman). Women speak of their honor as possessing shame. Shame is considered as a desirable attribute because it regulates conduct and prevents members from breaking the norms of rural society. This is particularly true for women. The terms for honor denote masculine values, and they signify one's ability to protect the patriline, the family, and one's women from dishonor. In speaking to outsiders, women and men often invoke these terms to describe their "essential" humanity, goodness, and faith as Muslims. The poor may be poor, but they are more favored by Allah because of their piety, humanity, and honor. Moreover, the poor keep their word: they do not break their covenant with Allah. Implicit in these discourses of spirituality is the embedded notion of class, and a reference to the lack of entitlements due to poverty.

While the discourse of shame is manifest in social discourse in rural society, shame as a category is mutable. The processes of shaming—who can shame whom, what counts as shame, and under what conditions is shaming possible—are continuously shifting and being rewritten. What was considered shameful a decade ago has over time become normalized and routinized. It is no longer shameful for women to be visible in public places, to conduct business, or to talk to non-kin men. I witnessed instances in which women would publicly humiliate a man for his failure to repay the loan money. This was socially acceptable female behavior because in this encounter the man was seen as breaching a financial contract in his inability to pay. These are new forms of public behavior for women, and in some instances, they grant individual women power and authority. In the past, Grameen Bank was called the Beggar's Bank (Fokirnir Bank), and joining it meant a lowering of one's status. During my research, I heard people call it the Loan Bank (Kistir Bank). It had lost much of its former social stigma, and middle-class women enthusiastically joined these NGOs to access capital. A friend recently sent me a popular ditty about BRAC, which translated to "Get yourself a BRAC or two, party and feast all day long" (ekta, duta BRAC dhoro, shokal shonda nasta koro). As the ditty shows, in popular culture, these institutions are now seen as ways to enrich oneself, and no longer as stigmatized institutions associated with the poor.

In conceptualizing my frame, I found that loans from NGOs circulated within a grid made up of kin and local elites. Loans with their accompanying obligations (whom to give them to, how much to give, what interest to charge, what payment schedule to agree upon, etc.) impinged on the interlocking grids of kinship and community relations that I have outlined here, and they were determined by, and determinants of, those relationships. Breaching a debt obligation resulted in far-reaching consequences for the individual borrower as well as the community integrated into these loan circulations. Microfinance loans circulated not merely as contractual obligations that must be met but also as social obligations within a wider field of reciprocities that hold rural societies together. In the next chapters,

I examine the multiple manifestations of microfinance, as women caught inside loans and debt obligations maneuver within a field intersected by the flows of neoliberal ideas, NGO governmentality, the economy of shame, and the obligations to their families and community.

Chapter 3   **The Everyday Mediations of Microfinance**

AS THE NGO sector expanded in the twenty-first century, Bangladeshi NGOs have diversified into financial services and social business enterprises (SBEs) in telecommunications, Internet services, solar energy, and packaged foods. As discussed in chapter 1, the Grameen Bank and the leading NGOs have created a consumer base made up of millions of poor borrowers and their families that remains dependent on these institutions for loans, jobs, and services that are channeled through the NGO sector. NGO governmentality operates through a careful exploitation of this relationship of dependency with their borrowers at the grassroots. Chapters 3 and 4 examine how these markets and market subjects are created through the work of NGOs and microfinance lending.

As the landscape of microlending has developed, the rules and norms that guided the conduct of microfinance institutions have changed, becoming standardized and operationalized among Grameen, BRAC, ASA, and Proshika. I introduce the reader to these changes below.[1]

First, there was a manifold increase in the number of NGO borrowers. Grameen Bank went from 2.7 million in 1998 to almost 7 million borrowers in 2007, a number that continues to grow to date. Second, the loan amounts have been dramatically increased. At the time of my research, the average amount of the loan was 5,000 taka. In 2007, these NGOs offered multiple categories of loans, and the average amount for a microenterprise loan was between 50,000 taka ($746) to 300,000 taka ($4,477).[2] In comparison, during my research, only three women in my survey of 158 had loans worth over 100,000 taka ($1,492 at 2007 figures). Third, the primary focus of these institutions was now on business enterprises, instead of their earlier focus on social programs. For example, Proshika had cut social programs in nonformal primary education, adult literacy, and cultural activities due to withdrawal of donor support. Finally, to make their organizations competitive to the borrower in terms of cost, these NGOs had all calibrated their interest rates close to 10 percent.[3]

Another area in which all these institutions had consolidated was in the loan-repayment schedules. The length of time to repay loans had been reduced from fifty-two weeks to between forty-four and forty-six weeks (Grameen, forty-four weeks; BRAC and ASA, forty-five weeks; and Proshika, forty-six weeks). A reduction of six to eight weeks resulted in intense pressure on poor borrowers, who had a shorter period within which to repay the loan at higher weekly installments.

The increase in loan amounts was quite stunning given that rural people's incomes had remained relatively flat. Loan amounts were increased due to the profusion of microfinance money in the 2000s, but also in an attempt to keep "worthy" clients from borrowing from multiple sources. Yet, my conversations with borrowers and NGO workers in 2007 revealed that borrowers continued to borrow from numerous sources, and they borrowed from one source to pay off another, a cycle that deepened during adverse economic times.[4] The significant development within these NGOs is the increased targeting of the middle-class borrowers, such as richer traders and farmers, a process I identified in my research in 1999. As loan amounts have expanded and new commodities—such as cell phones, packaged foods, and Internet services—are offered, a richer class of borrowers is sought. With the expansion of financial services that require more financially robust clients to bolster the profit margin, these NGOs continue to withdraw from skills training and literacy programs, adversely affecting poor women in their ability to negotiate the market.

Social Businesses: Grameen Danone and Polli Phone

As noted earlier, microlending is closely linked to neoliberal development. In his Nobel acceptance speech, Professor Yunus redefined the model of poverty eradication as one based primarily on private ownership. In this worldview, nothing is free, and everything from water to education to healthcare is regulated by the rules governing the free market. In his writings, Yunus has made it his goal to send poverty to the museums.[5]

> Almost all social and economic problems of the world will be addressed through social businesses. The challenge is to innovate business models and apply them to produce desired social results cost-effectively and efficiently. Healthcare for the poor, financial services for the poor, information technology for the poor, education and training for the poor, marketing for the poor, renewable energy—these are all exciting areas for social business.[6]

Through the careful execution of this neoliberal ideology, nothing is free, and everyone is a potential entrepreneur; it is not "poverty" but the entitlements of citizens that are being sent to the "museum." Socially responsible business combines "maximizing profit" with "doing good to people in the world" as mutually reinforcing instrumentalities. These new businesses signify moralism in development—a benign relationship between capital and altruism as multinational corporations target communities to generate profit, and concurrently, help the poor with income and social opportunities. In order to implement this diktat, Yunus's bank has been at the forefront of promoting socially responsible businesses. Below I discuss two social businesses, Grameen Danone and Grameen Polli (Village) Phone.

Grameen Danone

In 2006, Grameen Bank and Danone Corporation of France entered into a partnership with a 1-million-euro investment to produce a highly fortified yogurt in Bangladesh. In 2007, it introduced Shaktidoi, an energy yogurt that provides 30 percent of the nutritional requirements of a child. The Grameen Danone plant has created a chain link of people who are connected to yogurt production: Grameen cow owners who sell their milk to the plant, plant employees, and sales ladies whose earnings are from the sale of yogurt to rural customers. These sales ladies are assigned territories in Grameen Bank centers, at which borrowers gather weekly to repay their loan installments to the bank officer. The idea was that the fortified yogurt would bring health benefits to poor children, and profit to Grameen and the Danone Corporation. By targeting women borrowers who usually have some disposable cash on loan collection day, Grameen Danone has carved out a captive consumer base for their product among the clients of Grameen Bank. Similarly, the bank officer present could also exhort these women to buy a Grameen-owned product that would improve their children's health.

Yet, at 6 taka (9 cents) for a sixty-gram container, the yogurt was priced beyond the capacity of a poor family's subsistence income. A typical poor rural family of five has a daily average income anywhere between 125 and 200 taka ($1.86–2.98) based on the economic activity they are engaged in. The family's subsistence is around 60 taka (less than a $1) per day for cereal consumption, which in the past was supplemented by foraging for firewood, fish, and vegetables on public lands and water bodies. In recent years, these properties have become privatized (a point I discussed in chapter 1), which poses a serious threat to the livelihoods of economically marginal people. At this income level, a parent would have to pay 18 taka (27 cents) per day to meet the children's daily requirements of vitamins and minerals from Shaktidoi.

Failing to recover its costs by selling to the poor, Grameen Danone began to target the urban middle class at a higher price in 2009. While its penetration in Bangladesh was motivated by a social business concern of providing healthy food to the poor, Danone had not ruled out the possibility of conducting business the conventional way, that is, by making profits from the sale of its yogurt.[7] Although Bangladesh is a desperately poor country, its middle class of 20 million has modern consumption needs. Whether by design or accident, it is this group that has become the consumers of the yogurt.

If one reads Professor Yunus's *Creating a World without Poverty*, it becomes evident that these ideas are hammered out as corporate deals behind the scenes, and then presented to the women and the public as innovations in bringing income-generating opportunities to women.[8] In chapter 7 of his book *Creating a World without Poverty*, Yunus devotes three pages to the comments made by Guy Gavelle, industrial director of Danone Dairy–Asia Pacific in front of the first generation of yogurt sales ladies. Only two brief paragraphs are devoted at the end of that chapter to the women who discuss the lack of spoons to eat the yogurt—and the solution is for Grameen Danone to sell plastic spoons for fifty Bangladeshi pennies each! This is offered as an illustration of open dialogue between management and its female sales force. Interestingly, none of these women discuss whether poor rural families that have between three and five children will have the capacity to purchase these cups of yogurt, what should be the price of the yogurt, whether selling the plastic spoons at an additional charge is a marketable idea, or how often rural families will consume an item considered a luxury, questions that should be of paramount interest to any group of salespeople. Yunus closes this discussion by offering the final word to a woman whose voice is heard only once. She endorses the yogurt to say, "We all had a chance to taste this yogurt, we like it. . . . This is going to be a popular product."[9] I do not have to remind the reader that this woman's voice is managed and scripted by Grameen officials.

Grameen Polli Phone

In the creation of these new markets that target poor people in the developing world, "wireless telephony is one of the most rapidly expanding ICTSs (Information and Communication Technologies) worldwide."[10]

The Grameen Polli Phone program has generated tremendous enthusiasm among NGOs, corporations, and individual investors alike. It has been replicated in Uganda and Rwanda. In his visit to Bangladesh in 2000, former president Bill Clinton remarked, "I want my fellow Americans to know that the people of Bangladesh are a good investment. With loans to buy cell phones, entire villages are brought into the information age."[11] These are exhilarating images of an information-based society built by entrepreneurial rural women.

In Grameen literature, the access to cell phone technology is recast as access to economic and social opportunities, and Bangladeshi women are manufactured as the paradigmatic entrepreneurs of telephony. These transactions between buyer and producer are crafted as a seamless exchange between demand and supply.

> [Grameen's village telephone program] offers a relatively inexpensive model for connectivity and with it, access to the world's information resources for populations that were hitherto isolated and information poor. It reminds us, too, that empowered by only voice connectivity people can and will take advantage of information to better their lives and improve their economic situations.[12]

According to this script, the farmers make a phone call to find out the price of rice in different local markets, and then make the rational decision to sell it at the highest price. Yet, what is not revealed is whether the farmer has the means—social, monetary, and infrastructural—to get to the town where rice is selling at a higher rate. "Neoliberal policy constructs people in poor countries as 'entrepreneurs' who simply had to bring their wares to 'the global market'—often via the Internet."[13] There is no doubt that telephony has provided rural people with access to information. But it is equally important to consider whether access to information technology by itself is the leveler of other inequities within which these social relations are inscribed. The existing research on Grameen phone ladies tends to focus on outcomes measured in incomes, and it construes the women as willing entrepreneurs. These studies do not analyze how Grameen Phone sets prices of phone services and how these loans are recovered from the borrowers.[14]

The Grameen Polli Phone program began in 1997. Polli Phone is a subsidiary of Grameen Phone, of which Telenor, the Norwegian telecommunications giant, owns 62 percent and Grameen Telecom, which is a not-for-profit subsidiary of the Grameen family of enterprises, owns

38 percent.[15] In 2006, the company received 19 percent of its profit from its Polli phone ladies.[16] While this high rate of profit is recast as the entrepreneurial potential of these phone ladies, one could equally ask why the cell phones were sold at such high prices to rural clients. At their initial offering, the phones were priced at $390.[17]

In its early years, the Grameen Polli Phone was an extremely lucrative venture. Poor borrowers could only purchase the phones by taking loans from Grameen, hence increasing the profit base for the bank. The program largely benefited the Grameen Bank, which had a profit of $110 million in 2002.[18] However, by 2005, the revenues had leveled off with the incursion of cheaper cell phone services in rural areas.[19] In my conversations with Grameen cell phone operators in 2007, all of them noted that although they had initially benefitted from renting out the phones, increased competition from other companies had dried up their profits. This led to many women giving up their cell phone business.

In a news story, BBC reported that the number of Grameen phone ladies shrank from 300,000 to 210,000, a decline of almost 30 percent in 2008. While income for these phone ladies may have leveled off, Grameen Phone subscribers had climbed to 21 million, which helped the company achieve "a staggering 68 percent profits," posted in 2008. This 21-million-strong group includes middle-class and urban subscribers. Grameen Phone is set to sell 65 million worth of shares in an initial public offering (IPO).[20] Given this scenario of women's loss and the corporation's gains, more independent research on the women and Grameen Phone needs to be conducted to evaluate how rural women were instantiated as "entrepreneurs" into the making of this highly profitable company. These economic arrangements between corporations and NGOs have consolidated and entrenched the microfinance lending practices that were set in place in the 1990s.

The Grameen Bank Model of Microcredit

The story of microcredit begins with the Grameen Bank of Bangladesh.[21] The Grameen Bank (or Rural Bank) was started in 1976 by a local economist in Bangladesh, Professor Muhammad Yunus.[22] The Grameen Bank model is centered on poor women's income-generating potential as entrepreneurs. It supports group formation, mandates group responsibility for individual payments, and enforces strict fiscal control and peer pressure in loan recoveries. In its early days, a technical determinism shaped the interactions between the bank and its borrowers through the recitation of the Sixteen Decisions that emphasized capitalist norms of individualism, hard work, discipline, hygiene, and savings. However, by the time I did my research, this model had been largely abandoned at the local level, although it existed as rhetoric.

In 1979, the Bank relocated its offices from Chittagong to Tangail, a relatively prosperous town close to the capital city, Dhaka. Tangail is the center of the weaving community in Bangladesh. By targeting weavers who had disposable income, and who could therefore pay the weekly installments on time, the Bank was able to show quick results in its loan recovery program to its potential backers. It was this success in high repayments that led to its formalization as a bank for the poor under the banking rules of Bangladesh Bank in 1983. At the time of its formalization as a bank, Grameen Bank received financial assistance from the Ford Foundation to the amount of $800,000. The International Fund for Agricultural Development (IFAD) gave a loan of $3.4 million, which was matched by a loan offered by the Bangladesh Central Bank.[23]

In 1979, Grameen membership had stood at 28,000, only 11,000 of whom were women.[24] When in the 1970s gender became tied to aid programs worldwide through the U.S. Percy Amendment and the United Nations Decade for Women (1975), the Bank was able to capitalize on rural women as its beneficiaries. From their initial field operations, Bank officers had recognized the difficulties they faced with male borrowers. The men who worked during the day were unable to attend their mandatory weekly meetings, and it was difficult to force them to pay on time. Rural men also recognized the need of loans in their occupations. This mutual recognition by both parties led to a tacit agreement between the Bank and rural men to let women be the bearers of loans while the rural men remained the primary users of the money lent. Bank officials found the women were more pliant and easier to work with. This gentleman's handshake fed into global gender initiatives and helped the Bank to reinvent itself as a bank for poor women.

The Bank operated on the following principles.[25] Forty women formed a Center, which was housed in a female member's house. The women had to locate a member from their group who was willing to provide the space voluntarily for the Bank's weekly meetings. The meeting place was called a *kendro ghar* (center). In the financial culture promoted by the Grameen Bank, nothing was free for these women. If members wanted to have a roof or any other facility in their center, they had to raise the money themselves. These forty women formed smaller groups of five women that made a total of eight groups within the center. Each week, the women met in the center and handed over their weekly installments (kisti) of the loan to the bank officer who collected the money.[26]

The women elected a leader for the group, chosen among themselves, called the group leader (kendro prodhan). The role of the group leader was to maintain group fiscal responsibility, discipline, and attendance at the weekly meetings. The group leader made loan proposals on behalf of the members of her group to the Bank officer. Her role regularized a strict line of accountability and hierarchy within the group. These rules created an authority figure within the group of women that the Bank officials could hold accountable. In his research, Rahman found that women from dominant lineages in the village became the leaders within the group and controlled the resources.[27]

The loans, usually between $100 and $200, were given for a year on a fixed interest rate of 20 percent (1998 figures).[28] According to a 1995 World Bank study, high interest rates have resulted in the Bank achieving near self-sufficiency.[29] The actual interest rate paid by the Grameen borrower included hidden costs of group fee, mandatory savings, entrance fees, cancellation fees, and agricultural loans that came with product tie-ins (packets of hybrid seeds) that raised the rate to a much higher de facto rate.[30] But despite these hidden costs, the interest charged was much

Women borrowers calculating loan payments.

lower than the prevailing rate charged by rural moneylenders, which stood at 120 percent. According to the director of Credit Development Forum (CDF), members themselves subsidized almost 35 percent of the NGO loan fund.[31]

Although the Bank claims that it does not require a collateral, there were three types of unstated collateral written into their practices: (1) built-in financial safeguards; (2) the community as fiscal enforcers; and (3) the instrumentalization of shame as a loan recovery technology. For Grameen Bank management, the individual savings account and the group fund acted as safeguards against potential defaults. While on paper Grameen borrowers could withdraw their money any time, I found from borrowers that they could not withdraw their savings at will. If they wanted to leave the bank voluntarily, they had to find creditworthy members to take their place before they could access their savings. All borrowers were mandatorily required to put "0.5 percent of every unit borrowed into an emergency fund" to be disbursed in times of death or natural calamities, and an additional 5 percent of the loan into a group fund account.[32] Members were not allowed to withdraw these enforced savings even after quitting the Bank. After 1995, withdrawals were allowed, but only after the Bank had recovered all outstanding debt.[33] Some of these rules have been relaxed in recent years.

According to NGOs, peer monitoring is the care that each individual member of a group of women supposedly takes when they become jointly responsible for the loans. Brigg identified the NGO loan center as the dense gathering of the hierarchies of the Bank and its disciplinary technology. Brigg suggested that "the operation of power is more diffused as microcredit recipients go about their daily lives, the loan center is the site where the lines of force of the disciplinary technology of Grameen microcredit are gathered together and are most dense."[34] However, my research suggests that the practices of daily life are the sites of dense supervision and surveillance, as individual group members monitor each other constantly to safeguard their financial investments. NGO governmentality is exercised against individual women through the capillaries of the community. This has led to a proliferation of social disciplinary technologies, with poor women policing each other, notifying managers of defaults and problems, and evicting probable defaulters from the group. Thus, NGO peer monitoring in reality performs as the policing of women by women. The women occupy the subjectivities of auditors and enforcers of NGOs, becoming their eyes and ears, and act as the financial police of the NGOs.

By keeping daily surveillance of its women members through others in the group, I found that women routinely reported to managers about individual women and their families regarding behaviors that would breach their financial obligations to the Bank. The women notified the managers when they found out that someone's husband had a drinking problem, or was cohabitating with a second wife in another village, or that the family consumed excessively by rural standards. More financially able women also evicted poorer members from the group because they feared that they would default in the future. These acts of telling on one's neighbors have been reported in some BRAC and Grameen Bank studies as instances of women becoming empowered and fighting patriarchal norms within their communities.[35] Yet, these behaviors are not as innocent as they appear. They often become toxically synergistic with kin and financial obligations, and produce effects that are contradictory to the stated goals of these NGOs of "helping the poorest women." I found that these micropractices of surveillance resulted in increased strife and antagonisms among the women borrowers and between them and the wider community, a fact that I analyze through case studies in chapter 4. In the following pages, I examine the transforming rural landscape that has become densely mediated by NGO loans and new rules of conduct exhibited by all groups of people brought inside the practice of microlending.

Routinization of Microcredit Operations

Increased competition among various NGOs for creditworthy members had forced them to dispense with background checks, relax their rules and regulations, and increase the amount and number of loans. This led to serious membership overlap, as the Badal Shah case showed in the previous chapter. In my research area, at least 50 percent of the borrowers belonged to more than one NGO. Many women belonged to five or six NGOs. Often women borrowed from one NGO to pay off another. The emphasis on microcredit as the model of development had increased the pressure on NGO officers from their headquarters to fill their quota of new members.[36] Thus, NGOs abandoned their earlier model of reaching out to the poor, and instead focused on members who were moderately rich, and therefore, less risky. In Pirpur, ASA, in operation for only two years, had begun to give loans to rural merchants and the middle class to increase its member rolls with less risky borrowers. The fact that microfinance NGOs have turned to richer clients to reduce their risks has been well documented in more recent studies.[37]

Often, richer women would hire poorer women to act as proxy members. A large number of poor women had become professional proxy members, joining as many NGOs as possible to get loans. The job of these poor women was to travel from one NGO meeting to another to collect loans on behalf of their richer clients. The members would get the loans in their names, and transfer the money to the person who had hired them. The fee these women charged was a small sum, usually around 100 taka ($2). In some instances, they could keep the savings that accrued through NGO savings plans. In 1998, this amount was usually between 2 and 5 takas on every 100 takas. So, a loan of 5,000 taka would come to 250 taka in savings. The NGOs paid between 7 and 8 percent simple interest on the members' savings funds. The government interest on savings accounts was 12 percent in 1998. NGOs predominated in rural life, to the extent that some women borrowers remembered days of the week by calling, for example, Monday BRAC day, Tuesday Grameen Day, and so on.

Grameen Bank and BRAC had a list of social awareness issues that their members were required to learn and recite at the beginning of each meeting. For example, women at the Grameen and BRAC meetings I visited no longer recited the Sixteen Decisions (Grameen) or the Seventeen Rules (BRAC). When I mentioned this fact to the field-worker, he made them perform for me, but many of the women no longer remembered the rules; they had to be prompted. I found that newer members had never learned these rules in the first place. In some of the loan meeting centers, the processing was focused on financial transactions. The women wanted to hand over the money and return home to do their housework, and the officer was busy counting the money. If all transactions went smoothly—that is, if everyone was able to pay without a hitch—he would pack up and leave for the second loan meeting place.

At the field level, I observed that the field-workers of these NGOs had little time to devote to training or to other social issues, although on paper all these NGOs claim to do so. The field-workers spent the bulk of their time distributing and recovering loans. While NGOs like Grameen, BRAC, and Proshika claim that they teach and organize their borrowers against gender discriminatory social practices—such as dowry, multiple marriages, abandonment of married women, maintenance, custody over children, and spousal abuse (mandates set up by donor countries)—I found very little evidence of such programs in the villages. In his research, Fernando found that the local field officer had only spoken about skills training and empowerment twice in five years of service, once during training and then with researchers such as him.[38]

At the Grameen offices I visited, the processing of loans was routinized. The women borrowers were all asked the same five questions. The transaction took the following format, with a bank official prompting the borrower when she forgot her rehearsed lines on the loan application's purpose.[39] The following five questions were asked in sequence: What is your name? What is your husband's name? What is the loan for? What is the loan amount? How much is the loan installment? And then the money was handed over. The speedy disbursements of loan requests indicated the bureaucratization of microfinance itself, with little time or incentive for managers to oversee what the borrowers did with the loans.

NGOs in Rural Society

In Pirpur, Grameen was very strict about timely collections and maintained a tight control over fiscal discipline. Grameen officials noted that lax behavior would be taken advantage of by poor people, and they did not allow late payments to accumulate. Local people had their own script of these organizations in terms of their oppression of rural people. Grameen was termed "ruthless" when it came to loan collection, and borrowers paid Grameen

Manager with BRAC women borrowers at a meeting.

Women at a Grameen center.

before they paid the other NGOs. BRAC was second in terms of applying pressure to recover loans. BRAC employees were described as the most "rude people, who used vulgar language" in their interactions with the borrowers. Proshika was a poorly managed organization in my area. Many of their former field-workers had been fired for misappropriation of funds and for a large number of defaults. Consequently, they had resorted to police and court cases to recover money. In 1998 Proshika had seventy-four court cases pending against its members in Pirpur. ASA had come into Pirpur in 1996. The problems faced by ASA were those of a latecomer arriving at a local credit market that was already saturated with NGOs.

In Pirpur, CARITAS was the only large NGO that emphasized a savings model over a credit model, and its leader, Jeffrey Pereira, was outspoken about the harmful effects of credit on social life.[40] I did not hear a single case of violence perpetrated by CARITAS against its members. Given the different cultures of loan recovery tactics, local women made calculated, rational choices. For example, they said that they would "pay to Grameen and BRAC before we pay to CARITAS because their managers are not so bad." But as some of the CARITAS managers pointed out to me, they could not remain "soft" in a market in which other leading NGOs act tough. They either had to abandon the credit model or become transformed as an institution. As noted in the Introduction, Catholic Relief Services (CRS) initiated a divestiture of all microcredit operations.[41]

One of the major contributions of NGO work is the introduction of urban, educated people and social identities and ideas into rural communities. The ability to control enormous resources has allowed the largest NGOs to become a new class of institutional elite. NGO leaders are not tied to land or to industrial growth for their status and power. They are elites in the development industry who derive their status and power from contacts with Western donors and their ability to grant loans, jobs, research grants, and consultancies to different groups of people. Their meteoric rise to power has to be understood in relation to the economic stagnation and unemployment facing the majority of people in Bangladesh. These elites maintain the power of their institutions through interlocking networks of dependencies created between the NGOs and different target groups—in particular, the rural beneficiaries and the urban and rural middle-class members who depend on NGOs for jobs and succor in a very tight employment market.

Similarly, the names of NGO leaders and of their organizations—Yunus of Grameen, Abed of BRAC, and Qazi Faruque of Proshika—are household names in rural Bangladesh.[42] NGOs have thousands of branches and field-workers and millions of clients, and they are able to efficiently implement various programs at the grassroots. NGOs recruit college graduates to work at the field level. In 1998–1999, these NGOs employed roughly 200,000 young men and women as full-time and part-time field-workers. Of this number, BRAC alone had hired 57,000 full-time and part-time employees. In 2008, BRAC had over 100,000 employees.

Rural people come in daily contact with NGO officers, whereas many of them have never met a government official. Rural NGO offices have a steady stream of people engaged in financial transactions, which is in contrast to government offices, where absenteeism is rampant. Such daily contact keeps the NGO worker informed about the intimate details of the borrowers' lives and helps in the management of their lending business. From the perspective of poor villagers, coming in contact with college-educated men and women creates new flows of ideas and also infuses them with a sense of pride. Writing on this trend, an author noted, "This going to the poor breaks down some of the threatening distance between the urban educated and the poor, that is so much a part of rural social stratification."[43] Given the permeation of NGOs in rural life, it is not surprising then that during my research, people referred to the NGO as *sarkar*, or government.

Proshika field office in Pirpur.

The NGOs symbolize the onrush of modern ideas, technology, and capital into the rural economy in concrete terms for a population that is largely living on a subsistence economy. The NGO offices are brick buildings in a landscape in which most dwellings are either thatched or made of corrugated tin. The offices have electricity and running water, modern office equipment, communication technologies (computers, phones, and fax machines), and residential quarters for their employees. NGO workers are provided with motorbikes and bicycles to do their work. Two of the NGOs, BRAC and Proshika, have also introduced radical ideas about women's social roles. Women field-workers of these NGOs ride bicycles and motorbikes.[44] Many of these female NGO workers have achieved limited practical freedoms. They are salaried and can use some of their income for their personal enjoyment. They live in NGO housing apart from their families, which gives them more freedom. The women also have contact with non-kin men. The NGO female workers serve as role models for rural women who see them in leadership roles with autonomy, money, and power. My research did not focus on NGO female workers, but based on my observations, I would say that the transformation of social roles is occurring among this category of women.

NGOs and Rural Women

Within the patriarchal structure of rural Bangladesh, there was grudging admiration toward women who had become successful through proper investment of their money. I found that women who generally benefited from microcredit loans were the following categories of women: women whose husbands had steady incomes from petty trading or who owned several acres of land; women who were widowed or abandoned and who did not have a male relative who could make a claim on their income; women who had marketable skills; and women with husbands who were ill or less controlling and who allowed them to participate in income-generating projects. These women were more outspoken about their autonomy and made comments such as, "I go wherever I please," or "My husband doesn't understand money." I found that a majority of these women did not live with their in-laws, and that increased their independence and decision-making power within the household.

There is no doubt that NGOs have increased the visibility of rural women in public spaces. NGOs have provided women with legitimate reasons to be in the public sphere—that is, to travel to loan meetings and NGO offices. However, a rural woman's social mobility is a complex issue, and the researcher has to be careful to analyze these gendered circulations. One has to distinguish between a local woman (ghorer meye) who has married within the village, and a woman who was brought into the village through affinal ties (bayirer meye). The women who were ghorer meye, because they were considered daughters of the village, had fewer restrictions on their mobility, and were usually more visible in public spaces.[45]

One such woman was Anowara Begum, who was a member of Proshika and a group leader. She had loaned money to a local rice trader who had not paid her. When I asked her how she was going to recover money from a man, she said to me, "Come with me, Apa." She took me to the market near her house and went up to the rice trader and told him loudly in front of his customers that he had to pay her immediately. This incident occurred with two female outsiders watching his public humiliation while the other traders smirked. The visibly embarrassed man who was trying to conclude a transaction said that he would come to her house that evening to pay. The ability to control capital had also given women such as Anowara the ability to "scold" non-kin men in public, but it did not grant her security. If she fell behind on her payments, she too would incur the wrath of her fellow group members and NGO officers in public.

When I went to the homes of the majority of NGO borrowers, I did not see any visible changes in their living conditions. Most of the time the women and children were eating watery rice with a little bit of bitter gourd and chilies.[46] The women wore saris that were old and often torn. The children were equally poorly dressed. These women had been members of the leading NGOs for ten or twelve years, and yet one did not see material improvements in their lives or in their dwelling quarters. Moreover, within the households, I found that women were also least likely to eat well, get new clothes, or have medical attention in times of illnesses.

The women told me that their major concern was how to pay back the loan installments, and they sold whatever they could get their hands on to stay abreast of their payments. These women, once they got the loans, had to reorganize their resources to pay back the installments.[47] Although poor borrowers temporarily acquired some assets through NGO membership, I found that many of them could not hold on to these assets for a longer duration. These women often had to sell their accumulated assets to pay off the NGOs. Fernando also concluded that women's deep immersion in microcredit had led to a reduction in their leisure, education, and welfare.[48]

Moneylending and Women

I found that instead of curtailing the exploitative work of traditional moneylenders and weakening their hold on rural people, microcredit operations had effectively widened the net of moneylending and introduced more stresses into the community of borrowers and lenders. Traditional moneylenders do not target the very poor because they do not own assets or land that the moneylender can repossess.[49] Through membership in NGO loan programs, the formerly asset-less poor have accumulated some assets. The moneylender now sees the poor as "creditworthy" risks. Thus the net of usury is cast much wider, bringing in the formerly poor and asset-less people inside its web. Contrary to arguments made by Professor Yunus of Grameen Bank that his bank is reducing the power of the traditional moneylender, the Grameen Bank enhances the profits of moneylenders. A BRAC report has made a note of this point by quoting women who mentioned that "BRAC involvement has increased their worthiness in the eyes of the moneylenders.[50] More recent studies have corroborated that moneylending is a lucrative and ongoing trend.[51]

The moneylenders in Bengal were traditionally Hindus. With the partition of India in 1947, the majority of landed Hindu aristocracy left for India. Between 1947 and 1964, many prosperous middle-class Hindus left the country, especially after the 1964 Hindu–Muslim riots in former East Pakistan. In the aftermath of the war in 1971 and the military takeover in 1975, there was another Hindu exodus. At present there are very few Hindu moneylenders left in rural Bangladesh, although Hindus remain associated with the profession. In the ensuing vacuum created by the departure of prosperous Hindus, an emergent class of wealthy Muslim farmers and traders rose with the formation of Pakistan, and later Bangladesh. Many entered the profession of moneylending. In public, they shied away from being identified as moneylenders because of the social and religious stigma associated with moneylending for Muslims. Some Muslim moneylenders tend to give up moneylending once they have performed the Hajj due to fears of repercussions of their worldly profession in the afterlife.

In my research, I found that, for Muslims, moneylending was dissociated from their self-presentations because of Quranic injunctions against usury. Thus, it was not surprising then that the women did not reveal this aspect of their lives to outsiders. I would often be sitting in someone's courtyard talking to the NGO member who had just vehemently denied that she is a moneylender when a woman would appear asking her for money. In such circumstances it would be explained to me that this was not usury, but *shahajya* (help, assistance).

I also met a traveling moneylender who used to sit under a tree about twenty feet from the NGO meeting place. On the way to the meeting, NGO members would often stop and get loans from him. At the conclusion of the meeting, he would pack up his belongings and move on to the next meeting. Another moneylender, Mosharraf Bepari, would sit inside the Grameen Center (kendro) with cash. The Grameen field-worker would often turn to the moneylender and ask him to cover the default amount for a member who could not come up with the full payment on that day. This acceptance and routinization of moneylending among formal and informal networks of people—the NGOs, the traditional moneylender (mahajan), women moneylenders (chhoto mahajan), and kin—show the extent to which institutionalizing debt ends up reproducing multiple interdependent actors. These actors were also integrated into reciprocal obligations, and a breach by any one actor affected the larger group of linked individuals.

I found a rise in moneylending among the women borrowers as well as the emergence of a market subject: the *chhoto majahan,* or the small female moneylender. Most of the women I met participated in some small form of moneylending, and they loaned at 120 percent rate of interest. This was implicit social knowledge for these women, and not a mathematically calculated figure. In their social world, they had knowledge of two forms of interest, that of the NGO and that of the traditional moneylender. As rational market subjects, they opted for the higher one. One also began to see the dislocation of the behavior of lending without interest toward conceptualizing money as a commodity. Women proudly said, "*Amra taka khatai*" (we invest money). When I asked some women how they reconciled charging interest with the prohibitions in the Quran, the women retorted sharply, "You (meaning NGOs) are the ones who have taught us about *shudh* (interest). You make money off us. So, if we do anything wrong, it is because rich people have taught us to do that."

Dowry and Women

Given the preferential treatment of women as the key to access to capital for rural households, it should not be surprising that loans acted as a form of dowry for women. In a recent study of microcredit, it was found that dowry exchanges had risen to 82 percent of all borrowers.[52] Dowry is the payment of money and goods to the groom's family by the bride's family at the time of marriage. While dowry is a Hindu custom, and Muslims are supposed to pay a bride price, dowry has been universally accepted by Muslims in rural society since the 1970s. With increased contact with India after the independence of Bangladesh in 1971, and the integration of Bangladesh into the global economy, rural men now demand dowries to help defray their costs of starting a business, finding employment, or going overseas.[53]

With the high availability of NGO loans, dowries were no longer tied to the tangible assets of the family (the land they could mortgage to pay the dowry) but rather to the loan-generating potential of the women in the family. Several times I heard NGO officers encouraging poor people to borrow loans to pay off their daughters' dowries instead of begging. While these were individual managers acting on their own, their words underline a shift in NGO discourse from charitable ethos to market principles. Once a poor man had approached me for some money to help pay the dowry for his daughter's wedding. The NGO officer sitting next to me told the man, "Why are you asking her for money? If you come to us, we will give you a loan." When I asked him why he would extend loans to support dowry payments, he replied, "It is better than begging." When I visited Tangail as a guest of Grameen Bank in the early part of my research, I found that among the Hindu weaving community, the demand for dowry was very high, and in most instances, NGO loans subsidized dowry payments.

I did not come across any dowry-free marriage in my area, and the women explicitly told me that "this could not happen because of social expectations." Several NGO field-workers confided to me that their managers had ordered them not to get involved in the intimate lives of their borrowers because that could potentially disrupt their ability to recover loans. In a 1994 study Grameen Bank claimed that there were 30,000 dowry-free marriages among their members, but Rahman during his research did not find a single dowry-free marriage among the villagers in his area.[54]

In one Grameen loan meeting, I asked the women if they had given and received dowry. They said that they had to. Several women pointed out other women in their group who had recently paid dowries for their daughters' marriages. According to Grameen rules, members are not supposed to take or receive dowry. I said to the manager who was sitting there, collecting and counting money, that his members did not follow the rules of Grameen. In response, he said, "You can never teach these people anything." To show me that he did his duty, he then asked the women, "Why do you take dowry?" The women in turn questioned him, "Did you not take dowry when you got married?" The manager replied in the negative. Then one woman laughed and said, "Sir, you are wearing a large gold ring. Who gave you that?" When he did not reply, she went on to add, "That's a lot of gold. You educated people take dowries as well. What are you going to teach us?" Such social critiques often ran through the exchanges between the female borrowers and male managers.

Everyday Practices of the Economy of Shame

A central thesis guiding my analysis is the notion of honor and shame that women embody as the custodians of family honor.[55] I found that NGOs appropriated these notions of rural women's honor and shame toward their loan recovery program. Loan recovery technologies deployed by NGOs used public shaming as a form of social control. That is, if one is unable to pay, the NGOs have the power to shame that person in public to make one lose face. Women who were unable to pay their loans on time were often publicly humiliated, or the fear of a public humiliation hung over their heads, acting as a form of discipline in their lives.

The use of shaming as an instrument of social control of the poor, particularly of poor women, has a long history in rural Bangladesh. Women as the custodians of family honor remain particularly vulnerable to shaming. The shaming of men through their women (mothers, wives, and daughters) is an existing social practice. In a face-to-face society, one's ability to maintain honor (the protection of one's family name, the honor of the womenfolk, and the patriline) structures one's social acceptability. To lose face is the ultimate mark of dishonor. Every one will know the cause of his shame and point to his disgrace in public. Men and women told me that when a disgraced man walks through town, people taunt him as a person who has lost prestige.

Shaming takes many forms in Bangladeshi rural society, from rude language to regulation of women's sexuality to disciplining poor people through accusations of sexual infidelities. Public punishments and sanctions include the following: floggings, pouring pitch over bodies, tonsuring women's hair, hanging a garland of shoes around a person's neck, isolating someone's family in the village, publicly spitting on a person every time she or he walks by, making adults hold their ears as a sign of their guilt in a public forum, breaking apart one's house to recover money, and so on. Shaming by NGO borrowers ranged from verbal abuse in public to a group of women descending on the home of the defaulting woman to repossess the saleable assets of the family to taking away her cow or goat to hewing down trees as firewood. In extreme instances, the group of borrowers would demand that the house be sold off to recover the money. All these actions are intended to isolate the "guilty" party and to create humiliation in the public forum. I refer to this as the economy of shame, that is, the appropriation of these existing forms of shaming by a modern institution. The NGO instrumentally deploys various forms of shaming in its own capitalist welfare—namely, the recovery of loans—by governmentalizing the concept of shame to guide the conduct of rural people toward certain ends.

Women borrowers circulated within webs of indebtedness to multiple NGOs, kin, small moneylenders, and the traditional moneylenders. I discovered that NGO and Grameen Bank officials effectively transferred the social and administrative costs of loan recovery to the community. When a default occurred, officials applied pressure on the group members to recover the money from the defaulting woman: they had to pay up for her or they would lose access to future loans. The women, who were struggling themselves, were unwilling or unable to pay for a defaulter in the group. If they failed to recover, their husbands would get angry with their inability to bring them new loans, on which they depended. By holding the group liable for individual borrowers, the group of borrowers functioned as the collateral for the NGO.[56] At the exhortation of NGO officials, the group of borrowers publicly shamed these defaulting women and men in order to recover the money. In these strife-ridden conflicts over loan repayments, I did not come across any instance of loans that were forgiven by the NGOs.

According to the notions of proper conduct for women, a woman dishonors her husband and family when outsiders come into her house and verbally abuse her for her husband's inability to pay up, causing her husband to lose face. In such situations, husbands frequently threatened, and in rare cases, divorced their wives for bringing shame and dishonor upon them through NGO memberships. In such circumstances, husbands made sense of blaming the woman by saying, "She brought the NGO into my house. If she had not joined the NGO this would not have happened." When I pointed out to some of these men that they had used the loans that their wives had provided, they retorted back, "But why should our wives bring the NGO into our homes?" Within the patriarchal structure of the home, the boundaries of acceptable conduct were strictly enforced, and at times of crisis, these women were individuated from the family as "outsiders."

Rural women are the custodians of family honor. When a woman loses her honor, she loses face in rural society. The NGOs shamed rural men by shaming their wives. When NGO people and the group of borrowers came into a woman's house to demand money, they effectively broke the distinction between private and public, and the husband's honor was violated, as he could not protect his family and patriline from the external world. In these situations, the husbands in turn accused their wives for shaming them by bringing strangers into their house. The husband, through his angry words, separated the woman/wife from the family, making her an outsider who had brought shame on him through her actions, although it was the husband who used the money she brought home from the NGO. These behaviors speak to the vulnerable location of women inside the home and the NGO. The women were always at risk of losing face and bringing dishonor on themselves and their husbands. The men too were afraid of losing face if they failed to return the money to the NGO. These social codes were appropriated by the NGOs to safeguard their economic investments in the community.

In my research, I found that 95 percent of women borrowers gave their loans to their husbands or other male borrowers.[57] While the control of loans by men is not surprising within the social dynamic of Bangladeshi society, a more provocative task is to examine the social costs to women when they are the conduits through which capital is exchanged between the NGOs and rural men. Hashemi, Schuler, and Riley noted that even if women lost control of the loans, some of the money stuck to their fingers, and the women learned some basic principles of accounting and expenditures, which, in and of itself, was a form of economic and social empowerment.[58] Perhaps a more instructive way to conceptualize this relationship is to examine the production of a surrogate subjectivity among these women. In his pioneering work on Muslim women in the former Soviet Central Asia, Massell noted that the government manufactured Muslim women as a surrogate proletariat in the absence of a revolutionary working class.[59] Similarly, the loan schemes of various NGOs created a surrogate market subjectivity among the majority of women who, although not entrepreneurs, now circulated in a social milieu that was intersected by ideas of capitalist work ethic.

Women justified the transfer of loans to their husbands by terming such loans household income. Case studies and conversations with female borrowers also revealed that these loans repositioned them with increased vulnerability within the household and community, in what Rahman has termed "positional vulnerability."[60] On a personal level, these women were inside the patriarchal homes while their husbands controlled the loans; the husbands abused and threatened them if NGO group members came to their houses demanding loan payment. On a community level, they were up against the capitalist patriarchy of the NGOs, in which male managers coerced other female group members to come and recover money from them if they fell behind. When group coercion and public humiliation failed to recover the money owed, the NGOs would resort to police and courts to recover the defaulted sum. In 2007, I found that this system of recovery had become more operationalized. I write on this point at the end of the chapter.

The women borrowers did not always passively accept the coercive techniques employed by the NGOs. Women subverted the power hierarchies separating them from NGO managers. They deployed their own strategies to stall or delay loan recoveries. Their "weapons of the weak" consisted of small strategies of resistance such as making the manager wait, showing up late, quarreling, trying to trick the manager into embarrassing situations, and calling their managers' names.[61] The women also used the concept of dishonor to manipulate and embarrass NGO field-workers. The female borrowers watched NGO workers for any evidence of weakness. Often I heard women borrowers mention which NGO field-worker had a gentle side and could be manipulated. It was a contest of wills between the women and the NGOs, with the subordinated women trying to find small "weapons" with which to forestall the NGOs from repossessing their assets in times of financial distress.

In this respect, Scott's comment is essential in reminding us that "the relationship between dominant elites and subordinates is . . . very much a material struggle in which both sides are continually probing for weaknesses and exploiting small advantages."[62] However, these "weapons of the weak" were limited in their ability to transform the asymmetrical power relations between the NGO officers and their borrowers, and they should not be confused with "weapons" that could transform the bargaining power of the poor.

Since these women and their families were connected to the wider society, a large body of diverse people with competing interests and motivations was integrated into this process. This led to an increase in antagonistic relationships among the borrowers because they were often fighting against each other over loan repayments and the fear of potential defaults. For example, Hashemi and Morshed observe, "The Grameen system operates in a social milieu where women are willing and able to pressure one another to repay loans."[63] And in another context, Hashemi et al. note, "Women who miss meetings or fall behind in their repayments are publicly scolded, and may be visited in their homes by Bank Workers or members."[64] Yet, the social implications of such actions in the lives of women are not addressed by these authors. In a study of ASA, it was noted that 99 percent of default loans are collected by economic and social pressures that included local administrators and the chairman of the Union Council—people who represent the state in rural society to "create pressure on the borrower for repayment."[65]

In my conversations with women, they repeatedly used two words to describe what these NGO loans had come to signify in their lives, *chaap* (pressure) and *jontrona* (mental stress). In describing their mental stress caused by the loan recovery tactics employed by these NGOs, the women would often touch their foreheads or hold their heads in their hands. Holding their heads in their hands was symbolic of feeling *oshohai,* or helpless. It was symbolic of the world crashing down on their heads. For women, becoming bearers of credit has had multiple visible and invisible forms of stress and exploitation. As many of these women noted,

> Right after we take a loan, the worry sets in: how are we going to pay? Every day becomes a stressful situation. We usually set aside some money from the loan to pay a few installments. But we are poor people, we have so many wants. If we fall behind, then group members come and harass us. The NGO field-worker comes and harasses us. They insult us. They say, "You have taken

money from the NGO, and now you cannot pay. Do you not feel shame?" Our husbands and in-laws get angry with us. Our husbands say to us, "You are making us lose our *ijjat* [honor]." We have pressure from all around.

In the structure set up by the Grameen Bank, and one that was followed by the other NGOs, there was systematic pressure on each group involved in the loan-recovery process. When individual women failed to pay their installments on time, the group as a whole lost access to future loans. The group of women first applied pressure on the defaulting woman to recover the money. If they failed, the local NGO manager in turn put pressure on the field-worker. If the field-worker failed to comply, the defaulted amount was withheld from his paycheck. Publicly the NGOs denied that they financially penalize their field-workers for failing to collect the money. In private conversations, some of the field-workers confirmed to me that money was indeed deducted from their paychecks if they failed to recover the full amount of the outstanding loans. Too many defaults in his area resulted in the field-worker being fired. The manager was also under pressure from the regional office, which, in turn, reported to headquarters their monthly recovery rates. If the manager could not show a high rate of recovery, he would either be fired, or lose a promotion or a pay raise.

Field personnel worked six days a week, with only one day off. The stress on recovery was so rigid that BRAC, Grameen, and ASA field-workers complained that they could not return to their offices until they had collected all the outstanding dues, and sometimes it was 10 p.m. before they could return to their offices. Then they stayed several more hours in the office to update the accounts. While they were still out in the field, the manager and accountant had to wait for them in the office. Sometimes, these managers had to wait until midnight for a field-worker to show up.[66] There was little recourse available to these young NGO workers. They were not allowed unionization, which would help to improve their work conditions. The Grameen Bank manager in Tangail had expressed great distress at this state of affairs.

> All of you researchers focus on the women. What about us? Look at my workers. Their youth is being wasted by working for 14 hours a day. As a manager, I feel very sad for them. Write about them. They too have hopes and aspirations.

Most of the field-workers I interviewed said that the only reason they worked for the NGO was because of the "specter of unemployment." NGO officers routinely told members that even on the death of a husband or a child they had to pay their dues to the NGO first. When defaults occurred, NGO managers reminded the women, "Have we not told you that you must pay us before you even bury your husband?" NGO workers invoked these injunctions against late payments not because they were intentionally "bad" people, but because they were similarly trapped inside the institutional culture of strict loan recovery. These men and women, in many instances, complained about their coercive roles in extracting payments from poor people. But they saw no way out of this situation.

In each group meeting I attended, at least 10 percent of the women were struggling to meet payments every week. These women who were strapped for cash had the following options available to them: borrow money at usurious rates from the traditional moneylender; borrow from other NGO members who also lend at the prevailing market rate of 120 percent; take new loans from the NGOs to pay off debt; or sell their assets (pots, pans, trees, chickens, bed) to pay off their dues. If these women still could not come up with the money, they were subjected to verbal abuse and taunts by members of their credit groups.

Seventy-five percent of the women borrowers I interviewed noted forms of low-intensity verbal or physical abuse that were associated with loan recovery programs. The perpetrators were fellow borrowers, NGO officials, and spouses. Borrowers claimed that BRAC field-workers spoke to them in verbally abusive language, and that Grameen was known for its tyranny in Pirpur. These verbally abusive exchanges were a regular feature of loan collections. For example, the local BRAC female employee was notorious for her behavior. She was finally transferred during my research.

In one situation, the BRAC employee had told an older woman who could not pay her *kisti*, "Bring the money right now; otherwise I will throw hot water on your face." The older woman was extremely offended because "she was old enough to be her mother." When I went to meet the older woman in her house, initially she would not come out because she felt "shamed." After a while she came out and said to me, "We are poor so we take NGO money but that does not give the NGO people the right to insult us whenever and however they wish."

In another instance, a group leader had gone to the BRAC office to ask for some more time to pay her installment, and the same female BRAC field-worker had shoved her out of the office in front of others. I heard about this incident and went to see the group leader. At first she would not speak to me because of social embarrassment. Not only had she lost her self-respect, but

I, an outsider, had heard about that. She was unwilling to talk to me and would only say, "You are educated people. How can people like you behave toward us like this?" The same BRAC employee had confiscated the cooking utensils of another defaulting borrower and kept them in the home of a third borrower. The other borrower was supposed to hold on to the rice pot until the woman could come up with the money. Taking away a family's rice pot is a form of shaming for rural people. Losing one's rice pot was akin to admitting one's inability to feed one's family, which reduced one to the status of a beggar.

In another instance, Proshika management had locked up Achia Begum, who had defaulted on her loan. They had taken her to the Proshika office and had kept her locked in the kitchen overnight. When I met Achia, she cried and said that she was an old woman, so it did not matter, but now people were saying that her teenage daughter was also a "person of ill repute" (durnam). While I spoke to her, several of her neighbors came and taunted her by saying, "Why did you march with Proshika? Where is your Proshika Father now?" In the past, Achia Begum had gone on several Proshika-led social-mobilization marches that were seen acts of "shamelessness" by the women who now taunted her. These women and Achia had a complicated relationship. The women found Achia's behavior inappropriate, and I could tell that they did not like her. But there may have been a lingering envy toward Achia for her ability to break rural norms and have some practical freedoms, albeit for a short time.

Female employees brought inside the patriarchal structure of NGO operations often adopted more virulent forms of behavior toward the women borrowers. These NGO female field-workers were excessively abusive in their behavior. Women operating within the patriarchy of the NGO had to adopt a more aggressive style of interaction with the women borrowers precisely because they otherwise ran the risk of appearing "soft" and losing control over the group. A breakdown in fiscal discipline would make the women field-workers lose their jobs. Members who were struggling to keep up their payments were always looking for ways to trick the NGO field-workers. Any clue of their "weakness" would be used against these NGO female officers. The techniques of loan recovery imposed these behavioral constraints on the female field-workers. Caught between two patriarchal institutions, the rural family and the NGO office, these female employees were always at risk of losing their jobs because of their gender, and consequently, they overcompensated by applying harsher rules on their borrowers.

Of the four NGOs I studied, Proshika had resorted to the police and the courts to recover defaults. Of the seventy-four cases that Proshika had filed with the police in Pirpur Thana, I followed up on ten. In each case it emerged that the borrowers were, for multiple reasons, unable to pay, and because they had breached a contract, they were at fault. Many of the defaulters were not always honest people; often they frittered away the money in family expenses. But this "being at fault" has to be measured against how NGOs loaned to poor people without ensuring whether they had the capacity to invest the money.

Proshika's problems rose from the way it had distributed the loans and from its internal corruption. Proshika group members collectively decided who got how much of the loan, and they also decided the amount to be saved. While in theory it may appear to be an approach that empowered the poor because they made the decisions, in reality it led to pilferage among members who were often in collusion with the managers. Smarter and more educated members defrauded the not-so-smart ones. Sometimes, people defaulted because they did not have the skill to invest the money properly and thus ended up with enormous debts. In some instances, they had lent the money to kin members who in turn gave that money to labor contractors to find work for them in Malaysia, which did not materialize, and the money was lost.

The practice of an NGO resorting to the police—and the Bangladeshi police are known for their horrific crimes against women in custody—to discipline its borrowers was a disturbing trend. Women made to appear in court faced social stigma and ostracism from their families. These women had not only lost their honor by appearing in public, but they had appeared in a court of law as "criminals" (ashami) and brought shame on the family and their husbands. When these women went to court to make their appearance, everyone in the village knew about it. Their husbands were taunted by people who said, "Your wife has gone to court as a criminal." The wife became the conduit for the penetration of external laws (the courts, police) into the patriarchal home, in which the husband reigned sovereign.

In Enayetnagar, Proshika had a case pending against thirteen women. After their first court appearance, several of the women were asked by their husbands to leave because they were *be-ijjat* (shameless) women. While the actions of these men and the actions of the NGO need to be kept separate, it is important to recognize how the actions of Proshika management played out in the domestic lives of the women. These women were forced by their husbands' families to return to their parents' homes. I met with several of these women and their mothers, who were struggling with the consequences of the police action. Some of the women said that their husbands demanded that they pay additional dowry if they wanted to come back. These men who had demanded dowry were manipulating their wives' families to get additional income. Then there were other men who would not take back their wives because the women had been shamed, and they had in turn shamed the men socially.

Marital abandonment is a common phenomenon in rural Bangladeshi society, especially since the movement of rural men for work in urban areas and overseas. While Proshika itself did not create the practice of abandonment, its actions of reporting the defaulting women to the police contributed to the prevailing attitudes toward women, who were now blamed for "dishonoring" their husbands and families. Later, when I asked the local Proshika manager how they could on the one hand speak about "empowering rural women" and send them off to jail on the other, he retorted, "The best place for them is the police" (polishe-e jaoa oder jonno uttom jaiga).

When I heard of these incidents, I spoke with the woman lawyer who ran the local Madaripur Legal Aid Association (MLAA) about helping female victims of NGO abuses. She confided that several women had complained to her about loan recovery abuses by NGOs, but as an NGO her organization could not take legal action against NGOs. As she explained to me, "NGOs cannot work against NGOs. The clergy establishment is already against us. We have to keep a united front."

In 1998–1999, Proshika was one of the most important and high-profile NGOs that publicly demanded a pro-poor budget. The NGO and its leader Faruque had close links to the party in power, Awami League, and to the UK aid organization Department for International Development (DFID). He had become one of the major brokers of overseas aid resources for the NGOs. Legally, Proshika could not file police charges against the defaulting women because personal insolvency is not a crime in Bangladesh. But they could bend the rules toward their own ends.

As noted in the beginning of the chapter, by 2007, NGOs had synchronized their operations by calibrating their loan amounts, interest rates, and payment schedules. They have successfully incorporated elites and the law more systematically in their loan recovery techniques. For all of these NGOs, the basic system of loan recovery was still through the group of borrowers. But as loans programs have expanded sharply, NGOs have also taken additional risks in this vast outlay of money. In order to ensure their investments, they have turned to the inclusion of rural elites, such as the Union Council Chairman, to hold individual borrowers accountable. By brokering power with rural elites, NGOs work in tandem with the traditional power structure. NGOs bring money and resources to the villages that rural elites can share in when they assist in the smooth functioning of NGO operations. When elites that hold power and authority in society discipline defaulting members, this produces a heightened sense of shame and powerlessness for women in a hierarchical and face-to-face society.

Between 1999 and 2007, what had changed on the ground was the bureaucratic proceduralization of NGO activities in loans and social business enterprises. NGOs engage in a form of rural governance that Foucault termed the "right disposition of things, arranged so as to lead to a convenient end."[67] NGOs, through their work with rural women tend to organize resources and behavior toward certain ends, not always fully, but substantially. This is because NGOs are not fully sovereign in rural society; they operate within Ong's "graduated sovereignties" alongside the competing forces of government, clergy, and rural elites that all claim adherence of rural subjects.[68] Women who are NGO loan recipients were thus located within dense imbrications of loans and obligations that circumscribed their human possibilities. In fact, what we begin to see is the refined articulation of the collective powers of rural society into a disciplinary instrument that is exercised by these NGOs against the "errant" female members.

Chapter 4 **The Social Life of Debt**

THIS CHAPTER ANALYZES the relations between microfinance and women by examining eight case studies. Taking governmentality as a formal structure of analysis, I examine how NGO loans with their accompanying norms intersect the lives of women who are also governed by rules and obligations. While debt ties multiple people together in mutually reinforcing reciprocities, it simultaneously reconstructs the fields within which individual borrowers are situated, and circumscribes the forms of conduct within these intersecting domains. In this integration of dependencies, the actions of distant people can and do have effects on the livelihoods of individual borrowers and their families. Thus, a breakdown at any point in this structure of linked lending produces multiple ripple effects on a dispersed group of people.

The following eight narratives are intricate relationships of debt within a constantly changing landscape of rural social conditions that I identified in the last chapter: increased moneylending, proxy membership, inclusion of the middle class as beneficiaries, the weakening of social solidarity, failed market subjects, and heightened tensions over loan recovery. These case studies show how women borrowers were constrained within two competing dynamic structures—the loan-giving NGO and their families and kin groups, who also made claims on their loans.

Narrative 1: Grameen Phone Ladies

My first case study is from my research in 2007.[1] The cell phone is the most ubiquitous symbol of modern technology in Bangladesh. The introduction of cell phone technology has revolutionized telecommunications in Bangladesh. In 1996, Grameen Bank was one of four companies authorized to sell cell phones in Bangladesh. By 2007, Bangla Link, Aktel, Warid

Telecom, City Cell, Grameen Phone, and Teletalk all competed with Grameen Phone for rural consumers.

As noted in chapter 3, the Grameen Polli Phone program is a joint venture between Grameen Phone and Grameen Bank, which cost-share different aspects of the Polli Phone operations. Grameen Phone has the responsibility of getting the network available outside of Bangladesh. They activate the phones and send the bills directly to Grameen Bank. Grameen Bank remains responsible for identifying the borrowers and collecting the payments on the loans. By outsourcing its administrative costs—the selection of borrowers and the recovery of payments—to the Grameen Bank, Grameen Phone has kept its operating costs low and has remained a very profitable institution.[2]

Grameen Phone ladies are carefully screened by Grameen Bank personnel. The following three factors were considered in choosing an applicant: payment history, location, and some fluency in English.[3] Women with successful loan payment history—and whose husbands or family members were in retail business, or owned a shop in the market—were selected. At least one member in the borrower's family must possess some knowledge of English to recognize the letters and numbers on the phone. The selection process tended to benefit the better-off members within the group.

The Polli Phone program operated on the following basis. With the loans, the women purchased the cell phone, battery charger, SIM card, antenna, etc. These phones either stayed with the women in their homes or, if the family owned a retail shop in the market, the husband or an adult son handled the phone business. The women with the cell phones in their homes operated as rural telephone kiosks. The customer came to them and rented the phone by the minute to make calls. They also received calls from people who wanted to talk to their relatives in the village. In those cases, the phone operator asked the caller to call back within a stipulated time while she sent someone to locate the person. For this additional service of locating the person, she charged a small fee. In the early days of the program, phone ladies often had customers coming to their house late at night to make phone calls to their relatives living overseas. This trend has declined as more rural people have access to mobile phones, and fewer have to travel any distance to make phone calls.

In the peak of Polli Phone between 2001 and 2005, the women I met had run successful businesses. I found that these women shared features that I have noted as autonomy within family and a certain market savoir faire. Either they were heads of their households or their husbands had granted them autonomy in decision making. One of the women I met had a successful tailoring shop in town with seven employees and five sewing machines, and she used the phone as a private line. Below I discuss two such women, Rohima Akhter and Monowara Begum.

Rohima Akhter was a long-term member of Grameen. She had a tenth-grade education. She became a Grameen phone operator in 2002. Initially, she and her husband had rented a shop in Tangail for phone services. Later, her husband left to work in Malaysia, and she became the head of the household. Without her husband's assistance, she could not run the shop. At the time of the interview, she worked as a health worker for BRAC, carrying the phone with her on her rounds. In the early days, she could charge 6–7 taka per minute (10 cents); in 2007 she could charge only 2 taka (2 cents). Since the competing cell phone companies charged much lower rates, she had to shut down her phone business.

Rohima gave the following breakdown of her initial expense of purchasing a cell phone in 2002. All prices have been calculated at the exchange rate of 67 taka. The prices charged by Grameen Bank have declined since 2002.

Phone Purchase Loan	19,000 taka ($283)
Mandatory Security Deposit	10,000 taka ($149)
Mandatory Grameen Pension Scheme	10,000 taka ($149)[4]
One-time connection fee	5,600 taka ($83)
Total cost of the phone:	44,600 taka ($696)

Rohima's cost for running a phone operation was as follows: a monthly cost of 450 taka that included electricity ($6). She had to pay a phone line rent of 40 taka (59 cents), plus Value Added Tax (VAT) of 20 percent and service charge of 20 percent. Her weekly installment for the phone was 500 taka ($7) for a total of 2,000 taka ($29) per month. If she failed to pay her bill on time, the line was disconnected, and a reconnection fee of 200 taka ($2.90) had to be paid. According to her, they had to pay an additional 100 taka ($1.49) to Grameen for an itemized bill that listed all incoming and outgoing calls. This additional cost prevented many women from getting an itemized bill, but it also made them suspicious that Grameen was overcharging them. According to her, when she asked for her security deposit of 10,000 taka ($149), the Bank withheld it, saying that they would give her back the money if they could find another buyer for the phone. Rohima mentioned that the Bank had charged her 5,600 taka ($83.50) for an antenna that was priced much higher than the prevailing market rate.[5]

Rohima felt that, although she had received benefits from Grameen Bank membership, she had become heavily indebted in trying to run the telephone business because she did not realize that market competition would force down the price of renting the phone. Although Rohima was more literate than most rural women, her knowledge of how markets operated was limited. As she explained, "Grameen officials told us that we would keep on making money from the phone business." Although Rohima was economically better-off with a husband working in Malaysia, she could not negotiate the terms of the contract with the Bank. The Bank could withhold her security deposit, and she had no recourse to get that money back. The relationship of inequality and power exercised by the NGO against the borrower had remained fundamentally unchanged since my research in 1999.

In Bolla, a village near Tangail, I met with Monowara Begum, who used to have a successful Grameen phone business. Her profitability too had suffered as more phone companies had moved in, but she had invested her money judiciously. Given her proximity to the local market, she invested in moneylending to rural traders. With her income from her phone business, she had purchased a TV, refrigerator, and new furniture. In addition

Grameen phone lady.

to the Grameen phone, she had obtained a Bangla Link phone, which was cheaper to operate.

Monowara was the head of her household. Her husband had worked in Saudi Arabia but had returned home due to illness. Monowara was a member of both BRAC and Grameen. She had borrowed 80,000 taka from Grameen and 18,000 taka from BRAC for a total outstanding debt of 98,000 taka ($1,462). When I asked her why she needed to join another NGO since Grameen would provide her with cash, she explained that she wanted to increase her benefits by belonging to more than one NGO. Monowara, like many women I had interviewed, borrowed from multiple NGOs. Monowara's confidence reminded me of Jahanara, the moneylender in Pirpur whom I write about later in this chapter.

While we talked, Monowara's husband sat in a corner. She ascribed her success to the weakness of her husband. Her husband could not repress her ambition. My male research assistant did not like her comment. He asked her why she blamed him since he allowed her to work. Monowara laughed and added, "Can you see him doing anything?" Turning to me, Monowara said, "My husband is weak, I can keep him under control." Monowara was an intelligent woman, but the core of her success lay in not living with in-laws or a repressive husband who would take away her money. Monowara was very comfortable in speaking with non-kin men. She mentioned that since she had taken over the running of the household, she had more contact with men. She had also married within her natal village (ghorer meye), and hence was known to local people, and could move around town without hindrance.

"The phone business was good because I could earn money without leaving my house." In fact, her expenditure on operating the phone business was zero since she operated out of her home. She mentioned that in her area bank officials preselected those women who were already successful within Grameen groups for the phone loans. Thus, the poorer women in the groups did not get the loans because they were seen as risky. In the past, she said, there was a line of customers outside her home. Now, on a good day, she had between six to seven customers. While we talked, a man arrived to make a phone call. Monowara walked outside to handle the business. At this time, Monowara's niece brought in a tray with tea, biscuits, and snacks. Monowara's home showed all the aspiring norms of a middle-class lifestyle.

Speaking of her group dynamics, Monowara said that her Grameen Bank group now had seventy members. This increase in the number of members was due to the expansion of microfinance after 2000. Grameen Bank membership had increased from 2.2 million in 1999 to 7 million by 2007, a number that continues to grow. In her area, existing groups of forty members were expanded to seventy to eighty members. According to Monowara, twenty of her group members used the money profitably, ten to fifteen made the payments but they could not earn profits, and the rest of the women, that is about 50 percent, were struggling with their payments. She noted that these women had too many wants, and that they consumed the loan money upon receipt. These numbers corresponded with what I had observed during my research. When I asked how the NGOs recovered the money from defaulting women, she said, "We put pressure on them. They have taken NGO money, they have to pay back."

From my conversations with the women, I realized that the poorer women did not get access to these new technologies; it was the successful women who received these loans and benefits. The rates that were charged by Grameen Phone were higher than the prevailing market rate. While it was true that Grameen Bank had to invest upfront in the outlay of tele-communications, the cost of the operations was borne by the poor borrow-ers through high prices. The women themselves had many questions about how they had been charged for various services, and some of them felt that Grameen had overcharged them. Some of the women had mentioned that there were tensions among group members when a second woman from the same village received a cell phone loan because it would potentially reduce the income of the first borrower.

These loans were bundled with other financial services. The women were required to buy Grameen Pension Schemes (GPS) as part of the expansion of microfinancial services to the poor. The GPS plans mature after seven to ten years, when the investment is expected to double. During this time, the women were obliged to contribute to the plan every month. The benefit to these women was obvious. They were ensured a pension, but the Bank did not offer the women a choice in shopping for the best rates for their money. By creating these financial dependencies, the Bank management preserved links to the women for a longer duration, and ensured that their clients did not leave for another NGO.

At the social level, the most important aspect of the telephony was the nature of the business itself. Husband and wife jointly operated the phone because their customers could come to them 24/7. Thus, if the husband operated a shop, the phone was kept there. In the evenings, the wife or an older son would operate the phone while the husband went home to take his meal. Men who worked as day laborers would allow their wives to operate the phone from the home. The operation of a phone business exposed women to new social discourses. The women said that becoming known as the phone *bari* (home) had granted them status among their peers. Their contact with men had also increased. Strange men came to their homes at all times of day to make phone calls, while their husbands might be away at work. Most women said they managed this private–public distinction by maintaining a separate room where the customer would use the phone. This required that the family have the financial means to have a separate room in the first place. Telephony allowed villagers to stay in communication with their kin in other parts of the world. Thus, the service itself was conceptualized as providing a social good, and the women I talked to in Tangail claimed that they did not face stigma.

Cell phone technology has revolutionized communications in Bangladesh, and it has had a positive impact on small businesses where owners (mostly male) could monitor their sales through phone communications.[6] What is less clear, though, is the extent to which these phone sales have genuinely helped to move women out of poverty. Speaking on this trend to sell consumer goods to poor women and to showcase them as entrepreneurs, Stabile and Sterne raise the point whether "Bangladeshi women, who certainly know their needs better than USAID, nongovernmental organizations (NGOs), and the multinational corporations that stand to benefit from expansion of markets for various new technologies, [were] consulted about their everyday lives and needs."[7] As Shaffer noted, "In Bangladesh today, the only one making real money on Grameen Phone's wireless service is . . . Grameen Phone."[8] Given this reflection on the contemporary moment, I would like to take the reader on a journey through my ethnography conducted in 1998–1999. The following seven narratives are from Pirpur Thana.[9]

Narrative 2: In Search of Richer Clients

In my area, ASA was a new entrant into microcredit operations, and as such, it was facing stiff competition to increase its members. New entrants into NGO loan operations often resorted to middle-income members as their subscribers. This trend toward higher-income rural subscribers was a consequence of the market pressures on NGO managers to show high recovery rates to their head offices and donor agencies. But this process comes with its own complications, as the following case reveals.

In 1997, ASA started a Bazaar Samity in Pirpur that was made up of twelve traders. These men had the following businesses: photocopy shop, auto shop, retail store, stationery store, photo studio, tea shop, shoe store, small electronics store, rice mill, and jute trade. They were given a total loan of 128,000 taka ($2,782) by the ASA field-worker in Pirpur. When the regional manager (RM) of ASA found out about the Bazaar Samity, he ordered the new ASA manager to cancel their membership. The new ASA manager decided to disperse the group because "they were not the targets of ASA. These were rich men." As he pointed out to me, a tea-shop owner does not need 10,000 taka ($217) to invest in his business; 500 taka ($10) is enough for his supplies. On August 20, 1998, the manager canceled the Bazaar Samity. In keeping faith with the original doctrine of ASA, he felt that only the poor should be targeted.

As a result of their loan cancellation, the men of the Bazaar Samity became very angry. They threatened that if ASA wanted to stay in Pirpur, ASA would have to give them the money. They publicly insulted the ASA manager several times. Then one day they cornered the manager and locked him in one of their stores. The manager told them that his supervisor, the Regional Manager (RM), had to agree to their loan. The Bazaar Samity men threatened to publicly shame the ASA manager. "We will make you take off your pants, then you can go naked to get the RM." These rich rural men invoked the code of public shaming—"We will take off your pants"—to regulate the conduct of ASA managers.

It was at this time that the ASA manager came to Tareque of ETP to find a solution to the problem. As a local power broker, Tareque would often inter-mediate in dispute resolutions with various NGOs. Given the status and power of the men who were threatening the ASA manager, Tareque contacted the local female member of parliament (MP) and asked her to intercede on behalf of ASA. It was the MP who mediated that ASA had to give these traders the loan. On October 15, 1998, their new loan was sanctioned.

Since the transition to democracy in 1990, politicians have depended on monetary contributions from local businesses during their campaigns. Given this dependency between the business community and the politicians, it is not surprising that ASA was made to subordinate its decision to the MP's rul-ing. Tareque later confided in me that the reason ASA had wanted to cancel their loan was that the manager feared that these men would not repay the loan. ASA managers had resisted the inclusion of rich clients because they felt that their existing modes of instrumentalities—domination through shaming and surveillance—would not prevail with richer clients.

One day I heard from Rina that the ASA manager was upset with a field-worker for allowing the wife of a local lawyer to become a member of their NGO in the next town. The field-worker had recently joined ASA, and he was having difficulty with increasing his members in an oversaturated market of NGOs offering microcredit loans. This new ASA member lived in a brick house with a refrigerator and a TV. These are symbols of affluence in Bangladesh. The woman got a 5,000 taka ($108) loan to buy her daughter a harmonium, a musical instrument with keys and air bellows used by Bengalis.[10] The ASA manager was angry that rich people were becoming members of his NGO, and went to see the field-worker who had enrolled her in the first place. When I later asked the manager about this member, he mentioned that he had to keep her on. Her status as the wife of the local lawyer gave her power over the poorer members. The members in her group listened to her, and she could censure them if they failed to pay on time. Her social position as a middle-class woman ensured that the other women in the group would pay on time. This was the critical factor in the manager's decision to allow her to stay.

Similarly, in Krishnonagar I came across a headmistress who had joined BRAC with her three sisters. The four of them were each going to take a loan for 5,000 taka, for a total of 20,000 taka ($434). At a weekly meeting, I pointed out to the BRAC field-worker that she had a schoolteacher in her group. To save face, the BRAC manager was forced to tell the woman in front of me, "I cannot give you money. You are a headmistress, why have you joined BRAC?" The headmistress became visibly annoyed and said, "Why should you only give money to the poor? What about us?"

Later the headmistress invited me to visit her house, which was made of corrugated tin. We sat on a sofa in the small living room. She offered tea and cookies in china cups. Over tea she said to me, "I live on a fixed income. By joining BRAC I can have some additional income. We want to start a small poultry business." This was highly unlikely given that poultry farming is considered dirty work, and it is done by very poor women with few income-generating options. When I pointed that out to her, she paused and then added, "How can my maid get loans and wear new clothes when I cannot do that?" Her membership was not canceled by BRAC. Later I found out that she took the loan to buy new furniture for her house.

One day a visibly upset Tareque came into my room. On that day two women had come to the ETP office, one the wife of the local college teacher, another the wife of the richest man from the neighboring town. Both of them wanted to apply for loans from ETP and insisted that "he give them the loans." A troubled Tareque asked me, "What is happening to NGO ideology if rich people want our loans? Who are we actually helping?" Tareque's momentary loss of control, and his hopelessness, gave me pause. NGO field-level workers were under increased pressure from the headquarters and their supervisors to create new member rosters quickly and show high rates of return on their loan programs. The financial sustainability of the NGO was tied to high-interest rates. A few days later I learned that Tareque had given the loans to the women. As he explained to me, in order for him to expand ETP operations in their village, he had to reciprocate the demands of the elites.

Social considerations also motivated rural middle-class women to seek membership with NGOs. Microcredit had blurred some of the hierarchal distinctions that held rural society together. Some of the younger women, whose husbands were able to use the money productively, now had some money and consumer items. NGO activities offered them social outings, giving them the opportunity to dress up in nice saris, to wear jewelry and makeup, and to visit relatives and exchange gossip. NGO membership also brought them in contact with officers who came from a higher social background. Compared to middle-class women, poor women have always had more physical mobility because of their need to earn a living, but now these poorer women also had more "places to go." In rural Bangladesh, these were coveted moments of pleasure for women. Their familiarity with NGO workers tended to increase their status among their village cohorts. Women who were considered creditworthy could broker new loans for other women and kin, and this ability enhanced the status of some women within these groups. Middle-class rural women wanted to participate in these new forms of practical freedoms as well.

Political considerations also motivated richer rural families to encourage their women to join NGOs. The Bangladeshi government had legislated that one-third of all Union Council seats (nine seats in total) would be reserved for female candidates. Rural men wanted to hold on to local political structures through their wives. Their wives joined NGOs to run for rural public office such as membership in the Union Council. The NGO meetings gave them a forum in which to train in political canvassing and to establish a client base with local women. These women soon took on leadership roles.

Higher-income members were included in NGO loan groups because NGOs found they were better able to invest and pay back the loan. But this shift had also caused discomfort among many older NGO workers. While the discourses of globalization and neoliberalism were overtaking these older discourses of working for the poor, the ethos of charity as a social good in and of itself still remained a vital structuration for older NGO workers such as Tareque.

Narrative 3: Jahanara's Story, a Female Moneylender

Moneylending was strongest in villages close to markets where local traders sought out the women borrowers for loans. In my research area, this village was Krishnonagar, located west of Pirpur Thana and next to a market (a bridge connected Krishnonagar to the market). In an informal survey of Krishnonagar, 100 households out of 230 NGO beneficiary households were engaged in moneylending. But the number was probably much higher because many Muslims do not openly admit to moneylending. As a result of the proximity to the bazaar, the women of this village had more physical mobility. NGO-related activities had added to that mobility and had created some new pathways for these women to interact with the larger community of Pirpur. Grameen Bank, BRAC, Proshika, and ASA offices were spread throughout the town, and access to these offices meant a trek through town for the women.

Within this community of women moneylenders, I found that very few operated on a professional basis; very few took legal precautions to protect their investments. The women remained vulnerable to market uncertainties compared to the traditional moneylenders, who extended money as legal contracts and had other forceful means of recovering money—for example, the use of hired goons.

My research assistant Rina and I went around one morning in 1999 in search of female moneylenders in Krishnonagar. I was told by people to talk to Jahanara Begum, the most famous moneylender in this area. Jahanara had over 350,000 taka ($7,608) invested in moneylending, and she intrigued me because of her reputation. What did it mean, I wondered, for a woman to have amassed so much money? How did she become such a successful moneylender?

We went to her house several times, but she was always "out on business." Finally getting frustrated, I sent Rina alone to make contact with Jahanara. At first, Jahanara said that she would not talk to me. She asked Rina, "What do I gain from talking to her? By meeting with her I lose potential income." Rina told her that I was writing a book on the village, and I wanted to interview her for that purpose. This answer satisfied Jahanara. It made her recognize that her work was important enough for city folks to want to interview her. After that she agreed to meet me.

A few days later, we went to Jahanara's house. Her husband ran a tea shop with Jahanara's money. Jahanara had two sons and two daughters. The daughters were older, with the eldest having studied up to seventh grade. However, none of the younger children was enrolled in school. Jahanara said that there was no point in schooling them since she could provide for all of them with her money. In her words, "What can they do with an education? Better to learn moneylending."

I had expected a brick building in keeping with Jahanara's new status. Instead, four tin-roofed houses faced a courtyard. At one corner of the yard was a shallow tube-well that supplied drinking water to the family. The local municipal corporation had provided the tube-well. The family used a pit latrine. Jahanara shared the family homestead with one of her husband's two brothers. Jahanara and her husband owned two of these four houses. Her son-in-law and seventeen-year-old daughter lived in one of the tin-roofed houses. It was a large single room with a bed inside it. Unlike some of the other successful borrowers I had met, Jahanara was very careful with her money. Her residence was not ostentatious, and her lifestyle was frugal.

When we arrived, Jahanara came forward to meet us. She was dressed in a red sari and wore substantial amounts of gold (nose ring, bangles, and a chain) for a rural person. Her teeth were streaked red from chewing betel leaf. A striking woman, Jahanara looked confident and well fed. She had already notified several of her neighbors that an older sister from abroad was going to write about her in a book that would be read by many people. Soon after we arrived at her house, several women came and joined us. It was obvious that they held Jahanara in high esteem. Later some of these women told us that they were in debt to Jahanara. For Jahanara, my presence was an acknowledgment in front of her neighbors and kin of her social importance. I heard her say a few times to the gathered women, "Look, now city people come to talk to me."

Jahanara invested her money in four categories: short-term trade, small businesses, middle farmers, and NGO borrowers, with most of the money being given in short-term trade that takes between three to six months to return a profit. The money was lent to traders who bought local produce such as paddy (rice, especially in the husk), betel leaves, jute, and timber, and took them by boat to other parts of the country where they would fetch higher prices. Local people consider this a safe form of investment. They do not lose the money unless the boat capsizes with the goods, which, from what I could tell, was rare in this region.

At one time or another, Jahanara had been a member of all the NGOs in Pirpur. In 1999, she was a member of the following NGOs: Grameen Bank (seven years), BRAC (five years), Proshika (five years), ASA (two years), Nari Unnayan Prochesta (three years), and Productive Employment Project (PEP for ten years). Jahanara's day was atypical for a rural woman. She did not stay at home to do housework. Most of her time was spent collecting money from people. She also spent considerable time going to NGO meetings to pay her dues or to collect new loans.

Jahanara gave the following account of her life:

"My life was not always easy. I was the third daughter of a family of eight. My father was a poor sharecropper. He married me off early, a year after my first menstrual period. [I put that age at thirteen.] My marriage was a simple occasion and there was no dowry involved, just a small sum of money. I was considered beautiful as a young girl, so my father was able to marry me to a family with more wealth than ours. My husband's family had some land that they leased out. My husband was the youngest of three brothers. The first few years of my married life were difficult. I had three children and they all died in childbirth. Over the next ten years, I had four more kids, two girls and two boys. Then after my last son was born, I went to the Family Planning Office and had a surgery. This was my decision. I told my husband, we have two sons, and I can have an operation now. I wanted to give my children a better life.

"My husband is a simple-minded person. He could not handle complicated matters of leasing lands and keeping track of records. He got into a lot of debt. I watched all this from inside the house. He lost the land he got from his parents to the moneylenders. Following that, he started to work as a day laborer but he could not earn enough to feed a family of six. During this period, life became very difficult for us. There were days when I could not even light the stove for three days. Nobody helped me. My in-laws lived well but they did not share their food with us. Their behavior made me very angry, and I was determined to change my fortune.

"I knew about NGOs in the area that I could join. They were giving loans to poor women like me. I decided that I would join a *samity* (NGO) and I would change our circumstances. I did not ask my husband's permission to join. The first NGO I joined was Social Development Project (SDP). I took 7,000 taka from them. I kept some money aside for repaying the loans, and the rest of it I used for sharecropping. For every 1,000 taka, I would be given 6 maunds [1 maund is equal to 37.5 kilograms] of rice. Once the rice was harvested, I sold the rice and made a small profit.

With that money and some other money I had saved, I invested the money in short-term trade.

"The same year, I took out a second loan from SDP for 30,000 taka. That NGO manager was a kind person. I told him if he gave me a big loan [that is, several loans lumped together] then I would give him some benefit. [This meant that Jahanara would give him a share of her profits.] I told him how I had invested money in short-term trade and had received a good income. I asked him to give me more loans, and in two months I would be able to pay him back. This manager took a risk with me. He did not force me to pay back the loan installments on time. The short-term investment gave me 1,125 kilograms of rice in addition to 30,000 taka. I sold half of the rice for profit, and paid my loan installments with some of the profit. I realized that this was a lucrative business. All I had to do was raise money and give it to someone else to invest. I decided to join different NGOs to raise money.

"I have also taken out loans in my daughter's name and in the names of other people. I am teaching my daughter my trade. I take loans out by proxy. I pay these women 100 taka each for letting me take the loan. Now the managers of all the NGOs give me the highest loans possible. If they do not want to give me the kind of loan I want, I say to them, I will cross out my name and go elsewhere. [Here she paused and laughed.] They need me more than I need them. They do not want me to leave. I am a good investment. I have money, so I always pay my installments on time. In this way, I have raised 350,000 taka. All my money is lent out to traders in town: short-term trade, sharecropping, and NGO borrowers.

"From this 350,000 taka, I spent a third of it on family expenses. With about 1,000 taka, I opened a tea shop for Hasina's father. [Hasina is the name of her eldest daughter. Rural women do not address their husbands by their names.] I have told him to run the daily operating expenses of the family from the income of the tea shop. I will invest my money and make us wealthy. Occasionally, I buy clothes for the family. Once eight months ago, I fed my entire extended family of about 100 people. I fed them well. They wanted to know how I was doing so well. Well, what do you know? I just smiled.

"What are my plans for the future? I will remain with these NGOs for another five years. By then I expect to raise 1,000,000 taka. After that, I will live off my earnings."

Jahanara had purchased land for 60,000 taka. She had also bought some gold ornaments and three cycle vans that she leased out to day laborers. These vans were used for carrying goods and people in villages. She had also lent 10,000 taka to NGO borrowers.

Jahanara pointed to one young woman who had entered the courtyard and stood in one corner. Jahanara said, "That is Shokina. Everyday she comes and pesters me for a loan. She wants 60,000 taka [$1,304]."

I asked Shokina, "What do you need that much money for?"

Shokina did not reply. She kept her eyes down. Jahanara laughed and said, "Her brother wants to go to Malaysia, so she wants to raise money. She has already taken 40,000 taka [$869] from Grameen Bank."

Jahanara then turned to Shokina and said, "I don't give so much money to one person. What is my guarantee?"

I asked Jahanara, "Why will you not lend her the money?"

Jahanara laughed and said, "Hah, what do you know? I give so much money to one person and then what if she cannot pay me back."

Upon hearing this Shokina got very angry and left muttering, "We are not dishonest people. We too have honor."

Rina turned to me and said, "She is angry because Jahanara commented that maybe she could not pay in front of an outsider."

Jahanara turned to me and said, "Tomorrow she will be back asking for money. I have to deal with many situations. I never risk putting money all in one place."

This is how Jahanara described her success:

> One has to run. If you sit around, nothing will happen. I go with the members to the NGO office when we have to get the loan. I get the money and leave. I don't stay in their office long. When I give money to NGO women borrowers, I have to be careful. These women are so needy. You cannot give them too much money; 1,000 or 2,000 taka [between $21 and $43] is about the maximum amount. If I give them too much money, then I have to walk around empty-handed later. They will not be able to pay back. I give them loans when they cannot pay their installments or when there is an emergency.

I was quite taken aback by her confidence. This was the first time I had encountered a woman who was so confident in her ability to continue to prosper. Curious to know if she had a plan to protect her wealth, I asked Jahanara what she would do if these men decided not to give her back the money.

Jahanara explained, "I only extend money on a contractual basis. If they were not to pay, I would file a legal case against them. The traders are afraid of me. When they pay money, my husband stays with me. But I count the money. Everyone knows me here. To date, I have not lost any money. But I sometimes take pity on people. I gave 6,000 taka to a woman and she was supposed to pay me back 10,000 taka, which included the interest on the principal. But she could only pay me 7,000 taka. I let her off. Poor dear, she could not raise the money."

At the end of our conversation, Jahanara said that she did not think that other women could become like her. According to her, "They do not understand anything except their husbands. If I gave my earnings to my husband, he would use it all up. And I just invest my money in business. In the beginning, I never thought of getting food, clothes for my children. I was very careful with my money. If you go to the homes of these women on the day they get a loan from an NGO, you will find that for the next seven days they spend the money on fish and meat. My husband is also not like other men. He lets me have my way. I bought land next to my father's house. He did not say anything.

"I married off my daughter early, at the age of fourteen. What will she do with an education? She will also become a moneylender like me. I told my son-in-law that if he could raise 150,000 taka, then I would give him an additional 200,000 taka to go to Japan as a construction worker. This has been my final word to him: if you find the money, I will help you get to Japan."

After this conversation, my research assistant and I left because Jahanara had to keep appointments with her clients.

A few days later, Rina and I went to the Grameen Bank loan meeting in Krishnonagar, where Jahanara was the Center leader. At this meeting, Jahanara proposed loans that would go into her own pocket for ten members. All these members were proxy loanees. This was done in front of the Grameen field-worker. Later, the field-worker said to me, "If I do not let Jahanara take the money, then I cannot keep discipline in the group. She controls the group. And my office puts pressure on me to disburse loans to creditworthy people. She pays back on time."[11]

At this meeting, one woman called Kashai Bou [butcher's wife] was not present. Kashai Bou lived several villages away, and the Grameen Bank officer and Jahanara went to collect the money from her. Rina and I went with them. On the way to Kashai Bou's house, Jahanara told us that she had broken many houses when members could not pay. "We know when they cannot pay, so we take a carpenter with us to break the house." House breaking, which is the physical act of taking apart a house to sell off the construction materials, is an old custom in rural Bangladesh. Richer landlords would break the houses of poorer tenants when they failed to pay their dues. The building materials were sold off to recover the sum owed to the landlord.

A smiling Jahanara (small moneylender) with Kashai Bou in the background.

The Grameen loan officer, who was listening to our conversation, smirked and said, "Just ask her. They are very organized when it comes to recovering money."

I asked Jahanara, "Why do you break the houses of kin?"

Jahanara became indignant at first. Her comment was, "Why should we not? They have breached their trust with us. If they cannot pay, then we will have to pay. Why should I pay for them?" Then she became quiet and after a while added, "It is not good to break someone's house, but we are forced to do it. This is how we get loans from Grameen Bank and other NGOs. They put pressure on us to recover the money, then we all get together and force the defaulting member to give us money."

At Kashai Bou's house, we waited for one hour. Kashai Bou said that her husband had gone to the market to sell the hide of the cow he had slaughtered that morning, he did not show up. Finally we left. On our way back, Jahanara asked us to stop at her mother-in-law's house. Once there, Jahanara said to her mother-in-law, "Look, they come from the city to interview me."

When I mentioned Jahanara to the manager of an NGO in my area, he laughed and said, "She is an excessively smart woman. You come back in a couple of years and you will find that she has lost her money. She is extending too much money too quickly these days. There are too many unforeseen factors that she cannot control."

Narrative 4: The Other Side of Paradise

While Jahanara was the most successful woman I met during my research, Bokul's story gives another side of the social spectrum of NGO loans. One day I heard about the suicide of Bokul's husband. I had heard rumors about NGO members committing suicide because of their inability to pay back the money. Bokul lived in Guccha Gram, a cluster of ten small houses which was set up by former prime minister Khaleda Zia (BNP) for homeless families. The families living there belonged to the hard-core poor. It took us twenty minutes by a cycle van to get to her house. We had to pass the Pirpur market and then cross a small river to get there.

When Rina and I arrived at her house, Bokul gave us the following account of her husband's suicide. Bokul had taken a loan for 8,000 taka ($173) from ASA. She had only two installments left to pay when her husband killed himself. Bokul's husband, Iskander Bepari, was a cycle-van driver, but he developed a severe case of hemorrhoids, and could no longer work. His illness had forced him to fall behind on the payments. His inability to pay resulted in the group members and ASA officials coming to his house and abusing him and his wife. Then the group members decided that Bokul had to sell off their bed (chowki) to pay back the money to ASA. According to Bokul, who was a member of both ASA and BRAC, they broke the fencing of the house and took away the bed to sell it off. Following this incident, eyewitnesses said that Bepari began to cry because "he could not protect his honor." He later committed suicide by drinking pesticide, which is easily accessible in farming communities. It was unclear, though, if Bepari committed suicide because of his public humiliation by the NGO or because of depression brought on from prolonged illness and inability to feed his family.

Bepari had left behind four children, ranging in age from one and a half to eight years. Bokul worked part-time as a mud cutter on a road-building project. She made between 10 and 50 taka (between 25 cents and $1) a day. At the time I met Bokul, her children often went without food. Bokul's story deeply moved me. She was a young woman with four small children. The wages as a mud cutter barely supported the family of five. I wanted to help her. But if I helped her monetarily, it would get around, and others in Guccha Gram and elsewhere would demand that I help them too. Some of the other women I had known much longer. On an individual level, there was not much that I could do. On my last visit to Pirpur, I took a large sack of rice, lentils, and cooking oil for her. A small gesture, and I naively thought that Bokul would be happy with the food. Seeing the food, Bokul said to me, "How long will this last? What I need is a job. Can you find me a job?"

I was embarrassed by my ignorant act. Unable to give Bokul any concrete hopes for the future, I finally told her that I did not have anything to offer her. There was an embarrassing silence. Momentarily, the lines that separated us were broken. Bokul saw me as a woman with no power to change her destiny. Then the lines that separated our lives were redrawn. Bokul said she would cook her evening meal. It was time for me to go. I said good-bye.

As I walked away from her home, I asked myself if the actions of the NGO officers were wholly to blame. There are millions of Bokuls in Bangladesh. Growing up, I had met many young women, such as Bokul, who had migrated to Dhaka to be domestic workers in the homes of middle-class families. The work conditions that they were subjected to were horrific. In this scenario of wrenching poverty, what were the options? The majority of NGO field officers I encountered were ordinary men and women who were desperately trying to make a decent middle-class living. With the scarcity of jobs for in Bangladesh, NGOs offered field-workers a better life than what they could aspire to in small, provincial towns. Commenting on

Bokul with her children and neighbor.

their complicity in these coercive techniques with their often tragic consequences, an NGO manager explained the ethical dilemmas facing them by
giving the following example:

> I once went into the house of a woman who could not pay her *kisti* [install-
> ment]. I went into her kitchen. There was a 5-kilo bag of wheat. I told her to
> sell that to pay her *kisti*. That was the only food she had to feed her children.
> I had to do it. Then I realized that her children would go without food. What
> am I doing? I said to myself. I am supposed to help these people, and yet I am
> taking the food from her children's mouths. I gave her eldest son 50 taka ($1)
> from my pocket and told him to buy some food from the bazaar.

Then the manager looked me straight in the eye and said, "Do you think
I like doing this job?"

Narrative 5: Umar Ghorami and Failed Loan Programs

In my area, I found that Proshika had developed into a poorly run organization, with member complaints, management excesses, and lack of oversight in operations. This was particularly striking given that Proshika had
started as a social-conscientization NGO in the 1970s. Many of the older
Proshika members I met had a strong social critique of rural dynamics,
which they had learned in the early days of Proshika, when it had organized poor people against the landed elites. During my research, I found
that the organization diverged at a great length from its earlier message of
peasant struggle. When I mentioned this to Proshika management, there
was an unwillingness to acknowledge these problems.[12] The following
story, of Umar Ghomari, illustrates the indifference on the part of Proshika
when extending loans to people. Flush with donor money that emphasized
rapid expansion of its microfinance program with little oversight, Proshika
management loaned without inquiring whether these borrowers had the
capacity to invest the money productively.

Umar Ghorami ran a small retail store in Pirpur Bazaar. Ghorami had
been a member of Proshika's Bhai Bhai Samity (Brotherhood Samity) since
1994. There were twelve members in the group. Most of the members
were unemployed and had never handled large sums of money. In 1997,
Proshika filed a case against all of them. Ghorami told me the following:

"Our Proshika field-worker said that he would sanction 15,000 taka
[$326] for a project. I took 4,000 taka [$86] from this fund. I asked Proshika manager and field-worker to help me design a project. They said, 'We
have twelve or fourteen motorcycles at the Proshika office. Why don't you

Umar Ghorami in his retail shop.

sell oil to us?' I decided to do that but soon ran into problems with Proshika workers who use the motorbikes because they doctor gas receipts and steal money from Proshika. If they spent 500 taka on gas, they show it as 1,000 taka [$21.70] on the receipt. So, that project fell apart because they would not buy oil from me.

"Then one Proshika Apa [who later lost her job with Proshika] gave us a 10,000-taka [$217] project for planting mulberry trees on the strip of land on the side of the highway. We said to her that we did not know anything about sericulture. She promised to train us. They delayed in getting us the saplings. We planted them in the wrong season. For 6,000 taka [$130] they gave us 14,000 to 15,000 saplings. Insects destroyed these saplings. Proshika management said that they were not responsible. They said to us, 'Insects have destroyed the trees, what can we do?' The manager later told us we would not have to pay back the loan of 10,000 taka. We are uneducated people: we did not think of writing it down. Then he was transferred, and a new manager came in. The new manager demanded back payments on this loan.

"We took out another loan for 10,000 taka and replanted mulberry saplings. However, the District Commissioner [DC] came for a tour of the area and said that we had illegally planted on government land. The DC had all our mulberry saplings hewed. Proshika management had told us Proshika had leased the land from the government for 3,000 taka [$65]. They took that money from our funds. I think there were some personal tensions between Proshika management and the DC. Proshika managers again told us, 'What can we do? The DC ordered for the trees to be cut down.'

"In the meantime, the field-worker who had organized our *samity* was fired. He had never disbursed the full amount to us. Some of the members said they would not pay Proshika because the field-worker had tricked them into signing a document showing that they had received more money than what he had disbursed. The document showed that Proshika had disbursed 56,000 taka [$1,217], instead of 35,000 taka [$760], to Bhai Bhai Samity. But we only received 35,000 taka (15,000 + 10,000 + 10,000 [$760]) over a three-year period. So Proshika started legal proceedings against us. This case has been ongoing for one and a half years. For every court appearance, we have to pay between 300 and 500 taka as court costs. In addition to that, we have to pay *kistis* to Proshika for the remaining 35,000 taka.

"After my three losses with Proshika, I bought a cycle van. I borrowed the money from a moneylender. Then I sold off the cycle van to start the retail shop."

I asked Umar Ghorami why he took on a second loan for mulberry tree cultivation when he had failed once, and he said, "They promised us a new loan. I expected to recover my losses. They said that on an investment of 15,000 taka we could make 100,000 taka."

Ghorami added that Bhai Bhai Samity broke about two years ago. "As a member of the group, I had broken homes four or five times. I even broke my own brother's house."

When I asked him why he broke the house of his own brother, he replied, "Proshika management would order us to go and break someone's house to recover the money. They would say, 'They are defaulters, you have to recover the money, otherwise you will not get any new loans.' Now when I reflect upon it, I feel bad. These people cried, they would hold our feet to spare them, but we would go ahead and break the house apart and sell it off piece by piece. Our Proshika sirs would sit at the local tea shop and drink tea while we broke the house."

While Ghorami indicated a sense of remorse at some of his actions, he also felt betrayed by his brother for not fulfilling his contractual obligations. Confronted by my question, Ghorami had said, "I should not have broken my brother's house." Yet, facing social pressure from the NGO and the group in the future, Ghorami would most likely once again break the houses of other borrowers.

By giving loans to people who could not invest the money properly, and by telling them that they would materially improve their condition, the NGOs induced poor people into risk taking that often had, in my experience, unforeseen consequences on their lives. The problems faced by Ghorami reflected the unregulated and rapid growth of the microfinance programs in Bangladesh that emphasized an increase in member enrollments, loan disbursements, and installment collections over training and social investment in the lives of the borrowers.

Narrative 6: Loan Recovery through House Breaking

In rural Bangladesh, house breaking is the ultimate stamp of dishonor. During my research, I heard of incidents of house breaking (ghar bhanga) by NGOs to recover defaulted sums from members. House breaking is a preexisting mechanism of disciplinary control that was appropriated by NGOs in the service of their loan programs. It has the dual effect of public shaming (loss of one's home) and fear of punitive action if one fails to live up to the contractual obligations to the NGO. By adding it to their disciplinary actions, NGOs had routinized house breaking as appropriate behavior against defaulters. In fact, rural people talked about house breaking by NGOs dispassionately. When I asked some NGO members what they would do if a member had no assets left that they could repossess, they replied indifferently, "They have their house. We will take that." NGO officers would justify their actions by saying that NGOs do not break houses, community members do. Yet, these decisions were made with full knowledge and implicit approval of NGO officers. In my research area, I heard of five or six such incidents of house breaking.

I began to find a pattern of defaulters leaving for the urban slums of Dhaka. I had asked Rina to keep track of people who were leaving the village due to their inability to pay off NGO debts. We heard a number of such stories of urban migrations. These migrations resulted from the condensation of adverse factors from financial loss due to land erosion, mortgage, dowry payments, family illness, NGO loan payments, and business failures, and no one cause could be isolated.

In a nearby village, Komela was a member of Proshika. Of the seventeen members in her group, four had left the village for the city. One day I heard that Proshika and ASA had repossessed Komela's house. I also heard that she had borrowed extensively from NGOs and her kin, and that she had left for the capital, Dhaka. When Rina and I arrived at Komela's home, an older bearded man came forward to meet us and introduced himself as Komela's uncle. He asked me if I represented an NGO. Obviously suspicious, he kept asking me which NGO I represented and whether I had come from Dhaka to find out where Komela had gone. After he was satisfied that we were not with any NGO trying to discover Komela's whereabouts, he spoke to us about her.

Komela had been a member of Proshika since 1990. Her husband's name was Babul. Komela, Babul, and Komela's sister had taken loans from Proshika for 21,000 taka ($456). Komela took another 8,000 taka ($173) from ASA and 15,000 taka ($326) from CARITAS. Several installments were paid to Grameen, Proshika, and ASA. Komela apparently did not pay a single penny to CARITAS. She was also a member of Grameen Bank, but her relatives did not know how much she owed them. Then, one night about a year ago, Komela's family left their village. They left behind an outstanding debt of 44,000 taka ($956) to Proshika, ASA, and CARITAS. In addition to this money, they had borrowed 80,000 taka ($1,739) from a moneylender. Komela's relatives broke the house about two months ago because the Proshika field-worker had come and threatened them: "Either you pay the money, or you find some other way." Showing me around the area, the uncle explained, "ASA took all household belongings, the trees they had planted, the bed, even the slab used in the latrine. The big house was made of tin. Proshika sold the tin for 10,000 taka ($217). I took the tin from the kitchen and the cow shed. Komela and her husband owed me some money as well."

I had asked Komela's uncle why they participated in these acts of house breaking against their kin. He looked me over for a few minutes trying to assess where my sympathies were. Then he added, "You are critical of NGO activities, so I will tell you this. People are leaving the village because of NGOs. NGOs are creating new wants among rural people. Suddenly the very poor have money, and they consume it all. NGOs never look to see how people will invest the money. They are only interested in recovering their money. It is a business. Sometimes poor people think, 'We are poor, they will forgive our debt.' If you take NGO money, you will have to pay back 100 percent. They do a lot of tyranny, but we do not know how to fight them."

From the details I could gather, Komela and her husband did not have good intentions. They had raised capital from various NGOs, relatives, and moneylenders in order to leave the village to start a new life in Dhaka. Most

Komela's plot after her house was broken. An earthen pot indicates where her house was formerly located.

of the families who leave their villages for the city do so because they have lost all hope of survival in their village. The slums in Dhaka comprise a floating population of the poor who have come to the city because of landlessness. These men and women eke out an existence by plying a rickshaw, driving a cab, hammering metal pots, repairing bicycles, selling fruits, working in garment factories, as hired help, and in a variety of similar occupations. In most situations, the women continued to send money home to their relatives to repay the loans. I was initially surprised to hear of the transfer of money from Komela to her relatives. Kin members participated in breaking houses of kin, but they remained "loyal" to each other by meeting their obligations. An NGO worker explained the contradiction of this phenomenon by saying, "You have to understand that one day they have to come back to village society. They have to marry their daughters off. They get temporary relief by escaping to the slums, but they still remain linked to rural life, and they have to meet most of their financial obligations."[13]

Narrative 7: Feroza's Story

One day I heard that Feroza of Guccha Gram was going to lose her house to ASA. Feroza was a member of ASA and BRAC. She had fallen behind on her payments to ASA, and now the manager of ASA demanded that she sell her house to pay them. Rina and I went over to meet Feroza. Feroza's mother and her sons lived in one of the houses. Feroza's husband was a day laborer. He plied a cycle van. Feroza was his second wife. Initially, Feroza had lived with her husband and his first wife. Then, the two wives fought, and Feroza's husband made a very small thatched house (*jhupri*) for Feroza to live in with her newborn baby. This house was in one corner of their property.

Close to Feroza's house lived Salam Master, who was the headmaster of the local primary school in Shikarmongol, an adjoining village to Guccha Gram. He had bought land at the edge of Guccha Gram and built a house. Salam Master and his family did not associate with the local people there because they considered the inhabitants of Guccha Gram "lower-class people."

The situation became complicated when Feroza's younger brother, a day laborer, saw Salam Master's fifteen-year-old daughter and fell in love with her. He then proposed to her. The headmaster's daughter refused him. Following the refusal, Feroza's brother came to the house of Salam Master in the early hours of dawn one morning. He had a syringe filled with sulfuric acid. The bedroom window was open and the headmaster's daughters were sleeping inside. He sprayed the girls with the acid, burning their legs.

Following this event, the girl's father filed a case against Feroza's brother. Fearing arrest, the young man and his family (mother and another brother) left Guccha Gram in the middle of the night. Salam Master had influence with the police force and asked the constable to jail Feroza's husband instead. By jailing Feroza's husband, he reasoned that it would force Feroza to put pressure on her brother to return to Guccha Gram. With her husband in jail, Feroza fell behind on her payments. When I talked to local people, they said that Feroza's brother would eventually return to the village. The family could not stay away from Guccha Gram indefinitely. In their opinion, Salam Master should have waited to arrest the brother.

Feroza's case was with Mizan, a new field-worker with ASA.[14] He had a difficult time maintaining fiscal discipline among his borrowers. With Feroza, Mizan encountered problems with loan repayments. Mizan discovered that the first wife's daughter, Khadija, was married and lived with her mother-in-law in another village, Minajdi, which fell under his collection jurisdiction. Within two weeks of joining the new ASA group in Minajdi, Khadija and her mother-in-law began to pressure Mizan to give them both loans. Mizan had initially declined the loan request because according to

ASA rules, members had to save for twelve weeks before they were eligible for loans. Each ASA member saved 20 taka a month, for a total of 60 taka in three months. The savings acted as collateral in case of defaults, and also taught members fiscal discipline.

In order to recover money from Feroza, Mizan tried to compel her through her kin. He told Khadija that she had to put pressure on her mother (Feroza's co-wife) to force Feroza to sell her house to recover the outstanding dues to ASA. Once Feroza repaid the installment, he would give Khadija and her mother-in-law the new loans. Despite this pressure, Feroza would not sell her house. Failing to procure the loans, Khadija's mother-in-law became very angry with her daughter-in-law, and asked her son to take Khadija back to her mother's (Feroza's co-wife) house in Guccha Gram. Khadija would stay there until her mother and stepmother Feroza could settle this matter with ASA. At the time of my visit to Feroza, Khadija was staying with her mother. As a result of the return of Khadija, a shameful incident in rural society, the tensions between the two co-wives were intensified.

One day we went with Mizan to watch how he would apply pressure on Feroza to get money. When we arrived at Feroza's house, she was sitting in her courtyard stitching a quilt. Feroza had loaned 600 taka ($13) to another borrower. Mizan knew about the loan and wanted her to repay ASA from this money. She owed ASA 125 taka ($2.70).

Mizan asked Feroza, "Where is my *kisti?*"

Feroza looked up from her stitching and said lightly, "Why are you speaking so darkly?"

"Hand over the money fast. I am tired of the two of you skirting this issue."

Feroza said to him, "You have put your cycle on my quilt."

Mizan said, "I will run you over with my cycle. You get 600 taka from one woman. Tell her to give me 125 taka."

Feroza retorted, "I will give that money to BRAC."

Upon hearing that, Mizan became very angry and raised his voice, "Oh, you will give to your BRAC father, and not to me? Have you forgotten that ASA is also your father?"

(Here Mizan compared the filial duty toward one's father with one's duty toward ASA, the benefactor/father that took care of its poor children.)

Feroza became very angry and said, "You are not my father. My mother is not married to you."

Then Mizan shouted, "Come with me, I will take you to jail."

Feroza said, "Fine, I will go with you to jail."

They started to walk toward the market, and Rina and I walked behind them. Right before entering the market, Feroza stopped in front of a local bookstore. Mizan pulled at her arm to make her walk. The sleeve of her blouse came off. The blouse was already torn, so it came off easily. At this point Feroza started to shout, "You are a non-kin man, and how dare you touch my body? You have dishonored me." Feroza had purposefully stopped in front of the shop to have some witnesses who would perhaps come to her aid and save her from going to the police station.

Mizan, a young man in his early twenties, probably did not realize how quickly the situation would get out of control. Several men who were sitting at the shop had witnessed the "arm pulling" and intervened. One of them happened to be Feroza's cousin-in-law. These men said that Feroza should return home to Guccha Gram. They said that she was "at fault" for coming with Mizan in the first place. Feroza insisted on going to the police station with Mizan to file a complaint against him for touching her.[15] Finally, the men made Feroza return home, saying that they would settle things. During this incident I said very little, and was complicit in what was happening to Feroza by not speaking out. In the past, when I tried to intercede on behalf of the women, they would use my words against their NGO managers, which made my work very difficult. I also did not want to embarrass and antagonize Mizan because I depended on NGO field-workers such as him to be my interlocutors.

After Feroza left for her home, we all sat down at the bookstore, and tea was offered to everyone as is customary in Bangladeshi society. The men collectively decided that Feroza would either pay the 125 taka from the 600 taka she was owed or sell her house and pay off the entire loan. Although Feroza was the borrower, her opinion did not figure in this male-dominated discussion.

We returned with Mizan to the ASA office. When we arrived, another field-worker who was sitting at his table looked at me angrily and said, "You are making our work more difficult. The women in my group said that two women came and took down all information. Now these women will file a case against you."

Sitting down, Mizan said that "his blood had boiled over" when he heard that BRAC would get the money from Feroza, but not ASA. Feroza feared the power and oppression of BRAC more than that of ASA because of ASA's relatively unknown status in their village. The ASA management team was made up of four young men: one manager and three NGO field-workers.

None of them were local, and none had yet built up a system of trust in the community.

The other NGO field-worker said to Mizan, "You made the mistake of fraternizing with Feroza. You took her son and put him on your lap. Once you breach the official lines that separate us from our clients, our ability to enforce the rules collapses. Now you have to pay the price. By breaking these rules, you make matters more difficult for all of us."

I knew that they would break Feroza's little thatched house to recover their outstanding loans, but they were unwilling to confide in me when they would do it. A few days later, I heard from the ASA manager that they had recovered the money from Feroza. When I got to Feroza's house, her little thatched hut was gone. Feroza was standing in the open yard hold-ing her child in her arms. When she saw me, she ran and hid behind some trees. I stood in the yard and called her name a few times. She finally came out. When I asked her why she ran away (did she fear that I would further abuse her?), she said that she was embarrassed because I had witnessed her inability to pay. I tried to explain to Feroza that she should not feel shame about her inability to pay; ASA should be ashamed about making her sell her house for 125 taka ($2.70)!

Narrative 8: Chicken "Entrepreneurs"

Female chicken breeders are one of the most showcased entrepreneurs of microcredit programs. The BRAC chicken industry was set up in 1978 with support from Western donors, most notably from the Netherlands. The BRAC chicken program expanded under the Income Generation for Vulner-able Group Development Program (IGVGDP), run by the World Food Pro-gram and the Bangladeshi government, with BRAC as the local distributor of this aid.[16]

At the time of my research in 1999, the BRAC Poultry Program was not self-sufficient. At the BRAC Head Office, I met with Golam Mostafa, the regional manager of the Poultry and Livestock Program, toward the end of my research. Mostafa informed me that BRAC had opened the poultry pro-grams with a view to creating income and employment for poor women. BRAC targeted the poorest women among their beneficiaries—the VGD women. These women are usually destitute, widowed, or abandoned, and they are considered at high risk of economic vulnerability. Mostafa pro-vided me with the following figures. The local currency is calculated at 47 taka to the US dollar.

During this time, BRAC operated three farms—one each in Savar Khamar, Rajbari Alladipur, and Bogra Sherpur—that provided day-old chickens. In April 1999, the total number of day-old chickens supplied to BRAC Chick Rearers was 1,021,930. Out of this number, BRAC farms supplied 538,022 chickens, and the rest came from government and commercial farms. In addition to its own production of chicks, BRAC had agreements with state-run and commercial farms for the supply of day-old chickens. BRAC also had two feed mills to provide chicken feed to the rearers. From figures given to me by Mostafa, the feed was a compound made of hybrid corn, shellfish meal, and sesame husk. One kilogram of feed was sold to the rearers for 10.75 taka (broiler chick feed) and 11 taka (egg-layer feed). In April 1999, the two mills produced 1,519,000 kilograms, which at 11 taka per kilogram came to 16,713,345 taka.

Through its poultry program, BRAC had created four linked categories of BRAC women workers: chick rearers, key rearers, pullet rearers, and poultry extension workers. Chick rearers bought day-old chicks from BRAC, and BRAC bought the chicks back when they were eight weeks old. Key rearers, who bought these eight-week chicks from BRAC, sold them after two months either to pullet rearers (those who raise layer chickens) or directly to the market and commercial farms. The final category was the poultry extension worker, who was trained by BRAC to vaccinate and offer curative care to the chickens. BRAC sold the vaccines that it bought from the government to the poultry extension workers. Vaccine per chick cost 5 taka. The extension worker's profit was 50 poisha (100 poisha = 1 taka) per vaccine. For vaccinating 100 chickens, an extension worker made 50 taka.

I did find some discrepancies between BRAC figures and the figures I collected in the villages in Pirpur. First, BRAC had an official chick mortality rate of 4.8 percent for April 1999. I found a mortality rate of 50 percent or higher in my area. Second, the women I spoke with had bought the feed at 12 taka per kilogram, and not at 11 taka, as claimed by Mostafa from BRAC. The local BRAC manager had also verified 12 taka as the actual

Key rearers	1,420,200
Poultry workers	45,853
Chick rearers	18,289
Day-Old chick distribution	36,815,081

BRAC cumulative poultry statistics from 1985 to April 1999.

figure. The local manager probably admitted to this higher figure because I had already gathered this information from the women. When I mentioned this fact to Mostafa at BRAC, he said that I must be "misinformed." In my estimation, the local BRAC area management team in Pirpur was making a small profit off these women by overcharging them 1 taka (or more) per kilogram of feed.

According to field officers and VGD members I met, BRAC chicken farms were set up in the following manner.[17] The VGD women were identified and given loans by BRAC to raise the chicken for two months. BRAC employees visited the women's homes and selected a room in her house for "chick rearing." BRAC managers often intimidated and coerced the women into accepting the poultry farm concept.[18] These women depended on BRAC for the wheat subsidies (the WFP Program) as well as the loans.

BRAC Chickens at the Field Level

In Pirpur, BRAC had 6,200 members in 162 groups. There were 2,040 VGD cardholders, all of whom were also BRAC members.[19] There were twenty Chick Rearing Units (CRUs) in Pirpur. In my research area, I found that there was a high rate of attrition among BRAC borrowers. I soon found out that BRAC forced all its borrowers to buy between three and four eight-week-old chickens as a product tie-in with their loans. On days when BRAC distributed loans, one could see women outside the local BRAC office holding these chickens. BRAC charged 250 taka for four chickens, that is, a per-chick price of 62.5 taka. This amount was automatically deducted from the loan. Through this process, BRAC had created an internal market of breeder chickens and chicken feed, with its poor borrowers as the captive consumers. This forcible selling of breeder chickens as tie-ins with loans was an unwritten practice of BRAC. When I asked Fazle Abed about this policy in my meeting with him in Dhaka, he categorically denied it as "not true."[20]

The local BRAC manager in Pirpur became quite incensed with me when I pointed out that they forced these chickens on unwilling women borrowers. He said that BRAC distributed these chickens to women through its Vulnerable Group Development Program (VGDP) as income-generating projects. These chickens lay between 150 to 300 eggs a year, whereas local or indigenous chickens lay only between 45 to 60 eggs a year. By selling the chickens to the women, BRAC was ensuring a source of income for them. However, these chickens, called "breeder chickens," are imported from abroad, and they require a special diet, temperature-controlled rooms, good ventilation, and artificial light to survive. Poor women in Bangladesh do not have the resources to keep them alive for long, and most of the chickens die within a short time, as the high mortality rate of 50 percent attests.[21]

For the women in Pirpur, these chickens were an investment disaster. First, they did not want the chickens; they were forced by BRAC to buy them. Second, by the time the women reached home, the chickens would be almost dead from the humidity of Bangladesh. In order to recover some of their losses, most of the women sold the chickens in the local markets, instead. On days that BRAC distributed the loans and the chickens, I saw women at the local market trying to sell the chickens to the chicken vendor. Moreover, the diet of rural Bangladeshis rarely includes meat or chicken, and chicken is not high in demand. Few people wanted these chickens as egg layers because they were expensive to rear by local standards, and they were reputed to "die easily." But for the women, by selling them at a loss, they could recover at least part of their cost, that is, the 250 taka they had lost to BRAC.

BRAC had two kinds of breeder chickens: Faumi (also called white Leghorn), of Egyptian origin and imported from Pakistan; and Nera, which was a Dutch breed. Their breeding cycle is between one and a half to two years. Faumi laid between 150 and 200 eggs, and Nera between 250 to 300 eggs a year. According to BRAC, the cost of raising the chicken for two months was 18 taka (price of chick not included). This included feed of 11.5 takas per 1 kilogram per chick and vaccine medicine of 5 taka. Day-old chicks cost 10 taka for Faumi and 16 taka for Nera. So, the cost of each type of chicken was:

Nera chick	16 taka
Faumi chick	10 taka
Cost of feed	13 taka
Cost of vaccine	5 taka
Total per Nera chick	34 taka
Total per Faumi chick	28 taka

This cost did not include electricity, housing, building the wire coops for chickens, cost of chicken feeders, and most importantly, the cost of labor of these women. The women, when they were questioned about the expenses of raising the chickens, never factored in the price of their labor. The poor women and their families had to give up a room or find some space on their property for chick rearing. The room where the chickens were housed had to be well ventilated and to get plenty of sunshine. The temperature had to be controlled at all times, which posed a problem for women living in thatched or tin houses. Many of the women lost their chickens when there was a drop in temperature in winter or during the monsoon rains. After two months, BRAC bought back the chickens at a rate lower than that of the market (they had a preset rate that they offered the women) and then sold the chickens to other BRAC borrowers as loan product tie-ins. In turn, these BRAC borrowers sold the chickens at the market.

The breeder chickens circulated within this NGO-created economy made up of BRAC as a supplier of chicken and chicken feed, and the borrowers as rearers and buyers of these products. By setting up these poultry cottage industries, BRAC externalized the costs of production onto a group of vulnerable women who could not resist the imposition of these conditions. These women saw themselves as "entrepreneurs," whereas they worked as dirt-cheap labor for BRAC to establish its chicken industry.

I met with ten of the women chick rearers in Pirpur to find out about their experiences with these income-generating projects. All of them said that they had lost 50 percent of the chicks before the two months were over, that is, they had lost 50 percent of their potential profit from the sale of these chicks. Below I narrate the experiences of one such member, Runu.

Runu, a BRAC VGD member, had received a 15,000 taka ($326) loan to start a chicken farm. She said that "BRAC sirs" came to her house and told her that they would give her a loan to raise chickens, and that after two months she would make a 5,000 taka ($108), or a 33 percent, profit on her loan. They brought over the chickens, with special chicken feeders, and sold her the vaccines and special chicken feed. One of the rooms in her house was set aside for the chicken farm, and electric lines were rigged to keep an electric bulb on for 24 hours a day. Runu and her mother raised the chickens. They would take turns sleeping inside the chicken room at night to prevent foxes from killing the chickens. The room was thatched. They had covered it with a tarpaulin to keep out the cold and water. When I went inside the room, the smell of chicken excrement was so strong that I had to cover my nose with a cloth. Neither Runu nor her mother liked to sleep in the chicken coop at night, but they had invested 15,000 taka on this farm. They felt compelled to sleep in conditions that were likely hazardous to their health.

Runu had received training for three days from BRAC, but according to her, she had forgotten "everything." Within several weeks, 50 percent of Runu's chickens had died. Another neighbor of Runu's, Achia Begum, said that she had purchased 225 chicks from BRAC, and within eleven days 100

Runu's mother in her chicken farm. The sari and the mosquito net shows where one of them sleeps at night to guard against fox attacks.

chicks had died.[22] The Proshika chick rearers had similar stories to narrate. Overall, in my research area there was a 50 percent rate of chicken mortality. But unlike BRAC, Proshika had not created an internal market that turned its borrowers into consumers and producers of the chicken industry. Below I illustrate the costs incurred by Runu in her income-generating enterprise.

As the above breakdown shows, the women with zero chick mortality would make a profit of 898 taka, and not the 5,000 taka they were promised. When I mentioned this fact to the women, they said that initially they had thought that they would profit because BRAC managers had told them that they would buy all the chickens for 20,000 taka ($434) after two months, and that they would make a huge profit after paying off BRAC. BRAC management did not take any responsibility for the high mortality rate among its breeder chickens. Instead, they transferred the blame to the women for "inappropriate care" and "their inability to recall training." I am not making the argument that the breeder chicken industry should not be started in Bangladesh.[23] To the contrary, one cannot be against poor women making profit, but one can be against the exploitation and appropriation of the labor and wealth of poor women because they are unable to resist the imposition of these conditions on them by BRAC or any other

A. BRAC loan plus interest

Poultry loan from BRAC	15,000 taka
Interest rate at 15% (for 52 weeks)	2,250 taka
Total amount due to BRAC	17,250 taka

B. Runu's costs

Cost of 500 day-old chicks at 16 taka each	8,000 taka
Vaccine for 500 chicks at 5 taka each	2,500 taka
Chicken feed at 12 taka per chick × 500	6,000 taka
Electricity per month 176 taka × 2 for two months (two 150-watt light bulbs were on 24/7)	352 taka
Interest to be paid to BRAC	2,250 taka
Total cost:	19,102 taka

C. Runu's income

Her revenues: after 50 percent, or 250, of the chicks died, BRAC bought the remaining 250 chicks at 40 taka	10,000 taka
D. Runu's adjusted income	10,000 − 19,102 = <9,102 taka>

Runu's total adjusted costs for operating a BRAC chicken farm. Runu had a loss of 9,102 taka. If Runu had not lost a single chicken, she would have made a profit of 500 taka × 40 taka = 20,000 taka (her income) minus 19,102 taka (her cost from B above). Revenue = 898 taka or $19 at the 1998 exchange rate of 47 taka to 1 USD!

NGO for that matter. The pattern that emerged from these narratives was that these women were situated in a relationship of inequality and power vis-à-vis the NGOs that could grant or withhold loans from people who were in dire financial straits.

Analyzing NGO Practices

The lesson that we can take from chapters 3 and 4 is that the lives of poor women were constrained not only by their poverty but also by hierarchies of gender and kinship, and together these structures constrained their human possibilities. These structures of inequalities and hierarchies connected in multiple and antagonistic ways in the creation of markets and market subjects. In this landscape, the NGOs have successfully inserted themselves into the fabric of the reciprocities that hold together rural social relationships by linking the economic fates of various categories of people—women, their families, extended kin, petty traders, local elites, moneylenders—together in a lattice of financial dependencies. The community, in turn, had internalized these technologies of governance such that breaches of contract by individual borrowers were considered breaches against the collective good of the community.

The "inability to pay" took on several levels of significance. First, women borrowers understood this "break" in payment as a breach against the group and their individual interests. If we replace the notion of the group with the idea of a community, we can trace the extent to which a single default becomes entangled in a network that can eventually become explosive. Second, because these women were related as kin members, failure to pay was seen as a breach against the family and kin group. In these breakdowns, a defaulting woman was individuated as a "culprit" and separated from the group (be it family or borrowers) for bringing shame and dishonor on her husband, family, and community of borrowers.

In this scenario, the interest of the group lay in opposition to the individual. If one replaced the notion of "the group" with the financial institution or "the market," one can see the shift toward a very important transformation: the making of market subjects who are caught between market principles and existing social expectations. In these microcredit transactions, individuals become segregated, and common interests become privatized. In the remaking of this relationship, the individual is far more vulnerable than the group to the pressures of the market.

The eight case studies presented above show the polarities of the market subject, the successful women as in the case of Grameen ladies Rohima Begum, and Monowara Akhter, and the moneylender Jahanara Begum, and those who were unable to negotiate the stresses of the market, such as Komela, Umar Ghorami, Bokul, and Feroza. The concept of shame was central in the way the relationships in these narratives unfolded.

Amartya Sen has emphasized that a woman's agency has to be measured in terms of her increased decision-making power within the household. He lists several categories such as women's education, ownership patterns, and their employment opportunities, but he also noted that these issues are embedded within "the nature of the employment arrangements, attitudes of the family, and attitudes of the society at large about women's economic activities."[24] While women in Bangladesh came out to work in public works programs following the famine of 1974, the idea of the out-of-the-home worker promoted by microcredit programs kept the majority of the women inside their home, and as I have illustrated here, dependent on their husbands, kin, and NGOs. Thus, we need to analyze carefully the "arrangements" within which NGO narratives of women's empowerment get produced, and examine the processes through which women are constructed as entrepreneurs and consumers.

NGOs are able to govern rural populations because they provide a wide range of services to the poor. This has brought the NGO and the rural poor into a mutually dependent, yet ambivalent, relationship. Rural people are the first ones to acknowledge that "[they] submit to the will of NGOs because [they] are poor and powerless." While rural people were often critical of the actions of NGOs in many instances, especially those that interfered with the social roles of women, they were unwilling to contravene their contracts with NGOs. Without access to NGO credit, healthcare, primary education, physical assistance during floods, and road construction, rural life would be seriously jeopardized. It was this realization that made rural people consent to NGO governmentality. Rural people regulated their conduct to satisfy NGO dictates in order to reduce the adverse effects of noncompliance in their lives. This is precisely how and why NGOs are able to inaugurate themselves as the "allies of the poor," not through coercion, but compliance in a world of limited choices for their rural subscribers. NGOs provide services that the poor desperately need. In exchange, the poor clients give up some of their autonomy to receive these services. It is this power over resources that has enabled the NGO to reign as a powerful, but partial, "sovereign" in the triadic relationship of sovereignty, discipline, and government in rural Bangladesh.

Chapter 5   NGOs, Clergy, and Contested "Democracy"

IN THIS CHAPTER, I examine a conflict between Proshika and the clergy of a prominent madrassah known as Jamia Yunusia Islamia Madrassah over rural women's right to participate in a rally. The madrassah (hereafter called Yunusia) is located in Brahmanbaria, which is 150 kilometers northeast of Dhaka. Pirpur Thana is situated far from Brahmanbaria, in the southwestern part of the country, and it had no role in this conflict. As my analysis shows, the ability of NGOs to steer their female clients toward NGO goals took a particularly poignant expression in this conflict with the clergy.

Since the 1990s, Proshika had actively promoted a political culture among its rural beneficiaries, organizing them to contest local elections and attend political rallies. Rooted in the notion of liberal democracy—that is, the protection of the rights and liberties of the individual, and the defense of those rights against the state—NGO-sponsored grassroots democracy seeks to popularize secular norms such as the freedom of speech, assembly, religion, and the right of rural women to run for public office in a predominantly Muslim society. These democracy discourses have brought a profusion of development dollars from Western agencies to the NGO sector to promote human rights and good governance.[1]

Alongside the democratic movement, the 1990s also saw the mushrooming of Islamic political parties of various ideological orientations in Bangladesh.[2] The clergy of the various mosques and madrassahs in the country are affiliated with different Islamic groups. The rise in the number of these political parties, and the consolidation of their power at the rural level through foreign contributions, Islamic NGOs, mosques, and madrassahs, led to a series of confrontations between these groups and the NGOs in the early 1990s. However, after 1999, the Islamic political parties developed a different strategy. Instead of frontal attacks on the state or NGOs, they focused on bombings that sought to destabilize democratic rule by targeting public intellectuals, cultural troupes, theaters, government offices, courts, and journalists.[3] This shift in tactic and technology showed sophistication in training, coordination, and planning that these Islamic groups had previously lacked.

The following three incidents are important markers of this radical change. First, the legal feminist NGO Ain-o-Salish Kendro (ASK) had brought a petition to the highest court to declare all fatwas extrajudicial and illegal. The judges of the High Court ruled in their favor in 2001. The ruling was received with massive public rioting instigated by Islamic Oikye Jote, a coalition of seven parties that eventually led to the suspension of the ruling by the Appellate Court.[4] Second, in 2003 a movement known as Khatbe Nabuwat (Seal of the Prophet) began public demonstrations that members of the Ahmadiyya Muslim Jamaat must be declared non-Muslims through a parliamentary decree.[5] Third, in 2005, three hundred small bombs were set off all across the country within the span of thirty minutes that targeted courts, government offices, journalists' clubs, and theaters. While only a handful of people died from these bombings, the planners executed this operation with enormous skill and coordination.[6]

By the early 2000s then, the Islamic political parties had become sufficiently organized to strike at the state, judiciary, and secular forces through a combination of tactics ranging from public demonstrations to terrorist attacks. Within these groups, there is a range of political discourses and disagreements over strategy. Some groups advocate violence to take state power, others eschew violence. But all these Islamic groups are united in their demand to reconstruct society according to Islamic laws, or the sharia. They proscribe all forms of cultural festivities that include un-Islamic conduct such as the intermingling of men and women, music, theater, and dance; and they command that women wear the hijab (head-to-foot covering) in public. The strongholds of these Islamic groups are in the poorest parts of the country. Not surprisingly, these groups often come in conflict with leftists and NGOs over rural adherents, as noted in chapter 1.

The more socially progressive NGOs (Proshika, for example) have interpreted the rural clergy as part of a deep-rooted conspiracy to create a Talban-like state in Bangladesh. While the majority of the clergy may find the Taliban model worthy of emulation, these NGO claims of putative links between the Taliban and the clergy do not hold under scholarly scrutiny. Instead, I argue that it is more instructive to examine how NGOs and the clergy are entangled in similar motivations. The NGOs and clergy both attempt to establish their governance over rural subjects. They both provide services such as education and relief to the poor. However, within these two competing groups, the Western-aided NGOs are better equipped to service the poor, and they have the support of the government, which heightens resentment among the clerical establishment, as the NGOs encroach on their traditional clientele. Given this competition over resources, clients, and rural authority, it should not be surprising that occasionally these two groups find themselves in conflict. Against this background, let me discuss the conflict between Proshika and the clergy of Yunisia Madrassah.

I left Bangladesh for the United States in November 1998 for the annual anthropological meetings in Philadelphia. Upon my return to Bangladesh in January 1999, I heard that there was a clergy-led attack against Proshika women members in Brahmanbaria. At this time, Bangladesh was undergoing a serious parliamentary crisis that was played out by Awami League, the ruling party led by Prime Minister Sheikh Hasina, and the opposition leader, Begum Khaleda Zia of the Bangladesh Nationalist Party. The opposition had boycotted the parliament, and the country was facing a series of *hartals* (the shutdown of vehicular traffic and commercial businesses) in January 1999. The political situation was complicated by the fact that the ruling party (AL) candidate had won the local elections for a parliamentary seat held in the province of Pabna on December 10, 1998.[7] This win gave the Awami League control of all four parliamentary seats from Pabna. The opposition party, BNP, had challenged the vote count by calling it "ballot stealing."[8] Following the Pabna elections, trouble had broken out in various parts of the country between the two national parties. The opposition had called for a series of *hartals* all through January 1999.

During the month of December, Bangladeshis celebrate their independence from Pakistan. The month is one long celebration of musical soirees, competitions, fairs, and public events all commemorating the country's independence. In order to bypass NGO registration laws that did not allow political work, Proshika had formed an alternative umbrella organization called Trinomul Sangathan (Grassroots Organization) to conduct its political work. Trinomul members were drawn from Proshika member ranks, but Proshika leadership publicly claimed that Trinomul was an independent people's organization.

Fairs were the traditional social gathering space for rural people, and Hindu landlords were the patrons of these fairs. With the migration of Hindu landlords to India after the partition of 1947, the tradition of fairs had declined in Bangladesh. Proshika has capitalized on the concept of a fair as a site of political training and enlistment. During the 1997 local elections, Proshika had actively organized 461 cultural fairs in urban slums and rural areas with dramatized performances that showed the clergy as opposing social justice issues.[9] Moreover, ADAB, under Qazi Faruque's leadership, had sponsored 44,138 rural women to contest local elections. The women had won seats in 4,298 Union Council elections.[10] These demographic changes in rural government posed direct challenges to rural elites, who had traditionally enjoyed the power and privileges that came with these elected positions.

In December 1998, Proshika had organized a women's rally and fair in Brahmanbaria, which is a conservative town that is dominated by the Yunusia Madrassah, located in the center of town. When the clergy of the local Yunusia Madrassah heard about the fair, they issued a fatwa banning any fair or rally in their town, declaring them "un-Islamic." On December 7, 1998, when the Proshika rally took place as planned, madrassah students physically assaulted the gathered women and NGO officers. Later the madrassah youths burned and looted NGO buildings and houses belonging to NGO women clients. It led to three days of looting and rampage in Brahmanbaria, and the local government had to impose a curfew to calm the situation. Following this incident, Proshika characterized the clergy as "anti-development" and responsible for creating "a bad image of Bangladesh abroad." In the following pages, I analyze how the story on the ground was a complex weave of local and national politics, secular and religious power struggles, status games, crime and moneylending, that was played out on the bodies of poor women by both Proshika and the clergy in order to claim their sovereignty over them.

Challenges to the Clergy: Changing Social Dynamics

In order to comprehend the reactions of the local clergy allied with various mosques and madrassahs, it is necessary to examine the cultural shifts that have occurred in Bangladesh since the 1980s. Bangladesh has a two-tiered social structure that comprises a small coterie of Western-educated urban people who advocate women's rights and issues of social justice (the NGOs belong to this group), and a large rural population who are poor, illiterate, unemployed, and who are not part of the nation-building project. Since its transition to democracy in 1990, two female leaders, Begum Khaleda Zia and Sheikh Hasina, have led the country as heads of state. The leader of the Ghatok-Dalal Nirmool Committee, a symbolic people's court that tried the collaborators of the Pakistani army in 1971, was also female.

In urban society, there are many professional women in public life. Bangladesh is one of the few countries with a Ministry of Women's Affairs, established soon after independence in 1971. The national women's organization called Jatiya Mahila Parishad (National Women's Federation) is entrusted with the improvement of women's conditions. Since 1982 women have been appearing regularly at public service examinations and are being recruited into the regular cadre services. There is also a government quota for the recruitment of women. In 1998, 10 percent of all government posts and 15 percent of all clerical and lower-level posts were reserved for women.

In addition, special measures have been taken to appoint women to senior administrative levels, to the posts of deputy secretary and joint secretary.[11] There are women ministers, MPs, lawyers, doctors, teachers, bureaucrats, pilots, writers, journalists, NGO workers, and activists. Women are enlisted in the police force and the armed forces since the mid-1970s. Urban women are visible in public spaces, political meetings, and poverty seminars. They are vocal about the rights of women. While the participation of women in public life is a visible discourse, the majority of rural women are untouched by the discourse of the urban feminists.[12]

Feminist organizations have a small but organized lobby of urban, educated women who seek to protect the legal and economic rights of vulnerable groups, particularly women, and ethnic and religious minorities. Demands by feminist groups have gained momentum since the World Conference on Human Rights in Vienna (1993), the Cairo Population Conference (1994), and the UN Conference on Women in Beijing (1995), all of which made women's inclusion in local-level governance an important mandate for all signatory states.[13] These demands have been supported by Western aid agencies, particularly Canadian and Northern European governments. Within this area of women's rights, one of the key demands is the establishment of a Universal Civil Code (UCC) that would strip the clergy of their authority over Muslim family laws and bring jurisdiction to the modern courts.[14] At present, "the personal rights of Hindus, Christian and Muslim women are based on personal laws reflective of the different religious traditions.[15] The aim of feminists is to standardize the civil code to grant all women equal rights and protections under the law.

Under pressure from feminists, the Bangladeshi government adopted the Anti-Dowry Law in 1983, but dowry-related cases are rarely filed in courts.[16] The Bangladeshi government introduced the Prevention of Women and Child Repression Act of 2000 (Nari o Shishu Nirjaton Domon Ain). Despite these positive changes, justice for women continues to remain mired in judicial bureaucracy and inaction. In a recent report, it was found that "18,000 cases [of violence against women] remained unresolved within the judicial system."[17] These changes have led to a rise in violence and fatwas against women since the1990s, because the traditional roles and authority of rural male elites have been challenged.[18]

While the feminists have visibility and power in urban, NGO-dominated spaces, the power of the clergy is organized around influential madrassahs and shrines of famous pirs (holy men) in Bangladesh. In some areas, the leaders of large madrassahs are charismatic figures. Brahmanbaria is one such place. Successive Bangladeshi governments have not attempted to displace this clerical authority; instead, they have brokered local power-sharing agreements with them, allowing the clergy to have their own territorial sovereignty as long as they pay allegiance to the state and the political party in power.

The power of the clergy is a moral power based on their authority to interpret the Quran, Sunnah, and Hadith; their ability to give fatwas; and their authority to guide rural society according to Quranic dictates and the sharia. The social and economic structure of their power is derived from officiating at social ceremonies—marriages, divorces, births, funerals, and circumcision rites—and the contributions they raise through such activities in the community. For example, rural people show their respect for the individual cleric who manages the local mosque by bringing him the first fruit their tree bears, the first egg the hen lays, or some paddy (rice) from the first harvest. Many families consider marrying off their prepubescent daughters to the elderly clergy an act of piety.

However, the power of the clergy associated with large and established madrassahs is derived from the students who are their constituents. These madrassah students are primarily rural, poor, and orphaned. Urban and provincial middle-class people do not send their children to the madrassahs; they send them to public schools, where they can get a modern education.[19] The children of the poor and orphans who attend madrassahs join at a young and impressionable age, and the clergy take on both religious and parental roles for them. Many poor families give one of their sons to the madrassah to be raised by the clergy. It is considered an act of piety to dedicate one's child to spread the word of Allah. But more importantly, this reciprocal relationship helps a poor family economically, and they transfer the cost of raising a child to the madrassah.

The clergy demand that Bangladesh be under sharia laws. According to them, the regulation of women's sexuality is critical to the maintenance of the social order, and Muslim women must strictly adhere to Islamic attire and conduct their activities with Islamic decorum. Only the rigorous imposition of Islamic law will assure the "safe" reproduction of future generations of Muslims. In rural society, a Muslim man's honor is measured by his ability to control the behavior of his womenfolk. Many rural women do not conform to the clergy's notion of proper Islamic behavior, but they consider themselves to be pious Muslims. Thus, some of these settled notions of rural authority have been displaced by the actions of NGOs that promote female behavior that the clergy regard as "un-Islamic and immoral." The comments of Delwar Hossain Saidi, one of the leading Islamic authorities in the country and a former member of parliament, is indicative of the status of women in the worldview of these religious men. Women who are visible in public are deemed as the source of social chaos. Saidi's speeches are tape-recorded, and widely distributed in Bangladesh and to overseas Bangladeshis.

> If you [women] live in accordance with the respect Islam has granted you, the child you will conceive will be a good Muslim . . . . Islam has purdah to protect women from the evil eye. If the eyes of thousands of men fall on an exposed woman, then the child she conceives will also be affected. Children of such mothers become thugs, terrorists, alcoholics . . . . Everyone says, "Allah, kill this bastard. *And cast out the mother who conceived this child.*"[20] (Emphasis mine.)

The NGO versus Clergy Conflict

The Yunusia Madrassah controlled fifty-four smaller madrassahs in greater Brahmanbaria. Yunusia was built in 1914 but local folklore put its age at three hundred or more years. The older mufti of the madrassah was Sirajul Islam. He was popularly known as Boro Huzoor (Elder Mufti) and was a highly venerated man in the community. He was reputed to be 138 years old. His supposed longevity was a symbol of his piety and religiosity. He and his son-in-law, Mufti Hafez Nurullah, also known as Chhoto Huzoor (Young Mufti), played important roles in the public life of Brahmanbaria Boro Huzoor was the religious patriarch of Brahmanbaria and its surrounding villages. According to local people, no social event (births, deaths, weddings, construction of new buildings, official inaugurations) took place in the town without the blessings of the Boro Huzoor. A local trader explained the charisma of this man by saying, "Boro Huzoor can easily gather 150,000 people in one place in two hours. Such is his power in the community."

Trinomul Sangathan of Proshika planned to celebrate a five-day developmental fair December 7 through 11, 1998, at the Niaz Muhammad Stadium in Brahmanbaria. The developmental fair would showcase rural arts, crafts, competitions, and agricultural products. The application for the developmental fair was made to the district commissioner on November 17, 1998. The local district commissioner granted permission on November 25, 1998. The poster for the fair featured the following events:

Viewing of Arts and Crafts
Discussion
Folk Theater
Patriotic Songs
Puppet Show

On December 2, 1998, preparations for the fair were underway on the stadium grounds. At this time, the clergy arrived and reminded the NGO staff that there was a fatwa by their Boro Huzoor against any fair on the stadium grounds. They threatened those who were overseeing the construction that fairs were "un-Islamic acts." According to the clergy, fairs encouraged gambling, drinking, and dance shows that were all against the teachings of Islam. They said that if the fair were held, they would "burn down everything." The clergy then visited the district commissioner and reminded him that there was a fatwa against holding a fair at this site. Following their visit, the district commissioner withdrew his permission for the fair. In an interview with local journalists, he said, "At first Proshika had planned to have folk theater, patriotic songs, folk songs, stick competitions. Later they added a puppet show, which incensed the clergy because it is considered as a form of idolatry."[21] After opposition from the clergy, Proshika brought out a new poster and renamed the developmental fair as commemorating the spirit of the independence struggle.

The fair sponsors held a press conference on December 3 and demanded that the district commissioner give his permission for the fair. In the meeting Trinomul and Proshika representatives said that "fatwas are against development work" and that "such activities damaged our country's image abroad." On December 4, 1998, several thousand men and women belonging to Trinomul and Proshika went to the residence of the district commissioner to persuade him to reverse his decision.

The district commissioner, who is the highest government official in town, requested Proshika to get permission from Boro Huzoor of the Yunusia Madrassah, instead of upholding the constitutional right of the women to free assembly. Several journalists, who were present during a phone altercation between the director of Proshika (Qazi Faruque) and the district commissioner, alleged to me that Qazi Faruque had threatened the district commissioner by saying, "If necessary, I can move governments." According to them, Faruque had repeated that it was their (Proshika's) constitutional right to hold a rally regardless of any opposition.[22] Whether or not Qazi Faruque actually said this is debatable. What is important though is the recognition by local people that the power of NGO leaders overrode that of the district commissioner, who in turn, conceded power to the local clergy. Governance in this case was a triadic balance of negotiations between NGO, state, and clergy that Proshika was unwilling to acknowledge.

On December 6, 1998, several thousand Proshika members and workers camped out at the Niaz Muhammad Stadium. To prevent the fair, Yunusia clergy announced that they would hold a *tafsir mahfil* (recitation from the Quran prayers for the martyred freedom fighters) for seven days at the same venue. To avert a confrontation, the district commissioner declared section 144 at the stadium. Section 144 is a British colonial law that prohibits the congregation of more than four people in one place. After section 144 was declared, the police chased away the Trinomul and Proshika members from the stadium. On the day of the fateful event, the district commissioner and the superintendent of police left town to attend official meetings elsewhere. Only two dozen policemen were kept on duty to protect the entrance to the stadium.

On December 7, 1998, between 4,000 and 5,000 poor women and men who were members of Trinomul Sangathan and Proshika gathered at a place outside the town of Brahmanbaria.[23] Busloads of people had been brought in from all the adjoining provinces of Brahmanbaria. At approximately 12:45 p.m. the women and men marched into town to attend the rally. Qazi Faruque and other high-ranking NGO bureaucrats from Dhaka led the march into town.[24] Shouting the slogan "Faruque Bhai-er agotom, shagotom, shagotom" [we welcome Brother Faruque's arrival], the marchers walked by the Yunusia Madrassah. The local police stopped the marchers at the entrance to the stadium. Then the marchers redirected and congregated at a local college ground adjacent to the stadium, where the director of Proshika and NGO bureaucrats were expected to address the rally and speak against the undemocratic actions of the clergy.

As soon as the first speaker started to speak, youths and clergy from the Yunusia Madrassah attacked those attending the rally with stones.[25] These attackers were armed with sharp sticks, axes, and large knives. They tore down the stage, chased away the bureaucrats and NGO workers, beat the women attendees with sticks, and publicly humiliated them. Qazi Faruque and NGO officers sought shelter in nearby homes. Several women had their clothes torn off, and they were verbally abused. Women who were victimized at the rally later said to me that the clergy who harassed them had shouted the following: "You are *be-ijjat* [dishonorable women], you have no *sharm* [shame], you might as well be *nogno* [bare]." They claimed that the clergy ordered madrassah youths to pull off their clothes.[26] Around 3:30 p.m. rumors spread that two clergymen were killed in the riot. Thereafter, the madrassah crowd attacked the police station. Subsequently, law and order collapsed in the city for two days.

On the evening of December 7, groups of roving madrassah youths and local goons roamed the town, looting and destroying commercial businesses and NGO property. One of the slogans they chanted was, "Morle shahid, bachley gazi" [if we die we are martyrs; if we live we are warriors]. NGO offices were the primary targets of the rioters. BRAC, Grameen Bank, and Proshika offices were looted and torched. These NGO offices were stripped bare, and even the grill bars on windows were taken out with crow bars. In a nearby village, Chaibaria, twenty-six houses belonging to BRAC members were burned. Managers at BRAC and Proshika alleged that several hundred BRAC and Proshika school centers were torched. Proshika listed its damages at 9.2 million taka ($194,745).

On the evening of December 7, the clergy of Yunusia Madrassah called a press conference. At the press conference, they read a prepared list of injured madrassah students that ran into several hundreds. They called for a dawn to dusk *hartal* on December 8 to protest police brutality against madrassah youths. While there were many contradictory statements about what was said there, reporters who were present mentioned that at one point Brahmanbaria was declared "an independent state under the rule of sharia," and the Yunusia Madrassah and various clergymen got up and named themselves ministers of the Islamic State of Brahmanbaria![27]

On December 8 hordes of madrassah men along with local goons roamed the streets armed with knives, Chinese axes, and sticks. No police were visible in town. In the surrounding villages, NGO offices, schools, and homes of NGO members were explicitly targeted, looted, and torched. The following day, on December 9, an influential local Awami League political leader and a former state minister, Humayun Kabir, intervened to bring the situation under control.[28] December 9 was the national celebration of Begum Rokeya Day.[29] The local female Awami League member of parliament (MP), Dilara Hossain, marched through town with about twenty middle-class women to celebrate the Bengali Muslim feminist's emancipatory vision for Muslim women. Not a single member of the clergy challenged her or the procession of middle-class women. Despite their rhetoric against un-Islamic conduct of women, the clergy are careful not to attack upper-class women or the representatives of the state.

My Arrival in Brahmanbaria

In addition to Rina, who worked in Pirpur, I had a male research assistant, Selim, to help me with research in Dhaka.[30] Selim worked for a local NGO. On January 24, 1999, Selim and I set out for Brahmanbaria. Upon arriving in town, the first problem I faced was with the hotel manager on duty, who would not let a woman stay at the hotel without her husband. We waited in the hotel lobby for Nasir Bhai, a local leader, to clarify matters. Within a few hours, however, word had spread in Brahmanbaria that a female journalist was in town investigating the events of December. While I did face some problems at the hotel, these problems did not prevent me from walking around town with several young men who willingly assisted me with my work. The long-term work of NGOs has led to certain attitudinal changes toward women in society. It is now grudgingly acknowledged by men that in order to do NGO work, women are often required to travel with non-kin men on official work. While this was not considered desirable by rural patriarchal norms, men conceded because women's wages were necessary to the family income.

Later, as I walked around the city with Selim, I saw very few women on the streets. Whenever I had a reasonable opportunity, I would stop and ask people about the attack on the women by the clergy. Although at first sight the town appeared to be a stronghold of Islamists because of the presence of the madrassah, I soon discovered a critical engagement with politics, Islam, madrassah education, and NGO activities among the people of the city. The local people had a strong sense of pride in their city and felt that Proshika (not the Yunusia Madrassah) was tarnishing its "tolerant" image. When I pressed them on this matter, it was evident that they were uncomfortable—a complex feeling of respect and discomfort—about speaking out against the clergy of Yunusia Madrassah. Their criticism was veiled. People on the street did not fully agree with the rally (Why should women come to rallies? For whose benefit?), but they were also critical of the clergy, who, in their opinion, did not act in accordance with Islamic decorum. And it was pointed out to me several times, "Why should the *huzoors* [clergy] touch non-kin women? Is that behaving according to Islam?"

Soon several other local journalists and members of political parties joined us, and we sat down at a local tea shop. Selim introduced me as "Apa from America" who was writing a book on Bangladesh. Initially, I was quite surprised by their readiness to share information with me, but then I realized that they did not view me as an outsider. I had used informal associational networks (a local party member known to them) to enter into conversations. Thus, there was already an implicit understanding of solidarity among us. As political activists and journalists, most of these men did not question the idea of my writing a book. What was important to them was that I did not misrepresent them or their town as backward and intolerant. I raised the point that NGOs had claimed that local moneylenders had instigated the clergy to attack because the work of NGOs in microlending had reduced the income and clients of traditional moneylenders. As I pointed out to them, in my research in Pirpur I had found the opposite effect. The availability of credit had made formerly asset-less people into worthy clients for the local moneylenders. In fact, moneylenders were able to increase their business because of NGOs lending to the poor.

After listening to me, a local businessman spoke his thoughts on the conflict, "This is not about Islam. There is an illegal wine shop next to the madrassah. In broad daylight, people drink there. What do the *huzoors* do about it? And I do not believe that local moneylenders are really behind this. In this town moneylending is syndicated. Several influential clans control commerce. Brahmanbaria is one of the main entry points of smuggled goods from India, including contraband liquor.[31] It sits twenty-five kilometers from the border with India. You can sit in my shop, and if I am your guarantor, within one hour you can raise 500,000 taka ($10,638) or more. The problem was that Proshika misread local power relationships. The organization ignored the local power dynamics such as seeking permission from Boro Huzoor. Flush with foreign money, some NGOs think they can change society overnight and ignore local power structures."

Selim joined in the conversation and said that the clergy also practice moneylending, but they do it in the form of barter. Citing evidence from his work in villages, he added that the clergy often lend money to people in exchange for an agreed amount of rice to be given to them after a stipulated time. "The market value of the rice that is agreed upon is much higher than the amount lent. That is how the clergy practice moneylending, but they are careful not to call it such."

Another man who was also sitting at the table raised the Taliban conspiracy theory. "Where did the students of the madrassah find guns?" Then he added that he had heard Chhoto Huzoor say to madrassah students to return the weapons from where they got them. Looking at us, he posed the question, "Where will these weapons be returned? This makes me think that they must have a storage place in the madrassah." On the part of this speaker, association with the Taliban was speculation, and not everybody present agreed. Locally, it was rumored that two Taliban men were seen in town during the looting of December 7, and they had disappeared as mysteriously as they had surfaced. None of the men present had seen them, but they had all heard through rumors that somebody (nobody knew this person's identity) had seen two tall and fair-skinned men with grey eyes among the madrassah students. These speculations carried weight because during the Soviet invasion of Afghanistan, men from Yunusia Madrassah had gone to fight the Soviets. While there was a link between Afghanistan and the Yunusia Madrassah, this did not necessarily prove that the Taliban was involved in the present conflict in Brahmanbaria.

According to Nasir Bhai, local politics played the single most important factor in the situation getting out of control. The local chapter of the Awami League had split into two factions; one was led by Abdul Hai Sacchu, the other by Amanul Haque Sentu. There was tension between these two factions over the local elections. A former state minister, Humayun Kabir, had planned to contest a parliamentary seat from Brahmanbaria. His candidacy was supported by Sentu's faction. Rumor had it that Humayun Kabir provoked the clergy to act out and tried to embarrass Sacchu by letting the looting take place before stepping in to stop it.[32]

Later I met a local civic leader who narrated the history of the fair in Brahmanbaria.[33]

"There is a long history associated with the word *mela* [fair] and the Niaz Muhammad Stadium in Brahmanbaria. The stadium was named after Niaz Muhammad Khan, a civil servant during undivided British India who was an advocate of education, sports and the arts. In Brahmanbaria, he was the first person to construct public spaces like stadiums, parks, and canals. Beginning in 1941, there was an annual month-long fair where local arts, crafts, and agricultural produce were displayed. At the fair, school children participated in debate and poetry competitions. . . .

. . . After 1968–1969, the fair began to lose its original purpose and we began to see gambling, *khamta natch* [vulgarized strip shows where performers pretend to take off their clothes] and drinking at the fair. The revenues earned from gambling went to support some development projects in the city. Then between 1971 and 1974, the fair was abandoned by the city. In 1974, the fair was reintroduced, and puppet-shows, dancing, plays, and gambling returned. All through this time the clergy did not raise any objections. In 1980, when the military came to power, the clergy became emboldened and complained about the fair. . . . It is not true when people tell you that fairs are not celebrated here. In 1987 the *Baishaki mela* [harvest festival] was celebrated here. . . . Between 1987 and 1992, we could hold harvest festivals here as long as we consulted with the clergy. . . . It is Proshika's failure to recognize local authorities that led to this riot."

What featured prominently in these discussions with the local community leaders were politics, Taliban conspiracies, and the arrogance of Western-aided NGOs. These people represent the Bangladeshi middle class, and their views spoke to the social formation of their class. The cultural politics of national political parties dominate conversations among middle-class Bengalis, whose economic lives are affected by policies undertaken by the government. When middle-class men gather for *adda*, they tend to discuss politics over sports. This class tends to be more secular in orientation. They equally cherish their Bengali identity alongside their Muslim identity. In towns such as Brahmanbaria, where the madrassah clergy influence the conduct of social life, they fear a Taliban-like revolution in their country, although they fail to offer proof to support their assertions. But most interestingly, these men felt slighted by the NGOs who conduct business in their towns without consulting them in development activities. NGOs are the source of money and jobs in rural society, therefore, not surprisingly, middle-class people in small towns wanted to be included in the sharing of the resources. I will return to this point later.

That afternoon, I met with Aksir Chowdhury, a lawyer and the local human rights representative, who was preparing the human rights report on the conflict. I had gone with Selim and another young man who was known to Chowdhury. At first he did not want to speak with me. He suggested that I should wait to read his report that would come out in June. When I told him I would be back in the United States, he left the room. Selim mentioned to me that Chowdhury was feeling insecure, and was afraid to speak about the riot until after his report came out. I asked Selim and his friend to assure him that I was not going to write anything until after his report came out. After almost forty-five minutes of sitting alone in his office, Chowdhury gave me a very brief interview that lasted fifteen minutes.

> Why did the *huzoors* [clergy] react so strongly to the fair? They see women gaining legal rights as a threat to the madrassah. To them, women are subhumans. How dare they think of coming to the city to have a fair? It is an outrageous idea! . . . At a press briefing, the *huzoors* said that they are not anti-NGO, but they are against NGOs that are anti-Islam. They showed four books published by BRAC and ASA.[34] These textbooks are no longer used, but they took an example from one of the books that said a man couldn't verbally divorce his wife. . . . The clergy are reacting to what they conceivably see as a threat to their traditional power.

Visiting the Conflict Zones

The following morning, Selim and I visited the local Grameen Bank, BRAC, and Proshika offices. The managers at both Grameen Bank and BRAC were very angry with Proshika management. They claimed that Proshika had acted inappropriately and created problems for their work. Even after one month, NGO officers were not able to go to some of the villages to collect on their loans because the people were so angry they had threatened to "beat up NGO officers." The local Grameen Bank and BRAC managers said that they had sent away their families for safety. Next we went to the Proshika office. The managers were subdued and depressed. An older male officer broke down in tears when I asked him about the incident. With tears streaming down his face, he compared the behavior of the madrassah men to that of the Pakistani army during the war of 1971, when Bangladeshis were killed indiscriminately, and women in particular were subjected to rape. Somewhat surprised, I pointed out to him that making a connection between the war in 1971 and the riot over the fair was an inappropriate analogy. I mentioned to him that Proshika leadership knew about the fatwa; yet, they did not take measures to ensure the security of the women they brought to attend the rally. At that time, the manager who was listening to our conversation intervened and said that their head office had asked them not to grant personal interviews. When none of them would talk to us anymore, Selim and I left.

Our next visit was to Chaibaria, where twenty-six families had been affected by the rioting. Chaibaria was close to the town of Brahmanbaria. Mohsin, a local youth leader, joined us. Upon our arrival at the village, we met some children who took us to one of the houses that had been burned.

One could still see the burned houses, hacked corrugated tin, singed wood poles used in house construction, and broken mud walls. Families had assembled their few remaining assets into some semblance of normalcy. Some families had constructed makeshift homes with saris stretched between two poles to give them some privacy. In places, women were cooking their meals with the few remaining pots and pans that the madrassah youths had left behind. Although it was a month after the event, ashes and burned timber were still scattered all over the courtyard. When we entered, the women stopped their work and came up to us. They gave their names as Asma Begum, Arju Begum, Hasna Begum, and Ayesha Begum. They were all members of BRAC. According to them, none of the women from Chaibaria had attended the rally. They indignantly replied, "We do not go to processions." An older woman was sitting in front of one of the burnt houses and cooking rice. She came over and asked me to follow her. She showed me her dented pots and pans. "We are already poor people. They have looted and destroyed the few possessions we had accumulated."

Walking through the village, we saw that specific houses were targeted and burned, while others remained untouched. Many families in the village

My research assistant with a woman whose house was burned. Chaibaria, Brahmanbaria, January 1999.

Woman preparing meal in front of burned house. Chaibaria, Brahmanbaria, January 1999.

belonged to NGOs, so why were specific families targeted? I felt that village factionalism had played a part in these attacks. When I asked the women if there was a conflict between them and the village elders, they would not speak. Pressed several times on this issue, the women said, "Local people showed the way to our houses. They asked for an NGO school and villagers pointed to our house." Although these women were angry about the loss of their dignity, homes, and assets, they were also afraid to speak openly, for it was evident to the women that if the clergy came back, no one—not the police, rural authorities, or the NGOs—would protect them.

The most outspoken among them, Asma Begum, said: "On December 8, around 9 a.m. at least 1,000 men armed with sticks, axes, and knives came toward our houses. They wanted to burn the BRAC school. We had leased land to BRAC for a school. Our men were working in the fields. When we saw them coming, we ran to the field next door. We left our cooking behind. The madrassah men started to hack at the tin structure. Around 11 a.m., they set the houses on fire. They burned all five houses adjacent to the school. Then they looted twenty-six homes in the village. They took everything. They took away the pot of rice that we were cooking. As they went away, we heard them say tauntingly, 'It is fun to eat NGO rice.'

They took everything; they even took the soap I use for washing." Asma Begum showed me the cut on her ear and said that the men had taken her gold earring by pulling at it and cutting her ear. Yet, just moments earlier Asma had said that "they ran to the field next door." There were inconsistencies in what Asma told me. However, given the violence of which the women were victims, I did not want to pursue this line of conversation and let it rest.

As I toured the village, I told people that I was a researcher interested in the events surrounding the fair. Very few people believed that to be my true intent. I was seen as an investigator sent by the government or an NGO to uncover the events and to perhaps collect evidence to punish the culprits. Alternately, I was seen as a journalist who had come to do investigative reporting. I was also seen as an aid worker who had come to assess the damage in order to calculate relief assistance for the affected families. Although I repeatedly told people that I had no power or authority to provide them with relief assistance, my pleas went unheard. Given the various ways I was positioned in these interactions with the women, the stories I heard emphasized more the victimization of women than the underlying rural factionalism within these villages, which may have played an important role in the targeting of certain families.

Asma Begum and her neighbors. Chaibaria, Brahmanbari.

Down the road from Asma Begum's house was Monowara's house. Her husband had opened a small retail shop next to their house with a loan from BRAC. Both had been burned. A month after the rampage, Monowara and her family were living in a makeshift shack with only a sari as a cover over their heads. She told me that the mullahs had burned all her possessions, including a copy of the Quran. Monowara wanted us to take pictures of her house, thinking that she would get assistance from some NGO. She and her children posed in front of their burned house for pictures. A young man who appeared to be educated was watching us from a short distance. He asked Monowara, "Why are they taking pictures?" In response Monowara said, "They have come from the city. They will give us *shahajya* [aid]." Although we had repeatedly told everyone that we were not bearers of aid, we became identified as NGO staff because NGO officials are the ones who come in daily contact with rural people.

As we moved from house to house, more and more people gathered. Soon they started to ask, "Are you from an NGO? When will you pay us for our losses?" Several women said that others had come before, but they didn't receive any help. The same young man said to the assembled crowd, "These NGO people make money off of you. They take pictures and show them to foreigners and collect money." While older people are unwilling to confront urban people such as me, the educated younger generation is aware of how their poverty is instrumentalized by aid organizations to enrich themselves. These educated young men and women are willing to speak back to urban people they see as manipulators of their poverty.

The more we tried to explain to them that we did not represent an NGO, the angrier the crowd became. Finally, one woman said, "If you are not going to give us help, then have you come to watch fun [tamasha]?" From every side I was being pushed and shoved. "If you won't help, then why have you come?" The conversation was rapidly spiraling out of control, when Asma, who was following us from house to house as well, told the villagers that they should leave *apa* (elder sister) alone. Asma and the women from the first household escorted us out of the village. Although relieved that we had escaped a potential beating, I realized my participation in voyeurism. I had turned my gaze on people whose existences had been seriously jeopardized, only to document their tales of suffering for my research. Unfortunately, since I did not conduct ethnography in this area, I could not uncover the deeper motivations underlying the conflict because I did not have a relationship of trust with the women.

The next village we visited had the highest number of women who were victimized at the fair. This was at a distance from the town of Brahmanbaria. The men in the village told us that although Proshika gave them loans, that did not give Proshika the right to take their women to the city and make them march publicly ("Poor people have modesty; they cannot do whatever they please with our women."). The women told us that their Proshika managers had told their husbands that in order to continue getting loans from Proshika they would have to let their women attend the fair in Brahmanbaria. None of the men and women interviewed knew about the fatwa or the conflict between the clergy and Proshika. All of them said that had they known about Boro Huzoor's fatwa against the rally, they would not have attended the rally. As they pointed out, they may be forced to take loans from NGOs because of their poverty, but that did not give Proshika the right to take their women to rallies and parade them in public. They were honorable people. In keeping with local custom, the women had taken "permission" from their husbands before they went to the rally.

We had heard that in the aftermath of the rally incidents of domestic violence had increased against these women. Some of the women confided that their husbands continued to abuse them physically and verbally. A few of the more outspoken women retorted by saying, "Why should our husbands beat us? Do they not take NGO money? How can they eat NGO money and beat us?" The husbands of the affected women had become objects of ridicule in the village. Other men taunted them in public in their inability to control their women. So, the men took out their anger on their wives. The women also said that they faced increased verbal abuse from relatives who call them "spoiled goods," and that also led to their husbands' anger. Even after a month, these women faced shame within the community.

Most revealing were the conversations with the women about why they had participated in the rally. Smiling shamefacedly, the women told me they were excited by the prospect of seeing puppet shows. Contrary to the clergy, they did not view puppet shows as a form of idolatry. They saw it as entertainment, something that was lacking in their daily lives because there are very few places that women can visit for entertainment. Among poorer peasants, serious distinctions are not made between Hindu and Muslim festivals, and they tend to celebrate each other's customs to some degree. In rural Bangladesh, there has been a long tradition of cross-fertilization between Hindu and Muslim religious traditions.[35] This behavior is a source of anger among the clergy who consider such activities as idolatrous and un-Islamic. Similarly, the clergy associate rural fairs with Hindu forms of worship.

To the women the fair meant a day off from the daily grind of their lives, a chance for leisure. Going to a fair was a special day when they could put on nice clothes, watch puppet shows, and have a reason to be away from their in-laws, husbands, and children. Proshika managers had told them that "very important people" from Dhaka were coming to see them, and it was mandatory to greet them. In the clientelist culture of Bangladesh, rich and important folks coming to visit them was an acknowledgement of their importance as people. It demonstrated that they mattered. As several women said to me, "Rich people were coming to see us, and we would not go. How could that be?" And finally, for many of these women the rally was a *darshan*—a pilgrimage to pay respects to a holy man, Qazi Faruque, the leader of Proshika, who was the new patron of rural society in their worldview.

Meeting the Clergy

I had requested a meeting with the madrassah leaders through the people I had met. I was informed that Mufti Nurullah (son of Boro Huzoor, the patriarch) was unwilling to meet with a woman, but he would send his son-in-law, Mufti Kefayetullah, to meet with me. In the evening, I sent Selim to meet with Mufti Nurullah, while I waited for Kefayetullah. Several young men hung around with us while we went to various places. These were local youth leaders, and many of them had contact with the madrassah clergy. They told me that Kefayetullah was the public-relations face of the Yunusia Madrassah. One of them suggested that I wear a burqa for my meeting with Kefayetullah. I asked him to fetch me one. Unfortunately, Kefayetullah arrived before the burqa, and I had to cover my head as best as I could with my sari. When Selim returned and we compared our notes, I found that Nurullah's and Kefayetullah's statements were synchronized. Let me begin with Selim's report, which is an abbreviated form of the interview.

Mufti Nurullah (As Reported by Selim)

Why do we oppose fairs? This is because at a fair adult men and women unashamedly come in physical contact, women speak in raised voices, they watch puppet shows and folk dance dramas, and they gamble. They engage in all sorts of anti-Islamic activities . . . .

On December 7, 1998, we heard that Proshika chairman Qazi Faruque was leading a procession of 8,000–10,000 men and women, and they were marching toward the stadium. . . . Religious-minded people came to us with the news that the NGOs were leading thousands of men and women together through the streets. In front of the procession there were between 100 and 150 women wearing *jeans-er half-pant* and *Sandoz genji*. [This translates as denim shorts and transparent men's undershirts that resemble tank tops. Sandoz is an established manufacturer of men's undershirts from British India days.] The women had dressed themselves up in all sorts of offensive ways. In front of the procession, there were about 200 armed goons on motorbikes . . .

From the NGO-led procession we heard women chanting slogans such as "fatwabaaz nipath jak"[down with fatwas]; "amar shorir amar deho, jake khushi take dibo" [I will give my body to whomever I please]; "bhanga ghore thakbo na, shamir kotha shunbo na" [I will not live in a dilapidated house, I will not listen to my husband].[36] When people of Brahmanbaria heard these slogans, they became infuriated. They came to us for help. Local religious-minded people had also formed a spontaneous procession. We were urged to join in . . .

We, of the Yunusia Madrassah, are not against NGOs, but we are against any NGO that works against Islam. We will always remain vigilant against anti-Islamic forces. Let me give you an example. BRAC has a poster that targets women, and it says "mukher kothai talak hoina" [women cannot be divorced verbally].[37] The Quran allows verbal divorce. These kinds of teachings are against Islam . . .

NGOs have started to convert women into Christianity by giving them loans.[38] A young woman in Brahmanbaria came to me to complain about NGOs. Proshika had offered her a loan of 12,000 taka. They later told her that she would not have to return the loan if she let them put a Christian seal on her *tolpeth* [lower abdomen]. The young woman then refused to take their money . . .

Do we not hear stories about rapes and sexual harassment of women by NGO workers? At the fair in Brahmanbaria, between 5,000 and 10,000 men and women were going to come. If all the hotels in Brahmanbaria were booked, we could accommodate only 2,000 people. So, where would all these men and women stay? Under the open sky? Where would they defecate and urinate? If men and women live together like animals, some unfortunate incident is bound to happen. This is why we spoke out against such a gathering . . .

Mufti Kefayetullah

Mufti Kefayetullah came to see me the same evening. When Kefayetullah arrived in my hotel room, it was clear that he was apprehensive. His demeanor was conciliatory. When we sat down to talk, Kefayetullah repeated verbatim much of what was said by Nurullah. It was clear to me that they had coached themselves so as not to reveal any information that might lead to further problems for them. Below I discuss only the more pertinent comments made by Kefayetullah.

"We, the clergy, want to protect Muslim khristi-culture [Islamic values and culture]. For a long time our madrassah has educated people about the proper way of Islamic life and Muslim culture. . . . We cannot always oppose anti-Islamic activities because we are not in political power. . . . [T]he fair organizers gave us a direct challenge by marching in front of the madrassah . . .

Women will move in public without purdah, they will dance and sing in raised voices [Islam forbids women from speaking in loud voices in front of men because women's voices are said to bewitch men], and they will mix with non-kin men. All these activities are outside the teachings of Islam . . .

We are not against NGOs as such . . . . But we are always vigilant against the destruction of Islamic values and culture through the work of NGOs. Look at what NGOs do. Grameen Bank gives loans to individuals and then they hold the group responsible for repayment of individual loans. That is not justice. NGOs are reproducing poverty instead of eliminating poverty. We want to see the elimination of poverty [his solution is the establishment of sharia laws because Islam is the perfect code of life]. . . . According to Islam, the maintenance of women falls on men. NGOs want to do away with that [here he is referring to the NGO demands for the establishment of a Universal Civil Code]. But it is written in the sharia that men are responsible for women. If we follow the dictates of Islam, then all social problems will disappear. If a woman falls sick, does it mean that she cannot travel to the hospital? It is a question of how she will travel. Will she travel modestly or immodestly?"

Before Kefayetullah left, he said to me, "You have traveled to Brahmanbaria; you know how a Muslim woman should travel." That innocuous comment took on an ominous form in the middle of the night. After Kefayetullah left, Selim and his friends told me that the clergy of Yunusia had become concerned. They were asked many times by Mufti Nurullah what we were doing in Brahmanbaria a month after the incident.

Those fears were borne out later, when hired goons attacked the hotel in the middle of the night. For almost two hours, between 2 and 4 a.m., the occupant of a room down the corridor from my room was assaulted.

His door was repeatedly kicked and banged by several men shouting in vulgar language that they would "kill him." I looked through the peephole but could not see a single person in the long corridor. Neither Selim nor I came out of our rooms during this attack for fear for our lives. In fact, not a single person came out to investigate what was going on. All through the night I heard only one set of voices threatening to kill the man. It took the police two hours before they eventually showed up at the hotel. I heard some voices in the corridor, and then things quieted down.

The following morning when I came out, I first went to check on Selim. He opened his door rubbing his eyes, and looked as though he had slept through it all. We checked the room where we thought the attack was and found it padlocked. Two hours of constant kicking should have broken down the door. There was not a single scratch on the door. It was unclear to me whether this was a staged event to frighten me, or whether there was actually a person in that room. In the morning, Selim went to fetch Nasir Bhai, who had put us up in the hotel. Nasir Bhai told us that the hotel management said that the men were trying to collect money from a defaulter (in the middle of the night!), and that they were not aware that I was staying in the hotel. Had they known of my presence, these men would not have attacked him during the night. This was an odd statement given that almost everyone in the vicinity knew that I was staying in the hotel. After consultations with everyone, I decided that it was advisable for me to leave Brahmanbaria. It was evident that someone wanted to send a strong signal to me that they did not like my presence or my questions. Facing threats, most presumably from the clergy, I had to leave Brahmanbaria earlier than planned.

Analyzing the Violence

How do we understand violence, particularly violence against women and the brutalization of their bodies, as I have narrated here?

The educated local people that I interviewed (local businessmen, bureaucrats, political activists, journalists) saw Proshika's actions as the breach of a social contract ("there was a fatwa against the fair") and as an affront to the moral authority of the clergy ("we have had fairs here in the past, but it is always done in consultation with the local power structure"). According to them, Proshika did not deem it necessary to build coalitions with local community activists, and instead "wanted to do it alone." These local leaders did not consider the clergy as politically influential, but they acknowledged the clergy's social power in their community. The fair was an important event in their town, with 5,000 attendees and many dignitaries from Dhaka. Local leaders expected both recognition and invitation to the event from Proshika. For them, it was a rare opportunity to meet Proshika leaders, to introduce themselves, and perhaps to become partners in the development agendas of Proshika. Yet, Proshika failed to acknowledge and include them in this process, thereby alienating a core group of local mediators.

The intersection of national and local politics also played a decisive role in the creation of the violence. According to local journalists and political activists, it was really BNP leader Humayun Kabir's hoodlums who had started the widespread looting. It was also widely known that Kabir had supported the Yunusia Madrassah and had spoken at their press conference on December 7, 1998. Local politics was already a tug-of-war between the two factions of the Awami League in Brahmanbaria, popularly known by the names of their respective leaders, Sacchu and Sentu. Sacchu was considered "an NGO-friendly person." In order for Humayun Kabir to get elected as an MP from Brahmanbaria, he had to consolidate his power with Sacchu's opponents, the Sentu faction. He attempted to achieve his objective by creating violence in the town.

During my fieldwork in Bangladesh, I noticed a rise in Taliban guerrilla conspiracy theories in the newspapers. There were many reports of Islamic guerrillas attacking secular and progressive people.[39] The national newspapers, NGO supporters, and progressive forces in society represented these acts as a threat to democracy. According to the proponents of this view, an Islamic movement backed by the Taliban would undermine the Bengali ethnolinguistic nationalism upon which the country was established in 1971. Detractors claimed that these constructed threats of Islamic fundamentalism would allow Bangladesh and India to form closer military alliance to putatively fight Islamic militancy, while in reality it would give the Indian military an opportunity to infiltrate Bangladesh. This fear that Big Brother India (that is, high-caste Hindus who had formerly dominated Muslims in Bengal as landlords and rent collectors) was taking over the country was shared by Muslim Bangladeshis who felt that, with democratization and the return to power of the India-friendly Awami League, Bangladesh was once again part of Indian regional hegemony.

Perhaps the most revealing comments came from the clergy themselves. The clergy were at the core of the conflict, and their superficial responses were laden with other potential motivations. Nurullah and Kefayetullah repeatedly made two comments that illustrated how the work of NGOs and economic globalization were undermining their conventional sources of authority. In the first instance, the clergy justified their actions against the rally by saying that these women were marching into town bare in "denim shorts and Sandoz undershirts," and on "motorbikes." As moral guardians, they were compelled to protect the Islamic life by intervening. In the second instance, they remarked that NGOs have started to convert poor women to Christianity by giving them loans in exchange for Christian seals, and that they had to stop the proselytization of poor Muslims by these "Western imperialist NGOs."

These statements have to be analyzed in terms of the changes taking place in rural society. The NGOs have brought perceivable change in local consumption patterns among the poor. In some instances, the poor were able to have some of the same commodities as the clergy, thereby gradually leveling some of the material distinctions that maintained a hierarchical society. Although the comment about Bangladeshi women in "denim shorts and Sandoz undershirts" may sound absurd on the surface, the clergy were critiquing consumerism and Westernization, and their loss of control over rural subjects, particularly women. In rural communities, elite men traditionally wore undershirts under thin cotton *panjabis* (a long cotton shift-like garment worn by Bengali men). Poor men either wore short-sleeved shirts or they kept their torsos bare. The use of the term *Sandoz genji* referred to the adoption of the norms of elite culture by the village people.

Similarly, jeans or denim trousers are synonymous in Bangladesh with the West and the garment industry in which poor women work as labor. With the introduction of garment industries in Bangladesh, women have been integrated into a global manufacturing economy. It has turned women into wage labor, given them an identity as workers, and brought them inside a new economic order that is not controlled by the clergy. Many rural women have left for urban areas to work in the garment industry. The reference to "denim shorts" indicates that rural women are now beginning to adopt masculine traits. The women work outside the home, they come in contact with non-kin men, they demonstrate in public in raised voices, and they refuse to subject themselves to rural authority. The use of bicycles and motorbikes by NGO female officers poses a conflict with the religious beliefs of the clergy, who deem these behaviors as blurring the distinctions between acceptable male and female conduct. In other words, rural women are moving into economic spheres traditionally controlled by male power and authority, thereby leading to a breakdown of the existing social order. All these changes radically disrupt the worldview of the clergy.

The clergy also alleged that NGOs were converting Muslim women to Christians by giving them loans, and then they were forcibly placing a "Christian seal on the woman's underbelly." The underbelly here refers to the female sexual organs, and "a Christian seal" is the sterilization operation that a woman undergoes. A woman who has been sterilized is irrelevant to the reproduction of future generations of Muslims. Moreover, she is an explosive sexual agent: she can fornicate at will. These women have strayed from the control of their husbands and the Islamic norms to the control of the NGO, which represents anti-Islamic values. The clergy in their sermons claim that the West is trying to reduce the number of Muslims globally through reproductive technologies, and NGOs as their agents perpetrate these immoral acts. This new sexual identity of women that gives them control over their reproductive bodies will lead to a total breakdown of the moral order, only to be replaced by a social order based on an absence of shame, that is, the NGO-sponsored capitalist order that integrates women as labor. In the words of Nurullah, "Where will they sleep, under the open sky? Where will they defecate and urinate?"

Interestingly, the public rhetoric of the clergy on poverty has become putatively similar to that of the left political parties. Both are against imperialism and both are against the work of corporate NGOs; but these groups come from different ideologies. The clergy of Yunusia Madrassah recognize the limits of their economic power. Pushed against the power and resources of an organization such as Proshika, which has identified them as "enemies of the poor," they have few options. Kefayetullah knows the power of the statement "NGOs are reproducing poverty instead of eliminating poverty" to provoke indebted and dissatisfied rural people against the NGOs, as I analyzed in chapter 1. It is important to note that the clergy of Yunusia Madrassah are not allies of poor women or men. They use the rhetoric of poverty strategically—"we want to eliminate poverty and establish the golden age of Islam"—to recover some of the power they have lost due to the work of NGOs.[40]

The conflict over the Proshika fair has been analyzed by aid organizations and Western scholars who took their materials from NGO press releases as evidence of the clergy's antidevelopment stance.[41] In fact, the clergy and mainstream Islamic parties are neither antidevelopment nor anticapitalist; they are against the lack of Islamic decorum for women in the public sphere. In recent years, the Ja'maat-e-Islami has softened its attitude toward the participation of women in public life, and has encouraged women to join public service but within the contours of proper Islamic conduct. I met many young hijab-observant women who work in offices in the city. These women did not see a contradiction between their religious beliefs and their professional lives, which brought them in contact with non-kin men, as long as they remained within the decorum of Islamic female comportment.

In the aftermath of the crisis, perhaps Proshika was the biggest winner. It received large grants from CIDA, a Canadian aid organization, to fight Islamic fundamentalism in Bangladesh. The Association of Development Agencies in Bangladesh, which Qazi Faruque headed, termed the event a "social disaster" and had a series of workshops and papers on "social disaster management." In NGO discourse, violence became a technical event to be managed through training offered by experts known as "violentologists."[42] The field staff attended special workshops in which they were taught how to predict and manage violence to reduce social disasters. In its discourse of pro-poor politics, Proshika identified poor rural women as the agents of history, who, when sufficiently organized, would rise up against the enemies of development, the rural clergy.[43] In order to concretize this rural women's latent revolution, Proshika leadership focused on public rallies and assemblies to organize the women as a political constituency.

Proshika conducted this mobilization of poor women under the rubric of "shadhinotar juddher chetona" (the spirit of the struggle of freedom) and called for an end to "Islamic fundamentalism" in the country. By conflating issues of social and economic justice with Islam, and a developmental discourse with the nationalist movement of 1971, such politics gets constrained by the limits of its conceptual frames. Bangladeshi nationalism emerged from the concerns of middle-class Bangladeshis and their struggle against Pakistani cultural, political, and economic domination. This nationalism did not address the needs of rural people, nor did it have a well-developed plan of economic transformation. The "spirit of the liberation struggle" in its most Utopian ideal was the establishment of a Sonar Bangla—a golden Bengal that existed in some mythical past (similar to the golden age of Islam), when Bengal was a land of abundance.

By invoking this discourse, Proshika played into the nationalist rhetoric of the Awami League as the "patrons" of this history of Bengalis' struggle for freedom. It also used this rhetoric of the freedom struggle to carry out a frontal attack on the militant Islamic groups in the country. Fighting Islamic militancy on the one hand and making the ideational framework of the liberation struggle meaningful to the lives of most Bangladeshis on the other are noteworthy efforts. However, Proshika engages in this nationalism-inflected politics of the poor through its power over the lives of its borrowers, thus eroding their ability to determine their own stakes in such issues. When such plans are drawn up in NGO boardrooms, neither Proshika nor its Western donors consult the women about their everyday lives and needs, which goes to show the hierarchies and clientelism that are woven into these pro-poor discourses.

Anu Muhammad has argued that NGOs have reduced the political participation of people to a form of technocratic management. He has labeled this vulgar bureaucratization of political culture by NGOs "Project Culture."[44] Muhammad argues that these gatherings are not spontaneous political events, but are choreographed projects conceived in NGO boardrooms with project names, budgets, proposals that show number of personnel required for mobilization and training, number of vehicles needed to transport people, flowcharts of events, and meals for attendees. Then these proposals are submitted to donors for financial support. The donors support these proposals in their efforts to prevent the creation of another Taliban-like country in South Asia.

In the final analysis, poor village women, who were neither informed nor (necessarily) willing subjects of the rally, were the real victims. Caught in the cross fire of the clergy's wrath, many of the women could not return to their villages for several days. These women were triply violated and brutalized: once by the clergy, who beat them and had their clothes torn off because they were *nogno* (bare and without shame); then by their community that called them *noshto* (spoiled goods); and finally by their husbands, who also beat them, and in many instances, refused to take them back because they had been touched by non-kin men. For these brutalized women, there was no social mechanism in place to redress their grievances—a process through which they could fight the violence perpetrated against them by the clergy and by Proshika leaders, who had talked them into participating in the rally, and had later left them in the turmoil, concentrating instead on fighting Islamic fundamentalism through seminars, workshops, and citizens' protest meetings in Dhaka.[45]

These two forces, Proshika and the clergy, express competing and conflicting ideologies about the nature of Bangladeshi society and women's role in that society. On the surface, the leadership of Proshika expressed more modernist and "democratic" impulses that came in direct conflict with the sharia-based impulses of the Muslim clergy. But as this case study showed, the "democratic" impulses of Proshika were grounded in its undemocratic clientelist relationship with its constituents—the poor borrowers—who were often coerced to act according to the dictates of Proshika leadership. And, paradoxically, both parties—whether champions of more progressive and modernist ideas of women's rights, or as "guardians" of Islam—ended up brutalizing the bodies and souls of the women they sought to "empower" and "protect."

Chapter 6   Power/Knowledge in Microfinance

What does it mean to say that development started to function as a discourse, that is, that it created a space in which only certain things could be said or even imagined? If discourse is the process through which social reality comes into being—if it is the articulation of knowledge and power, of the visible and the expressible—how can developmental discourse be individualized and related to ongoing technical, political and economic events? How did development become a space for the systematic creation of concepts, theories, and practices?

—Arturo Escobar, *Encountering Development: The Making and Unmaking of the Third World*

IN THIS CHAPTER, I return to an examination of the powers that hold together the discursive forms of knowledge production. In doing so, I examine the actors and institutions that participate in the making of poverty research. Let me begin then with the following observation: How did Bangladesh—a country of 150 million people with its long history of peasant movements, its nationalist struggle against Pakistani domination, the amazing capacity of its people to rebuild their lives every year after natural catastrophes, its Sufi culture, music of the Bauls, and the poetry of Tagore and Jibanonondo—become synonymous with abject poverty? And how did the NGO become the preferred path of social and economic welfare of its citizens?

The opening quote reminds us that development is a discourse of the social imaginary held together by the discursive power of the first world over the third world in the environment of decolonization.[1] The technical

163

management of poverty on a global scale was created after World War II, with the establishment of the World Bank and the International Monetary Fund. Poverty research, the signature of the discourse of poverty, is a particular way of knowing the poor that has been legitimized at the level of ideology through the collection of reports and statistical data on the poor. Given that, it is important to query how different forces, both within and outside the nation, colluded to invent this category termed poverty research. What are the implicit aims that this research serves? As Cruikshank notes, "How did 'the poor' become a group with a shared set of problems and interests? How did 'the poor' become an object of governmental policy? Why were people willing to organize themselves around being 'poor' rather than or in addition to race and class?"[2] This chapter lays out the sources of knowledge that led to the creation of Bangladesh as the heartland of the microfinance revolution and of its rural women as "entrepreneurs."

The discourse of development has been popularized by the apparatuses of development: the postcolonial state, Western governments, aid organizations, researchers, and NGOs. An army of researchers, dedicated NGOs, and donors has worked ceaselessly to produce the discourse of development. This discursive knowledge formation is held together by the power of monographs, poverty seminars, symposia, editorials, NGO-training sessions, workshops, surveys, graphs, charts, dissertations, and audiovisual representations. Local and international researchers, NGOs, and donors reinforce each other in the production and maintenance of the hegemonic ideas on development—women's empowerment, microfinance, NGOs, human rights, and good governance. Yet, as White has noted, the political implications of these discourses and practices get muted in development literature.[3]

Foucault's insight into how truth and power operate in the representation of social reality, and how they make certain constructs more intelligible than others, is an analytical frame through which we can analyze "how a certain order of discourse produces permissible modes of being and thinking while disqualifying and even making others impossible."[4] This production of knowledge is critical in understanding how the NGO poverty industry is invented, reproduced, and entrenched as an institution and as a body of scientific "truths" that, in turn, reorganizes knowledge and resources, and prioritizes particular research ideas as legitimate. My analysis aims to uncover how these developmental "truths" are invented, how different categories of people are inducted into the maintenance of this discourse, and how they collude to make it hegemonic and intelligible to a wider audience.

In the words of early philanthropists, the technologies of citizenship operated within a political rationality that enabled people's autonomy, self-sufficiency, and political engagement, and they were "intended to help people help themselves."[5] Poverty research reproduces the idea of poverty under multiple categories, such as the poor, hard-core poor, the marginal, the landless, women, and indigenous people. While these categories are ways to manage large segments of the population toward objective goals and to influence policy, they tend to obscure the structural conditions and class relations that produce poverty in the first place.[6]

While I was conducting my research, every day I read in the newspapers about a poverty seminar, the launching of yet another poverty study, or a discussion on the findings of a recently concluded poverty study. Local intellectuals and NGO bureaucrats regularly wrote in the local dailies about microcredit, women's empowerment, civil society, and good governance, all connected with NGO work. Most of the Western researchers who congregated either at Grameen Trust or BRAC were studying the "microcredit phenomenon," that is, the relationship between microcredit (now called microfinance) and x, y, and z factors, such as women's mobility, health, improved child nutrition, and so on. As Fernando has stated, most of these studies on microfinance are quantitative, focusing on measurable statistics (loan repayment rates versus the strategies of recovery that this book has demonstrated). Fernando also noted that "current studies have failed to explore its impact on social, economic and political processes beyond its immediate project environments."[7] In this discourse of microfinance and women's empowerment, loan programs meant the ability of poor women to access and organize resources at the household level with little attention to their imbrication in other social relations, kin obligations, and market uncertainties.

In my visits to the Programme of Poverty Alleviation Library at the Grameen Trust or at the Ayesha Abed Library at BRAC, I wondered about the purpose of so many dust-covered documents on poverty, microcredit, empowerment, gender, appropriate technology, and the environment. Who reads them? What and whose purposes do these documents serve? In my interactions with local researchers, I discovered that many were skeptical of these research monographs. In fact, these ideas were not hegemonic, but local researchers self-censored what they said in urban research spaces, thus maintaining the domination of NGO discourses.

Below I offer a set of tentative formulations that can be used as a guiding map to begin questioning what the Grameen/NGO research symbolized for local researchers and how that operated in building discursive formations.

- The discourses function as discourses of exclusion.
- Within the NGO discourse, alternative or oppositional voices are largely neutralized; when they are included, these critiques have no practical effects.
- Questions of economic survival inhibit actors deeply entwined in NGOs from speaking out.

I put forward the idea that there is an archive of intimate knowledge about the poor that is being created through poverty research monographs. While it is too early in its gestation process to know what uses this archive may be put to in the future, there is no doubt that the research wings of NGOs form a vast knowledge-making machine.

These formulations are explored through the following questions and settings in this chapter. Why do we need to know the poor? What are the ways in which we know them? And finally, how does the Grameen Bank function as a form of symbolic capital for Bangladeshi elites? These questions are addressed in specific settings. I explore them through formal and informal interviews with local researchers at poverty seminars; through an examination of research projects of BRAC and Grameen Bank[8]; and finally, by analyzing the micropolitics of a conference held in Dhaka on Professor Yunus's economic philosophy, termed "Yunusonomics."

In his work on redefining the art of ethnography, Marcus has noted that the anthropologist encounters forms of knowledge that have already been densely "represented, inscribed and written about." That is, there is no uncontaminated arena in which the anthropologist as a sole agent can conduct ethnography. Hence, the task of the anthropologist is to disaggregate these dense imbrications of representations; yet, the anthropologist is one among many critical interlocutors who are engaged in this process of unmasking representations. As my analysis here shows, ordinary citizens also critique the hegemony of NGO knowledge production—as the example of the retired doctor discussed later in the chapter shows—but critiques such as his, or mine for that matter, are silenced and made illegible within dominant development discourse. Thus, the problem is not that of an absence of critique, but of understanding how to identify the sites in which these discourses are inscribed, and to make them more legible in public debates.

Taking the cue from Marcus, I define the leading NGOs (Grameen Bank, BRAC, and Proshika) as discursive epistemic machines. The task is to unpack dense webs of significations within NGO institutional spaces where this writing is produced. But this writing is a form of advocacy (in development lexicon, it is called action research). It is writing with objectives: to replicate the program, garner more funds, increase visibility, and satisfy one's sponsors. Writing, thus, becomes one powerful apparatus among a set of available apparatuses of these NGOs. Much of this writing is about record keeping, accounting, and public relations, all of which are necessary components of modern bureaucracies. But this writing is also ideological and acts as a form of social control.

In the word-of-mouth culture of Bangladesh, where veracity is accorded depending on the status of the speaker, publishing neat "scientific" documents as "facts" ushers in a new era of technocratic knowledge. These NGOs publish newsletters, brochures, journals, annual reports on research projects, research monographs, dissertations, flip charts, posters, and videos. These researches are self-referential; the authors refer to their preexisting work to legitimize the development policy that funds their research. What is evicted from this discourse is the biography of the author. Is the author of the research paper an NGO or World Bank representative or an aid industry consultant? If so, what are the constraints on the production of knowledge? These overlapping conflict-of-interest issues get silenced in urban research spaces. The researcher who is hired to evaluate NGO projects often has worked as a freelance consultant for the same NGO in the past. In the clientelist culture of Bangladesh, past connections and goodwill with one's NGO sponsors garner present project grants. These intimacies of how knowledge gets produced and by whom can only be accessed through an immersion in the social life of NGOs.

In this case, research production is nestled in interdependent relations of hierarchies and social obligations. Rahman (1999) noted that Helen Todd, who wrote *Women at the Center* (1996), is a journalist and wife of a microcredit visionary from Malaysia. Todd conducted a study of forty women in two loan centers in the Tangail district, and the Grameen Bank sponsored her research. Todd worked through local interpreters, which present considerable limitations.[9] Alex Counts of *Who Needs Credit* (1996) was a former Fulbright Fellow in Bangladesh. He conducted his research in Tangail, and he then became the president of the Grameen Foundation in the United States. Shahidur Khandker, whose book *Fighting Poverty with Microcredit* (1998) is the most-cited evidence of the beneficial effects of microcredit, is a lead economist at the World Bank, the institution that has adopted microcredit as the new panacea against global poverty. Similarly, Hashemi, who wrote several well-cited articles on the benefits of microcredit, was employed by the Grameen Programme for Research on Poverty Alleviation.[10]

In the collected volume *Speaking Out: Women's Empowerment in South Asia* (1996), the authors (Gul Rukh Selim, Lamiya Rashid, and Muhammad Shahabuddin) who contributed the articles on the Bangladeshi NGOs, BRAC and Proshika were employed by these very institutions. Both of their articles supported the positive effects of BRAC and Proshika on income and organizational potentials of women involved in loan programs. While the editors acknowledged that "research was not undertaken by outside consultants [note the use of the term *consultants* over *scholars*] but by people who actually work for the organizations involved," they failed to question the conflict of interest that such scholarship poses.[11] In NGO research, the distinctions between the categories scholar, consultant, and NGO employee get blurred. The assumption is made that those who dedicate their lives to poverty alleviation write from uncompromised perspectives.

This hegemony over development knowledge in NGO-dominated spaces occurs through the functional peculiarities of Bangladesh. There are very few primary investigators writing in English, the preferred language of Western-aided development discourse, in Bangladesh. This small coterie of English-educated local researchers dominates development discourse and has carved out specific domains of expertise (for example, microcredit and women's empowerment, reproductive health and women, environment and rural poverty, and so on); and the gate-keeping of these domains is strictly maintained. The leading NGOs recognize the need for self-promotion and a positive media image; they organize conferences and produce glossy brochures to create publicity about their programs.[12] Seminars, workshops, and conferences help to secure that image. Through this public-image–making process, NGOs reinvent themselves as "development" partners in urban spaces. These seminars are conducted with foreign development economists, consultants, donor representatives, Western-trained local researchers, and an august body of senior and retired (male) government bureaucrats in attendance. These conferences on poverty research become a way of cementing the institutional bonds among donors, NGOs, and a small group of English-language–educated professionals.

Alongside their work in microfinance and rural development, all these leading institutions have dedicated research institutions with their own separate budgets. Grameen Bank has its Programme for Research on Poverty Alleviation, housed inside the Grameen Trust. The Grameen Trust was set up in 1989 to help in the replication of Grameen-type microlending programs worldwide. In 1998, the Trust had a $100 million budget, which included a $97.5 million loan from the World Bank.[13] At the end of 1998, Grameen Poverty Research had 104 ongoing research projects.[14]

BRAC set up its Research and Evaluation Division (RED) in 1975. By December 1998, RED had produced a cumulative total of 653 research reports and papers.[15] The research wing of Proshika, called the Institute for Development Policy Analysis and Advocacy (IDPAA), was started in 1994. It was launched with financial support from the Canadian International Development Agency (CIDA). In comparison with Grameen and BRAC, Proshika's research establishment was still in a fledgling state: in 1998 it had only 10 ongoing research projects, but they were all very large projects on topics such as NGO–World Bank collaboration in development, shrimp cultivation and environment, structural adjustment review initiative, analysis of women's workload, and women's control over their acquired resources, to name a few. ASA was the only leading NGO that did not have a proper research wing. Of these four institutions, ASA had maintained a strict profile in microfinance services and did not venture into other areas. Due to their well-developed status as research institutions, I analyze the research practices and documents from Grameen Poverty Research and BRAC's Research and Evaluation Division (RED).

The production of developmental knowledge takes place on several levels. On one level, it is a form of technocratic knowledge, the type of informational database necessary in the management and accounting of development projects. On another level, it is about the vested stakes in the self-construction of local elites. As postcolonial subjects, local elites see themselves as members of a global circulation of transnational elites. Keck and Sikkink termed this a global "communicative structure," a forum of dialogues rather than a global civil society defined by shared values and common discourses and practices.[16]

The transnational NGO facilitates this circulation of "third world" elites who gather at many global conferences on problems facing marginalized populations (women, indigenous people, children, refugees, AIDS/HIV patients) living inside nation-states. These ongoing global conferences are usually sponsored by the United Nations, Western governments, and in the 1990s, increasingly in partnership with the private sector. These conferences take up issues such as the role of NGOs and civil society in biotechnology, good governance, human rights, women's rights, refugee rights, population planning, and AIDS/HIV research, to name a few.

Research monographs and newsletters function not only as analytical and measurement tools of poverty reduction strategies but also as a social archive of knowledge about the poor. What uses this archive may be put to in the future is open to debate. The formative rules of this archive are emerging, transforming and adapting to new environments. Knowledge production as hegemonic control aids us in thinking through the emergence of the local NGO poverty research institutions as institutions with multiple consequences, both anticipated and unanticipated. Through the massive knowledge production of poverty alleviation, poverty is exacerbated, entrenched, and institutionalized.

Modern computer technology is key to the making of this archive. Technology enables NGOs to gather, organize, categorize, and select information. This technology assists in the marketing of one's programs in the wider world of poverty studies. It also fosters the building up of a data bank of information about the poor that gets permanently stored in computers. Once imprinted into microchips, this information can be accessed, sorted, and used in a variety of ways. The poverty research programs incorporate the poor as part of an electronic surveillance technology.

This social archive is a specific type of intimate knowledge about the poor—a collection and storage bank in which information concerning who they are, their habits, behaviors, manners, customs, leisure activities, living conditions, possessions, recreational choices, belief structures, etc., is stored. The way these people eat, drink, sleep, defecate, work, reproduce, and entertain, is documented in taxonomic schemes that are in turn used to produce developmental knowledge and to implement development policy. These raw data are malleable, and can be interpreted in various ways to bolster one's ideological position and to claim knowledge about what works in the amelioration of poverty. This knowledge can be used to sell concepts and products to, and about, the economically impoverished. This data-gathering process is also a pedagogical tool. It teaches present and future generations of researchers, planners, government officials, students, and NGO bureaucrats how to imagine and construct the poor, and how to manage them as objects of knowledge.

NGO Ways of Knowing the Poor

Research monographs produced by NGOs are a form of advocacy research. Perhaps the best known of these documents is Grameen Bank's collection of stories of rural poverty entitled *Jorimon and Others: Faces of Poverty* (1982). The edited volume is a collection of poverty stories about poor women and the transformation of their lives through their membership with the Grameen Bank. These are linear and simplistic stories about poor women. Poverty is shown as the lack of access to credit in the lives of women. These women achieve a renewed sense of meaning and purpose in life after joining the Grameen Bank. In contrast, *The Net: Power Structure in Ten Villages* (1983), published by BRAC, is a more thorough structural analysis of poverty and power relations in rural Bangladesh. For purposes of my analysis, what is more interesting to analyze is what types of research ideas are highlighted as necessary and important. Thus, NGO research also covers a wide ambit of views. The tactics of "empowerment of the poor" as a poverty research tool, whether from the right or the left, share a strategy found in Cruikshank's analysis:

> The will to empower may be well intentioned, but it is a strategy of constituting and regulating political subjectivities of the "empowered." Whether inspired by the market or by the promise of self-government autonomy, the object of empowerment is to act upon another's interests and desires in order to conduct their actions toward an appropriate end; thus, "empowerment" is itself a power relationship and one deserving of careful scrutiny.[17]

Access to credit has been lauded as the way to poverty alleviation, and there are many research documents that support this position. As I have shown in the Introduction, the microfinance industry has become part of Appadurai's "finanscapes" through its global partnerships; and for those connected to its research at the local level, these connections meant money, power, and access to global circulations.[18] It should not surprise us then that the researchers who were part of this process were unwilling to engage in criticisms of NGOs or microfinance or of alternative ways of organizing resources and poverty alleviation efforts. The art of government, as Foucault has said, is the art of the management of populations. The NGO archive then becomes a source of knowledge/power about the local population in a postcolonial country. What was distinctive about this knowledge/power was that this technocratic knowledge was available to a host of actors, both national and transnational, to be used in a variety of yet unknown ways.

On my visits to the Ayesha Abed Library at BRAC, I was impressed by the professional conduct of the library staff and the organization of information. The library staff was very helpful and responded quickly to my needs. One could find documents easily and photocopy them for a nominal fee. These libraries sold their own research monographs. They also kept newspaper clippings on file. At BRAC, I was surprised to note that there was not a single study listed in the catalog on the 1993–1994 conflict with the clergy. The only citation I found of the clergy question in the catalog lists I got from BRAC was a paper on "Can Imams Teach in NFPE Schools: Report of Survey from Four Rural Areas," by Fazlul Karim and A. M. R. Chowdhury. It was a one-page document. The survey was conducted in 1990, long before the 1993–1994 conflicts with the clergy. The librarian could not locate the document, and I did not pursue it further. How does one read this absence of interest in the clergy in BRAC documents?

In trying to find information about the 1993–1994 events against BRAC by the clergy, I ran into resistance. BRAC was not willing to share information since the attacks had seriously harmed their activities. I was surprised to find that not a single paper or document existed on the events of 1993–1994. When I pointed this out to the librarian, she said, "I am new here. I have never seen them. They have removed all those documents. BRAC is a large institution and they want to minimize trouble. But you can contact one Mr. X; he is a former BRAC researcher. He did detailed research on the crisis, and then he suddenly left BRAC."[19]

I was introduced to Mr. Abed, the director of BRAC, through a mutual friend. When I met Mr. Abed, I told him that a report existed on the 1993–1994 crisis, written by a BRAC researcher, and I wanted to read that document. To deny my request was embarrassing for Mr. Abed since I was introduced to him by a close friend. The fact that I knew about the existence of the document, knew the name of the researcher, and had already noticed the removal of all documents related to the 1993–1994 crisis suggested to him that he might as well give me the document. Mr. Abed instructed the director of BRAC Research to give me the paper. When I met with the director of research, he handed me the document saying, "I thought we were no longer going to circulate this paper." There are two archives then, one private and one public. Unless one is an insider, it is very difficult to access the private archive of the large NGOs. As the author of a recent monograph on NGO workers in Bangladesh noted, "Most NGOs in Bangladesh maintain a high level of secrecy about their documents, staff salary and budgets. This makes the concept[s] of 'participatory,' 'grassroots,' and 'development' advocated by the NGOs somewhat illusory."[20]

Looking over BRAC documents, I noticed a shift in research topics from the 1980s to the 1990s. In the early phase of BRAC research, the period between 1977 and 1989, BRAC research focused on power dynamics in rural society (for example, the causes of landlessness among the poor) and appeared to have a more holistic approach to understanding the causes of rural poverty and social relations. In the later phase, the 1990s, BRAC research focused more on human rights, gender empowerment, and income-generating projects, topics linked to Western-donor interest. In the late 1980s, BRAC had published several studies on rural power dynamics that analyzed resource allocation and advocated changes in rural power structures through group formations.[21] In the 1990s, BRAC RED had shifted its focus from studies on village-level structural analysis to research supported by donor mandates on human rights, good governance, and women's issues. Below is a short sampling of some of these new studies from 1997 sponsored by BRAC that focus on gender and human rights issues.

1. Impact Assessment of BRAC's human rights and legal education training (1997).
2. Backlash against human rights and legal education posters (1997).
3. Household violence against women in rural Bangladesh (1997).
4. Prevalence and correlates of the risk of sexual violence within marriage in Bangladesh (1997).
5. The law and the poor: BRAC's human rights and legal education program (1997).

The following list, compiled from Grameen Poverty Research Newsletters, 1995–1997, is a chart of the funded research proposals for the Programme on Poverty Alleviation, Grameen Trust. Grameen Poverty Research funded proposals on a quarterly basis. The funding amount was not released, but it was a large budget for Bangladeshi research institutions.

1994	15
1995	30
1996	42
1997	12

On a monthly basis, the key investigators of the projects discussed their findings at the Grameen Trust offices. These small seminars functioned as a training ground for future researchers. The Grameen research program hired outside consultants, many of them university professors and Bangladesh Institute for Development Studies (BIDS) researchers, to work on these projects.

In Grameen's Action Plan for 1998–2005, Yunus defined "a poverty-free life" as a world in which the poor possess the following: "(1) tin-roof house, (2) beds or cots for all members, (3) access to safe drinking water, (4) access to a sanitary latrine, (5) all school-age children attending school, (6) sufficient clothing for winter, (7) mosquito-nets, (8) a home vegetable garden, (9) not having food shortage even during the most difficult time of year, and (10) having sufficient income-earning opportunities for all adult members of the family."[22] These were listed as basic needs to which all people should have access.

Grameen Bank used this ten-point index to monitor whether or not Grameen borrowers have graduated from poverty to relative comfort. Based on this survey, Grameen Bank has claimed that 50 percent of their borrowers have graduated from poverty, and another 50 percent were close to achieving that goal.[23] The questionnaire makes a one-to-one correlation between Grameen loans and people's ability to purchase a mosquito net, drink tube-well water, grow vegetables, eat three meals a day, etc.[24]

In my area of research, the local municipal corporation had provided the tube-wells to the majority of the poor; it had nothing to do with Grameen loans. It was not clear to me how the Bank made the determination that if one of its members slept under a mosquito net, it was because of involvement with Grameen Bank. What about other NGO memberships, other sources of income? When I asked the local Grameen manager in my research area if they had checked this list against what the members already possessed when they initially joined Grameen Bank, and if they analyzed how these changes were the direct result of these members' involvement in Grameen Bank activities, he said, "No, that would be too time consuming." Then he added, "Our head office gives us this list, and we fill it up on a monthly basis." In other words, they filled out the bubbles corresponding to what their members possessed and sent that survey to headquarters, which in turn collated the field-level data to validate the beneficial effects of Grameen and microfinance. This is what I found in my area, and other areas may work differently. However, as I noted in chapter 3, field-level officers are overburdened in their daily work schedules, and are unlikely to spend time thoroughly verifying such data.

Encountering the Desi (Local) Researcher

The leading NGOs—BRAC, Proshika, and Grameen Bank—have their own research institutions,[25] and they produce reams and reams of research documents. University professors and researchers who work as consultants on

NGO projects enjoy considerable privileges in a materially impoverished country. In fact, working as a consultant on an NGO project is a source of much-needed additional income for middle-class people. Salaries of university professors cover the costs of minimal living standards in Dhaka. NGO income provides access to better housing, healthcare, private schooling for children, automobiles—that is, to all the accoutrements of Westernization and consumerism in a poor country. One cannot discount the importance of these symbols in the social life of the middle class.

The "professor as NGO consultant" situation had become so grave—university professors attended to the NGOs, and not to their students—that the authorities of Dhaka University issued an official warning in 1999 to professors who spend their time as "consultants" on various NGO projects instead of discharging their duties to the university.[26] Not surprisingly, this relationship between research and work has had its linguistic transformation. In conversations with me, local researchers described their research as *kaaj* (work), as opposed to *gobeshona* (research).

During my research I came across the following. One of the leading NGO research institutions gave a local university professor a one-year project funding for $15,000. The annual salary of this university professor was $3,000. In another instance, the sibling of a well-known bureaucrat was given the equivalent of $1,000 to write a few project proposals. In the context of Bangladesh, where the highest-ranking government officer made around $250 a month (1999 figures), these were very high figures. These lavish contracts functioned as a way of creating, and at the same time cementing, new dependencies between the NGOs and a cohort of local consultants.[27] These project funds enabled hired consultants to have materially comfortable lives.

It must be mentioned here that these figures paled in comparison to the earnings of Western consultants who had neither local-language skills nor cultural familiarity with the area, but who nonetheless passed as "experts" because they were citizens of the grant-giving donor nation. It is well known in donor circles that development money benefitted the aid-giving nation.[28] These poverty research monographs were produced to satisfy donor policies, but they generated a new need for knowledge about the poor, and along with it a market for such knowledge products. Donors paid local NGOs handsomely for the latter. The donors, in turn, need such data on the efficacy of different aid programs sponsored by them to justify to their governments the need for continued grants to Bangladesh. Within the development industry, the sustenance of the international donor community depended on the continuance of these grants to the developing countries. NGOs and donor agencies are extremely guarded about their contracts, salaries, and internal documents, and these are not made available to the public or to researchers who are not connected with these NGOs or aid agencies.

Another key group of people inducted into the NGO sector were high-ranking government officials who were put on two- to three-year deputations at leading NGOs. These government bureaucrats acted as liaison officers. Their function was to be negotiators between the state bureaucrats and the NGO leaders, dispelling myths about NGO intentions and creating complementarity between these two groups. Such NGO patronage tied up the future and livelihoods of a key group of people—academics, college-educated youths, and more recently, government officials. This structural incorporation of the educated middle class into the NGO circuit was an unexpected conjuncture between an expanding institution in need of English-language–educated talent in a country with a small group of English-language–educated people.[29] Furthermore, a stagnant economy forced local people to be very selective in how they conducted themselves vis-à-vis people with access to power and resources. To put it bluntly, there is a shortage of jobs in Bangladesh, and those who do have jobs often need a second, and sometimes a third job, to make ends meet.[30] Moreover, the structure of social dynamics in Bangladesh, which is kin-based and face-to-face, made it difficult for criticisms of NGOs to emerge in the urban research spaces. In such societies, manners are a way of conducting business, embarrassment is generally avoided, and people do not openly criticize those on whom they depend for future favors.

While the NGO establishment has been able to induct certain groups of people into its structure, there was nevertheless a growing and robust critique concerning the activities of NGOs among people who were identified as leftists or those who were not part of the NGO network. These critics argued that the NGO bureaucrats were not elected representatives of the people and that their operations were not transparent. Furthermore, NGOs did not pay taxes to the government, although many of them had profitable commercial enterprises. In addition, NGOs were beholden to their financial sponsors, who happened to be Western industrialized nations. Thus, even if well intentioned, their programs were restricted by the demands of their sponsors, and their nationalist desires had to be subordinated.[31]

I encountered two types of local researchers in Bangladesh. The first group comprised middle-aged males who were socioeconomically privileged and English-language educated. They were academically talented (most were developmental economists), and many had received higher degrees from American and British universities. A group of them had also received their higher education from universities in the former Soviet Union and Eastern Europe. In the post-1971 phase, the Soviet and Eastern European governments gave many fellowships to Bangladeshi students to study in their countries. Many of them were former members of the communist or socialist parties of Bangladesh. Some of them called themselves "reconstituted" Marxists, and expressed solidarity with welfarist policies, but in their everyday life they were "NGO researchers."

Their work with developmental NGOs kept them within the discourse of "working for the poor." There was recognition among scholars working in Bangladesh that the changed global circumstances of the 1990s required creative thinking about solutions and social justice within a capitalist framework. Thus, Professor Yunus's social capitalism was an attractive model that allowed them to mentally bridge the world of socialist ideas with the ideas of capitalism.

The second type of researcher was a researcher by default: she or he was a researcher because of lack of employment opportunities. These men and women came from economically modest backgrounds. They were not connected to elites; their knowledge of English was fractured; they did not have the much-valued foreign degrees. Thus, they had to negotiate with the first tier of researchers in order to secure employment and research funding.

It was the latter group of people who were the real raw researchers. They may not have had the credentials or known the latest theories, but they were the ones who went to the field to gather data and who put up with the discomforts (malaria, cholera, diarrhea, to name a few) of research in rural Bangladesh. These people had thick knowledge about what was going on in the field, and they were willing to share that with a researcher such as me. They often could not voice their more radical observations in their research monographs, and thus they had a thirst for an audience with whom to share their views.

There was an implicit criticism of the top researchers (their patrons) embedded in their conversations. Often one heard the refrain, "What does he know? Has he ever gone to the field? You go ask him when he stayed in the village last." Although these men and women were not the primary investigators named on the research projects, they knew more about the hidden transcripts of research than the high-theory researcher who seldom went to the field. I was fortunate to meet several such people, who helped me in my own ethnographic endeavors.

The funding structure in Bangladesh was a pyramid structure with interlocking dependent groups of people, each depending on the tier above them. The highest tier was formed of a select few who had access to donors and people such as Professor Yunus of Grameen and Fazle Abed of BRAC. In the hierarchical and face-to-face social structure of Bangladesh, this relationship between the two groups of researchers was characteristically clientelist, and these dependencies obstructed major criticisms of the NGO establishment.

One day, while I was in the office of the director of a research program in Dhaka, the exasperated director showed me a two-page proposal write-up. The applicant had asked for 250,000 taka ($5,319) for the project. One page was a rather meaningless graph. The other page said that only three people had ever worked on poverty issues: Amartya Sen, Professor Yunus, and "yours truly" of the proposal. The proposal, if one could call it such, was utter nonsense. The embarrassed director said that had the person asked for a small sum, he could justify it. But how could he justify such a large sum? As we spoke, the director received a call from a well-known economist and a patron of the proposal writer about the status of the grant.

In another instance, I was at the office of the director of the NGO Affairs Bureau, and a retired gentleman was waiting to talk to his old friend, the director. When I asked the older gentleman what brought him to the NGO office, he said that since he has retired, he wanted to start an NGO. Yet, he had not even considered what purpose this NGO would serve. The retired gentleman also wanted to participate in the resources of this new economy of the NGO. Not surprisingly, the rapid and unregulated expansion of the NGO sector has led to graft and the creation of fake NGOs in many cases. Transparency International Bangladesh in its 2006 report identified the NGO sector as "moderately corrupt," with police and education at the highest levels of corruption. The report found that "there are a few NGOs that receive 90 percent of the resources from the donors; NGO activities are inflated to the donors to bring money for addressing problems that are actually artificial; there are also some 'well-trained' beneficiaries who always speak of the positive aspects of the NGOs every time the donors go for field visits; in 85 percent of NGOs, members of the governing body are relatives of the executive chairman."[32]

One has to recognize that the desired life of a middle-class person living in Bangladesh resides at a great distance from his or her reality.

This contradiction between what one has to do in order to survive as a middle-class person and what one wants to do is very difficult to bridge in a postcolonial state. The increased commercialization of urban life and the prohibitive prices of most goods and services from housing to education have made it difficult for middle-class people to maintain their lifestyles. As I have already mentioned, the salaries of university professors barely cover the minimum expenses of living in the city. One needs additional sources of income to survive, and the NGOs provided that relief to a small group of people. The postcolonial urban subject has to be located and understood within this grid of contradictory self-constructions, the pushes and pulls of a commitment to socialist ideals versus what she or he has to do to put bread on the table.

Similarly, the reception of the NGO has to be understood in the wider context of the dismal state of the economy in Bangladesh. Bangladesh can be characterized as a failed state. The successive governments have been corrupt, politically divisive, and inefficient. The industrialists in Bangladesh are almost all "loan defaulters." They took millions in takas in industrial loans from the nationalized commercial banks to set up industries, and the majority of them have defaulted on those loans. The government has not taken any action against them because many government officials have taken bribes from these industrialists, and these "loan defaulters" were related through kin to highly placed government officials. Within this climate of rampant corruption and disorder, the NGOs have emerged as institutions that were efficient in delivering services to the poor, and that were less corrupt. Local people who live in Bangladesh recognize NGO contributions, and they judge the negative effects of NGOs against what they deem as NGOs' positive contributions to society.

At the research institutes, I began to see a pattern that disturbed me. One of the functions of the research institution was the manufacturing of people who were trained to carry out the mandates of the parent institution. Bright young university graduates were inducted into the poverty machinery as underpaid research assistants by their professors. Once in, they were trained to think in NGO-prescribed methods. For these young men and women, contact with these NGO research institutes meant a job in the future, and their eventual contact with the wider world. They wanted to build a good working relationship with the research institution, and would accept the rules that were imposed on them. Often they would come up to me and say, "We like talking to you because you say different things." These bright young women and men had a critical outlook on the work of NGOs, but most of them acknowledged that this could not be made visible as discourse. As one of the young women said to me once, "Grameen Bank talks about poverty alleviation. If it was really committed to the removal of poverty, should not the word be elimination?"[33]

Toward the end of my stay, I interviewed one of the leading economists of Bangladesh.[34] During our interview, which lasted over an hour, he did not ask me one single question about my research findings. This was a surprising lack of interest in someone who is a dedicated researcher. This was perhaps due to his machismo as one of the country's premier economists, and his view that as an anthropologist and as a woman, I was doing wishy-washy research. But I also read this lack of interest as a concern: he did not want me to unsettle the narrative about Grameen in which his stakes as a scholar were rooted. When I told him that I had found that men used the loans, and that women faced increased violence both inside the home and outside, he refused to engage with my critique. Instead, his comment was, "I need more robust figures in order to be convinced," although he did not reveal what "more robust figures" meant and how such "robust figures" were to be gathered. He clearly preferred a certain type of statistical research—exemplified by the archetypal number-crunching researcher—over ethnography. His behavior reflected the behavior of many scholars who were part of the local NGO culture.

In another instance, a well-known economist at the Bangladesh Institute of Development Studies (BIDS) said in response to some of my observations about NGO loan operations, "So what if men use the money? You are very negative. People are not passive. They maneuver within a field of possibilities. . . . NGOs are promoting an entrepreneur from below. In my opinion, we have capitalism-er bikaash [expression of capitalism] through the NGO/microcredit route. The NGO route is an alternative vision to develop the non-agricultural sector through small, home-based businesses."[35] He analyzed microfinance as the new phase in capitalism under globalization for agrarian societies.

In a third situation, a friend who had helped to set up my field site said that our mutual friends had asked him whether I was making up my "research findings." According to him, these researchers were convinced that I was so "anti–Grameen Bank/NGO paradigm" that I was searching around for negative data to support my ideological stance. What all these people shared in common, whatever their ideological orientation was that they all worked as consultants for NGOs. This scholar–consultant identity had become so prevalent, and hence normalized, that within this group nobody questioned how this subjectivity influenced their objectiveness and positionality as knowledge producers. Nonetheless, within this group there was a range of feelings and motivations toward this work. They were all well-intentioned people. Their constraints were the political and economic conditions prevalent in Bangladesh. As one NGO bureaucrat with openly leftist sympathies said to me,

> [T]he question facing us on the ground is, what do we do now? Look around yourself and tell me what works in Bangladesh. The government does not provide relief to the poor, the national parties are completely corrupt and clannish, and we on the left have nothing to say to the poor. In the midst of this dismal picture, Professor Yunus has given us a tool, a possible solution to poverty. Perhaps it is a Band-Aid solution. In my opinion, we need to grasp the potential good of that solution and try to make it work.[36]

Several European schools, and professors and research fellows associated with these schools, dominated the meta-narrative of development discourse in Bangladesh.[37] These centers of development were the Institute of Development Studies (Sussex), Institute for Development Policy and Management at the University of Manchester, Center of Development Studies at the University of Bath, Center for Development Research (Copenhagen), and the Institute of Social Studies at the Hague. Many of the senior researchers associated with these institutions had amicable working relationships with donor representatives of EU countries. They often served as experts on donor-funding meetings, and they worked closely with the local cohort of NGO researchers.

The heavy presence of donors and aid-related activity had resulted in Western consultants coming to Bangladesh on an ongoing basis. Since Bangladesh is considered by Western diplomats as one of the least favored countries to live in, the consultants sent to Bangladesh were often less accomplished scholars in their own countries. Thus, well-trained local scholars were often subordinated to less trained foreign scholars who were hired by Western aid agencies as consultants.

> I was working at the research division of the largest NGO. One day, the senior management instructed me that I had to assist a Western anthropologist who would apply a new participatory tool. . . . We soon discovered that I had seven years of academic training in anthropology from a Western University; and the Western anthropologist had only a six-month short course in anthropology . . . from a North American University.[38]

In my encounters with both local and foreign researchers, I was often told, "You will have a difficult time proving your thesis." Local researchers were aware of the power of these leading NGOs to silence dissent, and they felt that as an individual researcher, I was setting myself up for failure. This comment made sense in an environment in which research meant reports for NGOs and donors, but not scholarly practice. Many of these Bangladeshi researchers considered me a "consultant," a term and identity they were familiar with, and not a doctoral student whose research goals and self-construction were perhaps different from those of the hired consultants of NGOs. The poverty discourse had rules about what types of critiques could be heard as legitimate discourse, and hence my research was seen as transgressing the boundaries of acceptability.[39]

The work of Bangladeshi-born Canadian anthropologist Aminur Rahman is an illuminating example of the power of this discourse to silence oppositional viewpoints. Rahman wrote a critical ethnographic account of the Grameen Bank called *Women and Microcredit in Rural Bangladesh: An Anthropological Study of the Rhetoric and Realities of Grameen Bank Lending* (1999). Findings from his research were originally put on the Web site of the Institution of Development and Research Canada (IDRC), which had funded his research. It was taken off the Web site after a few days because IDRC officials felt that they might embarrass Canadian aid officials who were supporting microfinance initiatives in Bangladesh. Fearing freedom of expression allegations, IDRC officials later reinstated Rahman's findings on their Web site. In Bangladesh, Rahman fared worse. He approached the only English-language academic publishing house, called University Press Limited (UPL). Although the book had been published by a leading American academic press, Westview, the UPL editor decided against publishing it. In the context of a single English-language press of academic note, dissent against the Grameen Bank can be easily controlled.

Toward the end of my research, I met the local Canadian aid official of CIDA for an interview in 1999. CIDA was sponsoring Proshika in its social mobilization programs. When I mentioned to the Canadian aid officer about the Proshika-sponsored rally in Brahmanbaria and the violence committed against poor women in the name of democracy, he became extremely annoyed and terminated the interview. Western aid agencies and their officers were equally invested in the maintenance of these hegemonic scripts of microfinance and women's empowerment. They were the field representatives of their governments, which were trying to open up local markets through their good governance programs.

The ordering of knowledge and its power to silence dissent that I identify and critique was deeply entrenched within the production of development knowledge. Multiple actors had stakes in its perpetuation, and their self-constructions and livelihoods were caught up in its maintenance. Escobar has identified the making of the third world as an object of knowledge through "the creation of a vast institutional network (from international organizations and universities to local development agencies) that ensured the efficient functioning of this apparatus. Once consolidated, it determined what could be said, thought, imagined; in short, it defined a perpetual domain, the space of development."[40] In this space, it is difficult for alternatives to the NGOs' way of organizing people and resources to appear, or for them to be taken as a legitimate discourse of social critique.

The Poverty Conference: A Local Who's Who

Dhaka, the capital city, is the paradigmatic site for the study of microfinance. There were endless seminars on microfinance held in this city of ten million. Often as I went about the city to yet another conference on microfinance I would wonder what these conferences meant to the ordinary people of this city.

I found an implicit contradiction in these seminars. The subjects of these multiple conferences were the poor. Yet the poor only appeared as percentages, graphs, and charts, and they functioned as means to an end, where the end was the facilitation of future grants for the poverty researchers and the NGOs. A few high-priced consultants and development researchers dominated the local poverty research scene. Most of them were economists associated with the Bangladesh Institute of Development Studies (BIDS). An invitation to the more high-powered seminars, usually held behind closed doors and by invitation only, and often at the only five-star hotel in Dhaka city, was a much-coveted invitation for people outside this closed-status group who were trying to make contact with these difficult-to-access researchers.[41] The corridor talk at such poverty seminars was about who got the highest poverty research contract, what was the highest going consultancy rate, who would get to attend the next UN conference overseas, who was in with UNDP, USAID, DFID, CIDA, SIDA, DANIDA, or the World Bank and who was out, who may have need for some consultants, and so on.

Another telling feature of these poverty seminars and conferences was the prominence of English. The speakers usually delivered their papers in English and the discussions were carried on in English as well. Usually there were one or two Western-donor representatives in the room. The use of English as a mode of communication was done with two purposes in mind. The panelists and organizers were speaking to the donor representatives. In the conferences that I attended in Dhaka, donor representatives rarely ever spoke. They responded to these research projects behind closed doors with NGO bureaucrats. The English language, which in a former British colony is a mark of class, was used as a form of social control. Communication in these seminars was not domination free. The participants' use of English inhibited many people from engaging in these so-called "dialogues," which thus functioned as monologues. While organizers claimed that these conferences were democratic and open, in reality, there were implicit power divisions that separated the ordinary people from the elite researchers. Scholars who dissented from the dominant view—such as professors Anu Muhammad and Badruddin Umar, who are highly respected leftist theoreticians in Bangladesh—were not invited to these seminars because of their criticism of NGOs and microfinance.

The Conference as Domination and Dissent

When I arrived in Dhaka in 1997, there was speculation that Professor Yunus would win the Nobel Peace Prize. His advocates were two of the most powerful people in the world, former president Bill Clinton and Senator Hillary Clinton of the United States. Professor Yunus's name was synonymous with symbolic prestige for Bangladeshis, the nation of floods and famines in the Western imagination. Many middle-class Bangladeshis, who had been disturbed by negative representations of Bangladesh in the Western press, believed that Professor Yunus would singlehandedly turn the fate of Bangladesh around and make them feel proud as Bangladeshis.

In April 2, 1998, Professor Yunus delivered a speech titled "Towards a Poverty Free World" at an international conference of economists. In his speech, Yunus castigated neoclassical economics by saying that the "seeds of poverty are firmly planted in the pages of economics textbooks" and that we need new textbooks that make the poor the center of focus, although it was not clear from his speech what these textbooks would teach. Following the publication of the text of the speech in the local papers, several economists took issue with Professor Yunus's representations of neoclassical economic theory. One of them, Mahfuzur Rahman, wrote that "Professor Yunus's comments were the verbiage of an evangelical preacher" because he had no clue of what neoclassical theory was about, and how neoclassical theory is taught in "good universities."[42] In support of Professor Yunus, one of his admirers wrote an article in a local paper. Below I offer an excerpt from it.

> In humanizing economics and the economic world, Professor Yunus wants to move away from the pervasive world of alienation in modern world society stemming largely from the production of commodities and the prevalence of wage labor. It is this challenge of creating a new paradigm, a radical rupture of neoclassical economics, that Professor Yunus points to. It is our task as intellectuals, as people committed to the creation of a poverty-free world, to take on this challenge, to bury the old and articulate the new paradigm. At the very least we can discard the first principles of neoclassical economics, the individualistic, egoistic, profit-maximizing man, Robinson Crusoe, the homo economicus par excellence, and substitute it with the interests of the poor.[43]

On August 22, 1998, a roundtable conference was held on the topic "The Economics of Professor Yunus: An Alternative Paradigm in the Making?" at the local British Council Auditorium, sponsored by the Center for Alternatives and the newspaper *The Daily Star.* These roundtable conferences had become a popular space for more educated members of society to engage in lively debates. These roundtables were supported by USAID and several other Western donors interested in promoting a culture of good governance among the urban population. Between 50 and 60 people showed up for this conference. There were five speakers at the roundtable discussion: three university professors, one BIDS researcher/consultant, and the director of the Programme of Poverty Research.

The director of the Center for Alternatives advocated making Professor Yunus's "economics" into a new discipline called "Yunusonomics" that should be taught at the university. According to him, the paradigm of Yunusonomics rested on six principles: (1) self employment; (2) human right to entrepreneurship; (3) credit as a human right; (4) role of family in business; (5) social-consciousness–driven enterprises; and (6) power of institutions in fashioning minds and activities.

The first speaker delivered an academic paper in Oxbridge English for half an hour to an audience that for the most part could not follow his rendition. As noted earlier, the use of English over the vernacular acted as a form of social control over the targeted audience. Despite an effort made by the panelists to control the debate, below I analyze how dissent operated within this conference that was attended by many people who were not associated with NGOs.

When the floor was opened for questions, the engagement of the assembled people was energetic. The responses were robust and critical. The first speaker was an angry retired doctor who said that he had expected the discussion to be carried on in language that was accessible to him. He then added that he went to his village often. His experiences showed that most people were becoming poorer after several years of membership with Grameen. He had calculated the interest charged by Grameen to be well over 50 percent. He asked the speakers, how could they claim that this was a new paradigm to be followed? How was this high interest helping the poor? None of the speakers would engage with his questions. Failing to get any response from the speakers, the retired doctor left the meeting.

A student of economics pointed out that Ronald Dworkin and others have addressed the ethical dimensions of economics. Yunus's contribution was in the creation of an institutional structure and in the collection of data that the poor are creditworthy. Another student asked what would be the benefits of a course on "Grameen Theology" at the university, and what students would learn that they did not already learn in a course on development. Another person called microcredit an "advanced system of charity" and commented that development must be a macrolevel policy initiative.

Several people also questioned the efficiency of making self-employment the engine of economic growth. Who would buy all these eggs, chickens, puffed rice, hand fans, etc., made by poor women in the villages? It was observed that too many women producing too many products with few buyers would only depress the prices and lower their profits. When I raised the question that women were being charged exorbitant interest rates, a retired leading banker remarked, "She lives in America and has credit cards. Why shouldn't the poor have access to credit?" What was obscured is the fact that in America consumers have access to bankruptcy laws and legal protections, whereas in Bangladesh defaulting women were taken to the police and courts by NGOs. Within a short time, it became evident to the panelists that they could not pass off "Yunusonomics" as a new paradigm. The reception was critical. In this changed climate, the speakers said that Professor Yunus had not claimed that he was the founder of a new paradigm. Yunus's contribution lay in questioning the basic tenets of neoclassical economics!

> The texts of development have always been avowedly strategic and tactical—promoting, licensing, and justifying certain interventions and practices, delegitimizing others. An interest in how the texts of development write and

represent the world is therefore, by extension, an interest in how they interact with the strategies and tactics of their authors and of those who lend them authority . . . . What do the texts of development not say? What do they suppress? Who do they silence—and why?[44]

The documents and apparatuses of poverty research aim to make visible certain forms of knowledge as intelligible to its audience. The constructed world of the poor that is represented through these research documents aims to construct the poor in particular ways. Yet, these documents tend to silence the poor, and instead speak for them. These are very strategic documents that seek to promote a particular model, in this case the microfinance model, and to consolidate it through research in order to garner funds for the NGOs.

The conference on Yunusonomics demonstrates that the discourses of poverty, NGOs, Grameen, and microfinance are not hegemonic discourses. These discourses become hegemonic only in certain urban research spaces. But there is a world outside of these structures in which the majority of the people live. When an article of mine entitled "Demystifying Micro-Credit: Grameen Bank, NGOs and Neoliberalism in Bangladesh" was published in *Cultural Dynamics* (2008), I received several e-mail messages from people in Bangladesh who wrote, "Thank you for your courage!" This may seem odd to a Western audience because Bangladesh is not a totalitarian state; it has a relatively free press. The use of the word *courage* reveals the control by NGOs of research critical of their practices in Bangladesh.[45]

I found that thoughtful, intelligent, and socially conscious people, such as the retired doctor at the conference and these young people who had written to me, find it very difficult to have their voices heard in the dominant knowledge sphere—that is, the main English-language dailies, the sole academic English publisher of note (UPL), and the perennial NGO seminars. Yet, despite their marginalization, they remain engaged and troubled about the problems that beset their politically and economically bruised country.

In my recent trips to Bangladesh, I am beginning to see the emergence of alternative sites of engagement, such as citizens' groups and Web sites and blogs set up by individuals who write about politics and society. They are places to which more politically conscious people load pictures, homemade movies, and eyewitness accounts of events. While it may be argued that the blogosphere is more about personal opinions than critical scholarship, these are sites in which alternative voices are heard, and they could act as a venue for an independent practice of knowledge production.

This discourse of knowledge that I have analyzed in the preceding pages is held together by the symbolic capital that Grameen Bank and NGOs offer to Bangladeshis. For Bangladeshi elites, who represent one of the poorest populations in the world—Henry Kissinger's "bottomless basket"—the renown of Grameen Bank operates as a form of governmentality. It endows them with pride and meaning as global citizens and guides their speech and actions toward maintaining these institutions and their stories. It is not surprising then that when Professor Yunus declared his intention to start a political party in 2007 after winning the Nobel Peace Prize, a decision he recanted, his primary supporters were diasporic Bangladeshis. The miracle stories of poor women's empowerment through the work of microfinance NGOs have shifted the global discourse on Bangladesh from a "failed" state to a state that gives development ideas to the world.

Let me share an interesting story of the pride that ordinary Bangladeshis take in the Nobel Prize of Professor Yunus and the Grameen Bank. One evening, a friend who is a professor hired a taxi in Dhaka. On the way, the taxi driver asked him if he knew Professor Yunus. Surprised, my friend said yes. To that the taxi driver replied, "Since you know him, could you please tell Professor Yunus not to get into politics. He has brought a lot of respect to our country. But our politicians are corrupt. If he gets into politics, he will lose the respect of the nation and the world. Ask him to work on poverty alleviation instead." Even a taxi driver whose daily life was a struggle in the smoke-filled streets of Dhaka and who resided in a world apart from the global development scene, felt empowered by the recognition that the Nobel Prize has conferred on this nation of 150 million.

The majority of Bangladeshis take tremendous pride in the Grameen Bank, its legacy of rural women's empowerment, its winning of the Nobel Peace Prize in 2006, and in its bringing world recognition and global respect to the country. It should be mentioned that the Grameen Bank and the NGOs have brought a certain degree of female autonomy in rural Bangladesh, and have given the country a new global image of hardworking women. They have also supplied much-needed services from reproductive healthcare to primary education to poor people that the state has failed to provide. Bangladeshis judge NGOs at the nexus of a failed state and the positive work of these institutions. These leading NGOs have been able to service the poor primarily because of strong donor support, one that the postcolonial state did not receive.

Professor Yunus, a member of the Bangladeshi male elite, has given his country one of the highest forms of international recognition. Grameen

Bank thus becomes invested with a sense of national pride. It becomes part of a nationalist discourse of how Bangladeshis stake claims as equals with the West on a global level. Hence, those of us who critique this model, or argue for alternative ways of thinking about the economy, take on the mantle of "traitors within," and encounter entrenched criticism from vested circles. As I have outlined here, the conditions of research that prevail in Bangladesh made it easy for critiques to be silenced, or to be rendered as merely another point of view that did not require serious engagement. To reframe Foucault's invocation of governmentality, research then is a conduct among conducts that shapes and guides the production of knowledge. Let me now turn to final thoughts in the Conclusion.

Conclusion From Disciplined Subjects to Political Agents?

AS THE MICROFINANCE industry has expanded in the twenty-first century, it has created networks among NGOs, international development organizations, governments, multinational corporations, and rich investors and poor people, bringing them into closer alliances and dependencies. These developments in financial networking between northern and southern countries will have significant impact on economy, state, and the lives of their citizens. In this new economic arrangement where businesses and NGOs form partnerships, Bangladeshi NGOs and poor Bangladeshis have again emerged as the paradigmatic site and subjects for the testing of these relationships and products for the poor.

The four organizations I studied have all gone through critical transformations. Grameen, BRAC, and ASA have become more powerful in terms of resources, widened their services, and exponentially increased their member rolls. Only Proshika has rolled back its programs because of a loss in donor support. These NGOs serve nearly 20 million clients and reach over 100 million rural people. Their penetration rate is 90 percent in the rural economy. Given the huge increase in microfinance loans, the government of Bangladesh finally initiated a new Microfinance Regulatory Authority Act in 2006. This high level of presence and resources grants these institutions enormous power over the lives of their subject populations, enabling them to guide their clients' actions toward NGO mandates, and to shape the economy according to global neoliberal agendas. NGOs exercise a range of governmentalities, from complicity to fear of prosecution, over their targeted populations to ensure that their objective ends are met.

In the preface to *Jorimon and Others: Faces of Poverty*, Yunus remarked on the presence of capital as key to the alleviation of poverty: "Nobody needed to have any special training. They had either already received this training as part of the household chores or had acquired the necessary skill in their

field of work. All they needed was financial capital."[1] This notion is a fundamental idiom of Grameen Bank's philosophy of microfinance, and one that
was adopted in practice by the other three NGOs I studied. Yet, as the case
studies in this book have illustrated, the reality on the ground is far more
complex, and these loans are entangled in other relationships of power,
inequality, and obligations. The following two ethnographic engagements
illustrate these paradoxes from more recent field investigations.

In 2009, I spent four months in Bangladesh on a research trip, and
had the occasion to visit the families of two of the women who had helped
to make famous both Professor Yunus and the Grameen Bank as a model
bank for the poor. In November 2009, I traveled to Jobra, Chittagong, to
meet with the family of Sufia Begum. Jobra was the village where Professor
Yunus had begun his experiment with microloans in 1976. Sufia Begum,
now deceased, was the basket weaver about whom Yunus writes in his book
Banker to the Poor. Her story of entrapment by moneylenders for failure to
pay twenty-two cents helped make Grameen Bank a reality. Commenting
on her situation, he wrote, "It seemed to me that the existing economic system made it absolutely certain that her income would be kept perpetually
at such a low level that she could never save a penny and could never invest
in expanding her economic base. So, her children were condemned to a life
of penury, of hand-to-mouth survival, just as she lived it before them, and
as her parents did before her."[2]

I was curious to find out how the family of this "first lady" of microloans
had fared. When I arrived in Jobra, I found that Sufia Begum had two adult
daughters who were literally beggars, and a grandson who was a rickshaw
puller. They lived in a decrepit thatched house with a hole in the roof. Even
if Sufia Begum had fared better in her life after her association with Yunus's
loan program, she was not able to pass it on to her family. These microfinance lending practices do not necessarily generate intergenerational
wealth. The people in Jobra told me that Sufia's family was the poorest in
the village.

Her daughter said that since the Grameen Bank had benefitted financially by showcasing her mother's story to win the Nobel Prize, the bank
had a moral obligation to repay their deceased mother. The family did not
ask for much: they wanted a new house with a roof that did not leak, but
the Bank was not forthcoming. Local villagers said that Professor Yunus
and the Grameen Bank had a moral responsibility toward the family
because the story of Sufia Begum had helped the bank achieve global fame.
Sufia's family alleged that after the Grameen Bank won the Nobel Prize, its

Sufia Begum's daughter in front of her mother's house.

officials had brought foreign reporters to their house, and had showcased their neighbor's brick house as the tangible evidence of their mother's success through Grameen Bank loans. While this allegation could not be verified, the anger of the family and community toward Grameen Bank was palpable.

In the social reality of rural life, it was kin obligations that structured how the people of Jobra saw the role and responsibilities of Yunus and the bank. Nobel laureate Yunus was called Moneylender Yunus (Shudkhor Yunus) by local people. It was startling to note that the place where the Grameen experiment had begun saw Yunus, who was born in a nearby village, primarily as a moneylender and not as an altruistic person! If one probed deeper into this discourse of moneylending, it became evident that they saw Yunus as one who had "gone places" by exploiting the plight of the poor in their village, but he had not taken his "own" with him. One could dismiss this discourse as primarily a result of resentment at a son of the soil for abandoning his kin obligations to the woman and the village that had been instrumental in his success with microfinance. However, the fact remains that the Grameen Bank is not a charity. It is arguable whether these moral demands can be made on financial institutions that operate under a different logic of contractual obligations between lenders and borrowers.

The next ethnographic engagement offers a different interpretation of events. During my visit to Bangladesh, I had the opportunity to meet a young woman whose mother was one of the women featured in the book *Jorimon and Others: Faces of Poverty*.[3] The book, first published in 1982, documented the life stories of sixteen poor women who had joined the Grameen Bank after it opened in Tangail. These stories helped to humanize the institution for a global audience. The young woman I met was a high school graduate. She lived in Dhaka, and worked as office help for a local feminist NGO. Her education, combined with her exposure to a feminist NGO, had radicalized her views. She and I spent several evenings talking about the work of microfinance NGOs in her village. Her mother, Anowara Bewa, had formed the first group in her village, Maijda. A widow in her sixties, Anowara Bewa was the mother of four daughters. Three of them had remained unmarried because of the family's inability to provide dowries. The daughter told me that her mother and many of her group members had suffered financially through their association with the bank. This was due to a number of factors, and not all of them were the fault of the bank. However, in her opinion, it was the lack of supervision on the part of the bank that was largely at fault. As a follow-up to our conversation, I went to meet her mother in Maijda, Tangail.

Following is the story Anowara Bewa told me. When Grameen Bank came to her village in the early 1980s, bank officials said that they would give loans to landless women who could demonstrate that they were hard workers. Anowara Bewa, who was desperately poor at that time, had to work as unpaid labor cutting mud and clearing a pond of water hyacinths to be selected as a member. Then she was asked to recruit members to form a group. She had to travel long distances to enlist these members because at that time the bank was an unknown institution, and people were reluctant to join. The daughter said that her mother, who had built a network of local women, gave her time and labor to help make Grameen successful in her area; yet, her contribution has remained uncompensated by the bank.

To make matters worse, Anowara Bewa's business venture in puffed rice soon failed because of changed family circumstances. An uncle who had helped the family died. Her unmarried adolescent daughters could not go to the market to sell the puffed rice. Moreover, a trader who had borrowed money from her to buy rice did not pay her back. Unable to keep up with the payments, she defaulted. The default occurred almost ten years ago. While the family could not say what the exact amount was, they did not think it was more than 2,000 taka (in 2009 exchange rate it would be approximately $28). When I asked to see the booklet with payment history on the outstanding loan, they said the book was taken away by the bank officials. During this period, the daughter alleged that bank officials had harassed the family multiple times. They had once locked her mother in their office, had confiscated their cooking utensils, and had thrice threatened to break their house to raise the defaulted sum.[4]

The daughter analyzed her mother's lack of economic improvement as a form of structural oppression. "They oppress us poor people through indebtedness." I raised the question that the bank is not a charity, and if she could not repay the loans, the bank had a right to claim the debt. She noted:

> What about all those hours of unpaid labor from my mother that the bank received in its early days? My mother found members for the bank's first center in her village. She had to walk several kilometers to find women who would join the group. My mother tried her level best to start her puffed rice business. Yet, when it failed, the bank never helped her to find an alternative source of income. In the beginning, bank officials had said that they would give jobs to the educated children of its members. None of that materialized. Instead, bank officials came thrice to break our house to raise the amount due. When they came the second time, I said, "My mother and eldest sister have borrowed from you but the house belongs to all five of us [mother plus four daughters]. We did not take any loans from you. How can you threaten to break our house as well? Do you call that justice?"

In both instances, an argument was made for social justice based on moral obligations. In this discourse of justice, the relationship between the borrower and the lender lay outside of a financial relationship. Seen from their perspective, the women gave their life stories and labor in order for Grameen Bank to prosper and gain global recognition. Yet, what they gave, a moral gift, could not be measured by the balance sheets of lending institutions. In this algorithm of obligations and reciprocities, the loanees failed to assert their claims because their forms of giving were not recognized as legitimate exchanges in the banking world. Let me pose the question then: Do organizations that work with the poor, and instrumentalize that poverty to develop their organizations, owe a moral responsibility to the very people they seek to empower?

In his Nobel speech, Professor Yunus called upon global corporations to look upon the poor as an unrealized market for their goods, just as he had done years ago to call attention to the poor as "bankable." Once the poor were identified as "bankable" by the Grameen Bank, millions poured into various microfinance schemes. Social businesses are innovative configurations between capital and altruism—the current pathways through which multinational corporations enter local economies and create and corner new markets in developing countries. The marketing of Shaktidoi by Grameen Danone presents some critical issues that need to be rethought in a socially sensitive mode. First, as I pointed out earlier, why sell sweetened yogurt to children whose parents cannot afford to pay for rice? Who can really afford to eat this product?

Similarly, the joint venture between Grameen Healthcare with Veolia, a French company with water-purifying operations in Africa and India, raises similar concerns. The idea is to sell arsenic-free water to people in rural Bangladesh at a nominal price. Sixty percent of the groundwater in Bangladesh has been contaminated with arsenic. The problem of arsenic in water in a deltaic region has posed tremendous health issues and risks to Bangladeshi people. But herein lies the problem. Water is a public good. It should be freely available to all people in Bangladesh. In cities, there is no arsenic contamination in treated tap water. So, should the solution be bottled water or a national level effort to provide treated water in rural areas?

The question then is, where do we draw the line on what is free and what is not? Should we create a world where everything has a price tag, even the most basic necessities, and then extract wealth from those people who are least able to afford it? The middle class has disposable income to buy bottled water as a safe alternative to tube-well water. It is this large untapped middle-class market that triggers Veolia's interest. Ultimately, Danone Foods and Veolia are searching for new markets beyond their current territories—not necessarily among the poor, but among the middle class in the developing world. And in the process, if some good trickles down to the poor, the objective of a social business enterprise is achieved.

Authors writing from a critical stance on NGOs have noted these developments within the sector. At the cusp of the transition of NGOs to a profit orientation in the 1980s, Pronk had warned against the "corruption" of NGOs through their deviation from social transformation to other goals.[5] In a recent publication, *Microfinance: A Reader* (2009), Arun and Hulme wrote, "Microfinance is expanding the benefits of capitalism to the poor, and not the creation of alternatives to capitalism."[6] I have argued here that microfinance and corporate MFIs are the precursors of privatization, and they construct the poor as possible markets. There are those who firmly believe in the promise of neoliberalism for the poor; I do not. Poor and vulnerable people should not be brought into the market without safeguards and protections. And as the recent financial collapse in the United States has shown, transparency, regulation, and accountability are important safeguards that should be in place to protect citizens. In the developed world, in times of financial adversity, wealthy people have recourse to lawyers and bankruptcy laws. In Bangladesh, a country that is prone to natural calamities, safety nets for the protection of poor borrowers are curiously absent.

A lot could be learned from grassroots organizations in other developing countries. For example, the work of Bunker Roy and Barefoot College (www.barefootcollege.org) offers an alternative paradigm. Situated in the Rajasthan desert in India, Barefoot College emphasizes learning through practical knowledge and skills over paper qualifications. The difference between the Grameen and the Barefoot College model is that Barefoot graduates learn how to make solar panels, for example, whereas Grameen borrowers purchase solar panels manufactured by multinational corporations and sold to them through the bank. Many such small-scale models abound in the developing world that seek to empower poor people through skills that teach them to make products that they can use to empower their communities.

Given the above discussion, let me summarize my key findings discussed in the book.

(a) *Microfinance loans have resulted in new states of domination against poor women.* One of the main arguments I make is that the access to microfinance loans has created new forms of subordination and oppression for poor women both at the household and community levels. I have shown here that while the loans are given to the women, the real users remain the men. Hence, the men control and use the loan, while the wives remain contractually obligated for the payments to the NGO. This has constituted poor women as means to capital for rural men, and not as owners of capital. The ability to access loans has not radically altered a woman's status or given her increased security within the household. As Rahman (1999) noted, NGOs hold women responsible for the loans because of their "positional vulnerability," and not because of their entrepreneurial skills. However, if the family were dependent on wife's income from wage-labor or a productive skill, then her value to the family's income would be higher because her labor would be more difficult to replace.

In the uncertainties of the market, things do not always work according to plan. When husbands fail to pay because of illness, loss of business, or some other unforeseen calamity, it is the women who suffer the consequences. Moreover, the NGOs tie individual responsibility to group responsibility in their loan programs, and that brings the wrath of the community, who sees the individual women as contract breakers. When defaults occurred, NGOs used the group of borrowers to recover the loan. This created increased strife and antagonism among the targeted women and their families because the group suffered if an individual member defaulted.

Contrary to their claim that there is no collateral for the loans, it is the group and a Bangladeshi woman's honor and shame that operate as the collateral. I have analyzed how NGOs appropriated rural women's shame as a disciplinary technology in their loan recovery programs. Codes of women's honor and shame that guide their conduct in rural societies were instrumentalized by these NGOs to work in their capitalist welfare. Husbands/families fearing the loss of face if their wives get shamed in public, try to come up with the money, often by selling or borrowing from other sources. In recent years, NGOs finessed their loan recovery programs by resorting to the courts, the police, and rural elites to enforce payments. In the face-to-face environment of rural Bangladesh, these actions escalate fear and competition among poor women.

(b)   *Microfinance loans have benefited the rural middle class at the expense of the poor.* With the increase in microfinance loans, NGOs have turned to the middle class and less indebted people as their clients. These new clients are traders, richer farmers, and petty officials. As NGOs have increased their loans, they have also targeted the more successful clients within their existing groups. Moderately rich clients assure NGOs of regular payments, and they pose fewer risks. Their social status enables these richer clients to act as enforcers within the group of borrowers. Richer clients also received loans through proxy membership and moneylending that the female borrowers engaged in. In 2007, the Grameen cell phone ladies I met were the successful borrowers who owned retail shops, who had husbands working overseas, and who already had regular income from employment.

By the 1990s, NGOs had shifted from their earlier conscientization model to a market model that operated on financial sustainability by maximizing profits. In the process, NGOs have transformed from primarily working for the poor to increasingly targeting the better-off people. With this shift in their client base, the NGOs will provide more goods and services to the rural middle class than to the poor. From these trends I conclude that these NGOs now reside at a great distance from their original doctrine of helping the poor.

(c)   *Neoliberal subjectivities are beginning to emerge among those women who develop into successful borrowers.* I have shown that NGOs operate within neoliberal principles of competition, profit, and entrepreneurship. I found that the women who benefited from microfinance loans shared similar demographics—they were heads of households, their husbands granted them autonomy in financial matters, they lived independently from their in-laws, and many had married within their native village, which granted them more mobility. They were knowledgeable about markets and displayed a certain savoir faire. These women lived by the principles of competition and rationality. They always sought to increase their income not through a sense of community solidarity, but through competition. While NGOs construct female borrowers as entrepreneurs, the emergent neoliberal subjectivity that I encountered was that of the petty female moneylender. The female moneylender embodied all the competitive aspects of the neoliberal subject.

Contrary to the claims of the Grameen Bank and the NGOs that their work in microfinance curtailed moneylending, I found the opposite effect in society. In fact, these loans have reproduced moneylending among rural women. Given the lack of investment opportunities for women, moneylending is a profitable option. Women can conduct business without leaving their homes. This has led to a new mediation of local understandings of the importance of money as an investable commodity, and has altered existing notions of usury in a predominantly Muslim society. Often these successful women would remark that they would not lend to kin or a poor woman because they would "lose the money." Instead, they would loan to the traders who would be able to pay them back on time. While the market was replacing some of the traditional obligations to kin, women continued to be positioned within the constraints of family relations that impeded the development of the market subjectivity in peculiar ways. What remains unknown is the extent to which this market subject will approximate the autonomous subject of the Western model of neoliberalism.

(d)   *The introduction of microfinance into private life has led to the loss of social solidarity.* The insertion of finance capital in the form of microfinance loans into private lives has begun to dissolve the private–public distinctions that organized rural life, and it has weakened the powers of the community to forestall market penetration. My research findings indicate that the profit orientation of microfinance policies has begun to rupture deeply held notions of family and community solidarity, and has helped to create the market as a sovereign entity.

In Bangladesh, the extended family is the core source of social identity, care, support, and kin-based solidarity. By introducing loans into private life, NGOs have begun to weaken the kin-based bond of identification and family solidarity. While loans can offer a family economic opportunity to collectively work on a project, they can also pit individual members against each other when things do not work according to prescribed norms, as some of the cases discussed in chapter 4 demonstrated. At the core is the use of social collateral as a disciplinary technique against poor people. By using the group as the enforcer of loan repayments, these NGOs pit poor families against other poor families, and as I have shown here, it often has devastating consequences at the level of the family and community. By appropriating existing forms of rural behavior such as shaming and housebreaking as part of their disciplinary toolbox, the NGOs have institutionalized these forms of behavior. In recent years, NGOs have resorted to the police and rural elites to recover their money that can have destructive results in the lives of women as I have demonstrated in this book.

(e)   *The emergence of the NGO as a shadow state.* In Bangladesh, the NGO emerged as a critical broker in development that occurred at the conjuncture of global ideological trends and the economic and political conditions prevailing in the country. The Western governments supplanted the Bangladeshi state by channeling millions through the NGO sector. Building the NGO as an alternative to the state was part of the privatization effect of the World Bank and Western governments. The NGO sector stepped in for a weak state and became the primary provider of essential services to the poor and also the employer of the middle class. Services traditionally rendered by the state—from rural credit to primary education to immunizations to basic healthcare—have been outsourced to the NGO sector. At the national level, the large NGO executives sit with donors and government officials on all major development initiatives, and openly participate in nation-building decisions. At the rural level, NGOs and rural people have a relationship of dependency. The NGOs need the rural poor to carry out their development mandates, and the poor need the NGO to receive essential services. It is through these linked and dependent processes that NGOs in Bangladesh operate as a shadow state.

(f)   *The production of knowledge in development.* The NGOs have created a vast apparatus of knowledge through their dedicated research wings. In order to operate in the age of technocratic knowledge, NGOs also require a vast group of NGO researchers and consultants who are drawn locally and internationally. The NGOs I studied produce an enormous amount of development literature. The purpose of NGO reports and monographs is to authenticate the work of NGOs for their donors and for a global audience. But as I have argued, development knowledge is not innocent. The operation of knowledge in this sphere is primarily toward objective ends—to solve a problem, to raise funds, to develop a new program, and so on. This knowledge has political implications because it legitimizes certain types of interventions as necessary for "improvements" in the economic and social fields, while at the same time, it tends to obscure other ways of organizing resources and people. Given their enormous resources, clients, and global connections, microfinance NGOs create an order of power-knowledge about poor people's lives that becomes hegemonic in development-dominated spaces, which silences dissenting voices and thereby produces their "truth." But with growth comes challenges. I anticipate that NGO-sponsored research will also face scholarly scrutiny in the years to come as these institutions expand.

(g)   *Inventing markets and constructing the poor as consumers.* It is not surprising that in addition to microfinance loans, NGOs have expanded their services to financial products, pension plans, education loans, and health schemes. The latest expansion is in selling commodities from cell phones to packaged foods to hybrid seeds and new technologies. NGOs are routes through which multinational corporations and their products enter local markets, find buyers of these commodities, and export their revenues. Through access to loans, the poor are constituted as consumers, and new markets are opened up in developing countries. The point is, of course, that not all of it is bad. Many people, such as the cell phone ladies, are able to use these products profitably. Those who benefited from phones were the ones who did not consume their income but reinvested the money in another productive capacity—that is, those women who had the skills to maneuver in the market. Thus, when their incomes went bust after 2005, these women had already invested in another source of income. However, my study shows that the majority of the poor consumed the loans and did not have the capacity to reinvest judiciously.

This book has exposed a range of techniques, tactics, programs, and procedures that were set in place through these NGOs. I have shown here that this growth in microfinance has accelerated privatization, weakened the powers of the state, and diminished public-sector investments. Through careful ethnographic research, I demonstrated how access to loans created antagonistic relationships, weakened social solidarity, invented markets for multinational corporations/NGOs, and manufactured new market subjects. I have shown here how knowledge is produced within the NGO sphere for global consumption.

The book offers a cultural diagnostics of how these microfinance processes have been introduced, entrenched, and reproduced in Bangladesh. My intent is to create intimate cultural knowledge of how debt relations affect the lives of poor women, who have little power to negotiate the terms of their loans with these NGOs. It is equally important to note that what I have found in my research may not hold true for other places because the local conditions will vary. The point then is to have more critical research done by independent scholars who are not affiliated with NGOs, the World Bank, other development organizations, or the aid consultancy industry. This is not to discredit their work, but to create more space for alternatives to the microfinance paradigm to emerge.

In his writings, the Bangladeshi economist Anisur Rahman cautioned that "these systems (microfinance) intrinsically strengthen existing power relations that 'condemn the large majority to a lowly and subservient state of living'—in fact, power relations that create and recreate poverty."[7] As I pen these words, I am reminded of my first trip to the Grameen Bank in Tangail. As I walked around the village with the young man who had accompanied me from Dhaka, he mentioned, "If you listen to the NGOs' rhetoric, they want to privatize everything." The idea that nothing is free has now come full circle. Foucault cautioned that not everything is bad, but everything is dangerous. There are inherent dangers in the journey Bangladesh is taking toward NGO corporatization and privatization that will have serious consequences for the majority of its citizens whose labor, identities, and potentialities will become the sites of corporate greed and experimentation.

Inside the political culture of Bangladesh, the heads of the major NGOs sit on many boards with government officials. In Bangladesh's aid-dependent environment, NGOs and donors help to write the rules that govern the country. In order to have real transparency and accountability, citizens' groups have to take on the role of holding the NGOs' feet to the fire. Perhaps the points that I outline below could be used to begin a conversation about transparency, accountability, and the role of civil society. I offer these thoughts to initiate a conversation, and not as a set of guiding rules. I firmly believe that the people of Bangladesh, given the right environment, are capable of creating dynamic processes to address these issues.

- An independent regulatory framework should be developed to oversee the work of the Grameen Bank and NGOs that work with poor people. This should be made up of private citizens, those who are not aligned with the NGO/development organizations and who do not receive any income as consultants.

- The prices of products from cell phones to seeds sold by Grameen/ NGOs through their microloan programs need to be made transparent. Alongside a government price regulatory body, there should also be a citizens' watchdog group to monitor whether products are sold to borrowers at a fair price by these NGOs. This information should be made public through such media as informational posters in rural areas.

- There should be governmental oversight in the interest rates that these NGOs charge. Failure to do so allows many NGOs literally operate as loan sharks toward their poor clients.

- The independent media and human rights groups have an important role to play in disseminating information about the actions that NGOs take against their borrowers when they cannot pay. Human rights organizations at the local level should set up a legal procedure for poor borrowers to prosecute NGOs that abuse their power in their transactions (such as housebreaking) with their clients. Surely, poor women should not be sent to jail when the richest people in Bangladesh who are loan defaulters are not prosecuted by the state!

And finally, the great modernist question that I am always asked as an individual researcher: if not microfinance, what alternatives are there for the poor of the world? Given the economic conditions prevalent in Bangladesh and the lack of accountability of its government to its poor citizens, this question is difficult to answer. Based on my long-term research in Bangladesh, I do not believe that microfinance is the solution to the structural conditions of poverty for the majority of its poor citizens; however, it can help certain categories of people, particularly those with marketable skills or who already have successful small businesses. We need job creation over the creation of petty trading with microfinance loans. In this respect, the public sector ought to be invigorated to become a provider of rural employment. The two nationwide programs that provide public sector employment are in the areas of Food-For-Work (FFW) and rural maintenance program.

Ultimately, in order for solutions to be effective, they must originate from the people themselves through democratic discussion and debate. Hence, the answer lies in the potential of Bangladeshis to organize as concerned citizens to demand accountability from international aid organizations, microfinance NGOs, corporations, and their government. This people-oriented movement has begun to take shape in Bangladesh, as I discuss below. Yet, to what extent this people's movement can gain momentum and appropriate the processes of neoliberal development, and transform them toward the welfare of the poor people of Bangladesh, remains open to future research.

Citizen's Movement as an Alternative Discourse

I would like to consider social movement as a form of political engagement for social justice that sits apart from the development NGO sector. I am mindful that citizens are not born but created, just as politics is not given but is a process that is built by people and institutions through open critical debate and reflection on their practices. "While the NGO is an organization, a social movement is an aggregation of people and organizations with a shared set of ideals that seeks to bring about social change consistent with a professed set of values."[8] Social movements offer a positive site of political action because they are unlikely to be targets of donor intervention, as they cannot be controlled.[9]

In creating awareness about social issues, the role of human rights NGOs has been significant. Since the transition to democracy, the media have played a pivotal role in disseminating information to all classes of people. The role of the vernacular press has been significant in creating awareness among people about the corporate deals that the government strikes with multinational corporations. The media have created a flow of information between the city and the hinterlands, breaking some of the boundaries that defined these geographical spaces as self-contained units. The Internet has connected educated Bangladeshis within the country and overseas through the blogosphere and has become a political voice of dissent.

There is a range of scattered human rights groups that are emerging in the country organized around political and social issues. One could conceptualize them as small points of resistance. Most importantly, they offer a space of discussion, organization, and mobilization outside the dominance of NGOs and mainstream political parties. In this respect, the role of a small group of concerned scholars, journalists, leftists, and human rights activists that have organized a citizens' group called the National Committee to Protect Oil, Gas, Mineral Resources, Power and Port is worth noting. They have organized themselves as a citizens' watchdog group to prevent the theft of the country's natural resources under corrupt governments.

A native economist, Professor Anu Muhammad, is the organizational leader of the group. It is this citizens' group, among several others, that is at the forefront of holding the government's feet to the fire over privatization issues ranging from open-pit mining, to allowing a multinational corporation to build a second deep-sea port in Chittagong, to the sharing of gas revenues between the government and multinational corporations (www.meghbarta.org). This group has become a vigilance group of concerned citizens who hold public hearings on the secret deals cut between the government and multinational corporations. Moreover, they play a critical role in educating the public on how these deals may negatively affect the country. They organize people's long marches, meetings, and discussions about political issues.

In 2007, the group began a formal investigation of the World Bank, International Monetary Fund (IMF), and the Asian Development Bank (ADB) through a People's Tribunal. The group asked these institutions for a public accounting of their work in Bangladesh since 1972. In December 2008, in front of five hundred assembled people, the People's Tribunal finally indicted the World Bank, IMF, and ADB for acting against the national interest of Bangladesh. The judges demanded compensation for the people of Bangladesh for the destruction of different sectors of the economy in agriculture, finance, energy, jute, and industry. While this process may fail to fulfill its promises, the People's Tribunal has set a remarkable antecedent for future generations, and for political action in

Bangladesh. It has involved ordinary people as critical interlocutors in the processes that affect the economic conditions of their country. While this movement remains a marginalized process, the margins can offer solutions that mainstream processes cannot.

From over a decade of research in Bangladesh since 1996, I sense a growing awareness in which ordinary people are being shaken from their apathy toward national level politics. While leftist political parties continue in the forefront of these people's movements, their role has been challenged by nonparty affiliates on the ground. While this political process does not have a unified ideology, one begins to trace a social movement that could be initiated by citizens for more accountability among those institutions that run the country—the state, national political parties, corporations, business elites, international development organizations, and NGOs. I am optimistic that this is an ongoing process of revitalized activism and imagination that stretches beyond the limits of a neoliberal order. So, in answer to the great modernist question—what is to be done?—let citizens, and not subjects, write the future of Bangladesh.

Glossary of Bengali Words

Adda	a style of conversation enjoyed by Bengalis
Apa	a formal address for a non-kin woman
Ashami	culprit
Baki	to buy on credit
Bari	house, dwelling
Bazaar	market
Begana	half-naked, shameless
Be-ijjat	shameless
Bhai	formal address for a non-kin man
Borolokh	rich and powerful people
Burqa	head-to-foot covering worn by Muslim women
Bustee	slums
Chaap	pressure
Chotomahajan	small moneylender
Chowki	a bed with no headboard
Daan	charitable contribution
Darshan	to visit a holy man or a deity at a shrine
Desi	native
Dhaar	borrow
Durnam	ill repute
Fatwabazz	those who issue fatwas
Garib	poor
Ghar Bhanga	to break a house
Ghorer Bou	housewife, bride
Ghorer Meye	daughter, someone who belongs to one's village
Goriblokh	poor people
Gram	village
Gusti	lineage

Hartal	shutdown of offices and vehicular movement
Huzoor	honorific for clergy
Jhupri	a very small thatched dwelling
Jihad	struggle against anti-Islamic forces
Jontrona	pain, suffering
Kisti	loan installment
Korjo Hashana	to donate labor for community works
Lajja	shame
Maan-ijjat	notions of honor
Mahajan	moneylender
Maktab	religious primary school
Matabbar	village elder
Math Kormi	field-worker
Maulana	member of the clergy
Monga	drought
Mullah	member of the clergy
Mufti	a clergyman who is learned in the Quran and Islamic jurisprudence
Mukhchalu	outspoken, forward
Murubbi	respected older person
Nakh phool	nose ring
Nogno	bare, shameless
Noshto	spoiled, ruined
Oshohai	helpless
Para	neighborhood
Purdah	seclusion of women
Putul Natch	puppet show
Reen	loan
Salaam	Muslim greeting
Samaj	society
Samity	civic groups, NGO groups
Sangstha/Sangathan	organized groups
Sari	a garment worn by Bengali women
Shahajya	assistance
Shaheb	a formal address for an educated man
Shalish	village adjudicating board
Shami	husband
Shamman	pride, honor
Sharm	shame

Shasthya Shebikas	BRAC rural health workers
Shudh	interest, usury
Tafsir Mahfil	recitation from the Quran
Taka	unit of Bangladeshi currency
Taka Khatai	to invest money
Tolpeth	underbelly
Zaqat	mandatory charitable contribution incumbent on all financially able Muslims

Introduction

1. David Harvey, *A Brief History of Neoliberalism* (Oxford, UK: Oxford University Press, 2005), 64.

2. Marguerite Robinson, *The Microfinance Revolution* (Washington, D.C.: World Bank Publications, 2001), 9. She writes: "Microfinance refers to small-scale financial services—primarily credit and savings—provided to people who farm or fish or herd; who operate small enterprises or microenterprises where goods are produced, recycled, repaired or sold; who provide services; who work for wages or commissions; who gain income from renting out small amounts of land, vehicles, draft animals, or machinery or tools; and to other individuals and groups at the local levels of developing countries, both rural and urban."

3. In my analysis, I use these two terms interchangeably, although the term microcredit is used more often.

4. Jude Fernando, "Microcredit and the Empowerment of Women: Blurring the Boundaries Between Development and Capitalism," in *Microfinance: Perils and Prospects*, ed. Jude Fernando (New York: Routledge, 2007), 2.

5. Geoffrey Wood and Iffath Sharif, "Introduction," in *Who Needs Credit? Poverty and Finance in Bangladesh*, eds. Geoffrey Wood and Iffath Sharif (Dhaka: University Press Limited, 1997), 31–32.

6. Linda Mayoux, "Women's Empowerment and Participation in Micro-Finance: Evidence, Issues and Ways Forward," 2002, 1. http://www.oneworldaction.org.

7. Ibid.

8. "Microloans Championed by Nobel Laureate Top 110 Million," State of the Microcredit Summit Campaign Report, Washington, D.C., November 1, 2006. According to the campaign director of the Microcredit Summit, Sam Daley-Harris, his organization had extended loans to 113 million clients, of which 82 million were among the poorest. Loans to these 82 million clients have a multiplier effect that "affected 410 million family members, a number greater than the combined populations of the United States, the United Kingdom, Canada and Belgium." The Microcredit Summit is a program of the U.S. antipoverty group RESULTS Education Fund.

Professor Yunus serves on its executive board. http://www.microcreditsummit.org (accessed August 18, 2008).

9. Ibid.

10. International Year of Microcredit 2005. http://yearofmicrocredit.org (accessed August 18, 2008).

11. The Grameen Bank is partially owned by the government of Bangladesh and legally it functions as a bank. However, in my analysis, I conceptualize it as an NGO for the following reasons. The Grameen Bank (often referred to here as the Bank) is autonomous in its internal governance structure. It has ties to international organizations. The Bank does not allow its employees to unionize, whereas government bank employees are unionized. Unlike conventional government banks, Grameen Bank operates many commercial ventures. The Bank is owned by borrowers who hold shares in the bank. These features set it apart from government banks.

12. All of these NGOs work with slight variations on the Grameen Bank model. They all have millions of subscribers, and cover more than 90 percent of the rural population. See Varun Gauri and Julia Galef, "NGOs in Bangladesh: Activities, Resources and Governance," *World Development* 33, no. 12 (2005): 2045–65. The NGO Proshika has lost much of its power and resources since 2000. In 2004, charges of financial irregularities were brought against its leader, Qazi Faruque. He was arrested and later released. Julfikar Manik, "Allegation against Proshika: Government Yet to Build Conspiracy Case," *Daily Star,* May 6, 2003. The following are their official URL addresses: www.grameen.com; www.brac.net; www.proshika .org; and www.asa.org.bd.

13. Matthew Swibel, "The 50 Top Microfinance Institutions," *Forbes Magazine,* December 12, 2007. The *Forbes Magazine* list of the top 50 microfinance institutions in the world placed the Bangladesh NGO ASA at number 1, Grameen Bank at 17, and BRAC at 21.

14. Syed Hashemi and Lamiya Morshed, "Grameen Bank: A Case Study," in *Who Needs Credit? Poverty and Finance in Bangladesh,* eds. Iffath Sharif and Geoffrey Wood (Dhaka: University Press Limited, 1997), 218. In the book, I use the term *poor* to refer to the borrowers of these NGOs. The term is not used as an undifferentiated category, but one that refers to this economic characterization by NGOs, and also as recognition that these people lack the social power to control their destinies.

15. For example, Grameen has ties to international lending institutions, multinational corporations, and private investors, and has over twenty-five initiatives known as the Grameen Family of Companies. For a description, see Muhammad Yunus, *Creating a World without Poverty: Social Business and the Future of Capitalism* (Philadelphia: Public Affairs Book, 2007), 78–79. Eighteen of these companies are registered under the Companies Act of Bangladesh, and they pay all duties and taxes to the government. "Grameen at a Glance," at http://www.grameen-info.org. For a critical analysis of this corporate link-up, see Anu Muhammad, "Grameen and Microcredit:

A Tale of Corporate Success," in *Economic and Political Weekly*, 44, no. 35, August 29, 2009, 35–42.

16. Michel Foucault, "Governmentality," in *Essential Works of Foucault: 1954–1984*, eds. Paul Rabinow and Nikolas Rose (New York: The New Press, 2003).

17. Shahidur Khandker, "Microfinance and Poverty: Evidence Using Panel Data from Bangladesh," *World Bank Economic Review* 19, no. 2 (2005): 265.

18. Harvey, *A Brief History of Neoliberalism*.

19. Aiwah Ong, *Neoliberalism as Exception: Mutations in Citizenship and Sovereignty* (Durham, N.C.: Duke University Press, 2006), 4.

20. Arturo Escobar, *Encountering Development: The Making and Unmaking of the Third World* (Princeton, N.J.: Princeton University Press, 1995).

21. Aminur Rahman has also made similar observations in his ethnography *Women and Microcredit in Rural Bangladesh: An Anthropological Study of the Rhetoric and Realities of Grameen Bank Lending* (Boulder, Colo.:Westview Press, 1999).

22. Muhammad Yunus, *Creating a World without Poverty*, 24–25.

23. By targeting an immigrant community that is largely drawn from the diasporic Bangladeshi community in New York, the Bank is able to capitalize on the nationalist feelings that the Nobel Prize and Grameen Bank engender among immigrant Bangladeshis. It can be reasonably speculated that the immigrant Bangladeshi borrowers will police each other to ensure regular payments to the Bank so as not to bring disgrace to an institution from their native land.

24. News Release, "The MasterCard Foundation and BRAC Will Expand Financial Services in Uganda," November 18, 2008. The MasterCard Foundation is an independent private foundation based in Toronto, Canada. It is funded by MasterCard Worldwide. Its aim is to start innovative programs in the areas of microfinance and youth education. http://www.themastercardfoundation.org (accessed March 3, 2009).

25. Staff Reporter, "Bangladeshi NGO Goes Global for Commercial Lending," *Daily Star*, May 27, 2008.

26. Jonathan Morduch, "The Microfinance Promise," in *Journal of Economic Literature* 37 (1999): 1571.

27. Staff Reporter, "Grameen Bank Says 'No' to Joint Venture Biotechnology Project with US Co.," *Daily Star*, August 3, 1999.

28. For BRAC, maize cultivation goes into the diet of its breeder chicken industry. Despite newspaper reports on the adverse effects on farming from the introduction of these new seed technologies, there is little oversight by the state over their production and distribution. See Samudra Haq, "Controversy over Hybrid Use," *Dainik Jonokontho* [Bengali], November 30, 1998. Jahangir Alam Johnny, "Allah Bachaile Ai Dhan Ar KokKhono Korbo Na [If Allah Saves Me I Will Never Again Use This Rice]," *Chinta*, 8 [Bengali], no. 2: 5–7, 1998.

29. Personal communication to author by BRAC chairman, Fazle Abed.

30. BRAC has created the traveling pharmaceutical sales-cum–health workers to provide income and healthcare to the rural poor. BRAC's *shasthya shebikas* (rural health workers) are given basic instruction in how to monitor height, weight, temperature, etc. They buy over-the–counter packets of medicine (for pain, stomach flu, tuberculosis, etc.) from BRAC, which they sell to their rural clients for a small markup. According to BRAC, this has provided these sales ladies with income, and it has also helped to reduce tuberculosis because the medicine is now brought to the home of the patient.

31. Jim Igoe and Tim Kelsall, *Between a Rock and a Hard Place: African NGOs, Donors and State* (Durham, N. C.: Carolina Academic Press, 2005), 5.

32. Muhammad Yunus and Alan Jolis, *Banker to the Poor* (Dhaka: University Press Limited, 1998), 11.

33. http://www.opportunity.org/microcredit (accessed August 10, 2008).

34. Gina Neff, "Microcredit, Microresults," in *Aspects of India's Economy* 21 (October–December 1996): 68.

35. This comment is also based on my experiences with women-in-development experts working for NGOs and donor organizations.

36. This framing distinction was suggested to me by Farida Akhter of UBINIG in Bangladesh. Recovery contains within it the idea of coercion, whereas I conceptualize repayment as noncoercive and voluntary.

37. Yunus and Jolis, *Banker to the Poor*, 91.

38. Syed Hashemi, Sidney Schuler, and Anne Riley, "Rural Credit Programs and Women's Empowerment in Bangladesh," in *World Development* 24, no. 4 (1996): 649.

39. See the following: Rahman, *Women and Microcredit in Rural Bangladesh: The Rhetoric and Realities of Grameen Bank Landing* (Boulder, Colo.: Westview Press, 1999); Fernando, "Microcredit and the Empowerment of Women," 187–238; Lamia Karim, "Demystifying Microcredit: The Grameen Bank, Neoliberalism and NGOs in Bangladesh," *Cultural Dynamics* 20, no. 1 (2008) 5–29; Anu Muhammad, "Monga, Micro Credit and the Nobel Prize," in *Micro Credit: Myth Manufactured*, ed. Farooque Chowdhury (Dhaka: Shrabon Prokashoni, 2007), 165–74.

40. Hashemi and Morshed, "Grameen Bank: A Case Study," 218. In 1997, the board of directors of Grameen Bank was made up of two government nominated members (since Grameen Bank is a quasi-government bank) and nine rural women who were nominated by local Grameen managers from among its members. These nine women were selected by area branch managers, and they represent the most successful borrowers within the most successful branches.

41. According to the Grameen Bank's Web site in 1998, "Grameen group savings have reached 7,853 million Taka (approximately USD 162 million), out of which 7,300 million Taka (approximately USD 152 million) are saved by women." In 1999, Grameen had more than 1 billion taka in its investment portfolio.

42. "Grameen Bank at a Glance," 2009. http://www.grameen-info.org.

43. Professor Anu Muhammad, a long-time researcher on the microcredit policies of the Grameen Bank, brought this fact to my attention.

44. Anu Muhammad, "Grameen and Microcredit: A Tale of Corporate Success," 37.

45. Arjun Appadurai, "Grassroots Globalization and the Research Imagination," in *Globalization,* ed. Arjun Appadurai (Durham, N.C.: Duke University Press, 2001), 3.

46. Saskia Sassen, "A New Geography of Power," Global Policy Forum Speech (2002): 2. http://www.globalpolicy.org/nations/sassen.htm (accessed November 15, 2008).

47. Jael Silliman, "Expanding Civil Society: Shrinking Political Spaces—The Case of Women's Nongovernmental Organizations," in *Social Politics* 6, no. 1 (1999): 37.

48. Flora Lewis, "For European Jobless, Self Employment Might Work," in *Grameen Dialogue* 34, April 1998.

49. Harvey, *A Brief History of Neoliberalism,* 159.

50. Ibid., 64.

51. Ibid., 3.

52. Ibid., 4.

53. James Ferguson, *The Anti-Politics Machine: "Development," Depoliticization, and Bureaucratic Power in Lesotho* (Minneapolis: University of Minnesota Press, 1994), 15.

54. Akhil Gupta, *Postcolonial Developments* (Durham, N.C.: Duke University Press, 1998), 9–10.

55. Ong, *Neoliberalism as Exception,* 4.

56. See Farida Akhter for a discussion of the management of population control in Bangladesh. *Depopulating Bangladesh: Essays on the Politics of Fertility* (Dhaka: UBINIG Publications, 1996).

57. Fernando, "Microcredit and the Empowerment of Women," 4.

58. Linda Mayoux, "Tackling the Down Side: Social Capital, Women's Empowerment and Micro-Finance in Cameroon," in *Development and Change* 232 (2001): 421.

59. Khandker's study was jointly supported by the Bangladesh Institute for Development Studies (BIDS) and the World Bank.

60. Khandker, "Microfinance and Poverty," 266.

61. Ibid., 284. It is interesting to note that Khandker does not cite the article by Aminur Rahman that appeared in *World Development* (1999). This article had initially raised some questions among Northern European microfinance donors. One Scandinavian country had sent a consultant to visit the Grameen Bank to independently verify if Rahman's conclusions on increased strife and violence against women borrowers were widespread. I met with the consultant in 1999. Unfortunately, the female consultant had no knowledge of Bengali and depended on Grameen Bank officials and local BIDS researchers to help her determine the validity of Rahman's findings!

62. Yunus, *Creating a World without Poverty,* 240.

63. Jonathan Morduch, "The Role of Subsidies in Microfinance: Evidence from the Grameen Bank," in *Journal of Development Economics* 60, no. 1 (1999): 2–4. Morduch's analysis clarifies the role of subsidies to Grameen Bank in keeping it

financially sound during its formative years, 1985–1994. It questions the microfinance literature that "asserts (with limited evidence) the win-win possibility of poverty alleviation with full cost recovery." He recalculated figures from 1985–1994 using Grameen's annual reports, and found that repayment was somewhere between 92 and 95 percent during this period. According to him, "a default rate of 5 percent" led to remarkable "direct losses equal to 21.4 percent in total expenditure costs."

64. A senior economist (name withheld) in Bangladesh provided me with the following figures that Morduch refers to in his article. All the commercial nationalized banks (Janata, Rupali, Pubali, and Sonali) bought a total of 6,500 million taka in bonds from Grameen Bank. The rates for bonds were 4 percent for three-year bonds, 5 percent for five-year bonds, and 10 percent for ten-year bonds. In 1994–1995, the inter-bank lending rate was 5.5 percent. Thus, the rate of return on the GB bonds was lower than the prevailing market rate. During this time, Grameen Bank was keeping FDR (fixed deposits accounts) with Janata Bank that paid 10.5 percent interest on its fixed deposit accounts. The point is important because the Grameen Bank does not believe in government subsidies for poor people; yet, it took government subsidies for itself.

65. Aminur Rahman, "Microcredit and Poverty Reduction: Trade-Off between Building Institutions and Reaching the Poor," in *Livelihood and Microfinance: Anthropological and Sociological Perspectives on Savings and Debt*, eds. Hotze Lontz and Otto Hospes (Delft, Netherlands: Eburon Academic Publishers, 2004), 34.

66. Ibid., 36.

67. Milford Bateman, "De-Industrialization and Social Integration in Bosnia," in *What's Wrong with Microfinance?*, eds. Thomas Dichter and Malcolm Harper (Warwickshire, UK: Practical Action Publishing, 2007), 207–24.

68. Kim Wilson, "The Moneylender's Dilemma," in *What's Wrong with Microfinance?*, eds. Thomas Dichter and Malcolm Harper (Warwickshire, UK: Practical Action Publishing, 2007), 97.

69. Ibid., 107.

70. Muhammad S. Haque and Masahiro Yamao, "Can Microcredit Alleviate Rural Poverty? A Case Study of Bangladesh," *Proceedings of World Academy of Science, Engineering and Technology* 36 (2008): 8.

71. Aasha Khosa, "Grameen Bank Can't Reduce Poverty: Economist," *Business Standard*, April 2, 2007.

72. Linda Mayoux, "Questioning Virtuous Spirals: Micro-Finance and Women's Empowerment in Africa," in *Journal of International Development* 1 (1999): 1.

73. Hashemi, Schuler, and Riley, "Rural Credit Programs and Women's Empowerment in Bangladesh," 650.

74. Mark Pitt and Shahidur Khandker, "The Impact of Group-Based Credit Programs on Poor Households in Bangladesh: Does the Gender of Participants Matter?" in *Journal of Political Economy* 106, no. 5 (1998).

75. Rahman, "Microcredit and Poverty Reduction," 33.

76. John Caldwell, Barkat-e-Khuda, Bruce Caldwell, Indrani Pieries, and Pat Caldwell, "The Bangladeshi Fertility Decline: An Interpretation," in *Population and Development Review* 25 (1999): 80.

77. Anne-Marie Goetz and Rina Sengupta, "Who Takes the Credit? Gender, Power and Control over Loan Use in Rural Credit Programs in Bangladesh," in *World Development* 24, no. 1 (1996): 45–64; Rahman, *Women and Microcredit in Rural Bangladesh;* Qazi Kholiquzzaman Ahmad, *Socio-Economic and Indebtedness-Related Impact of Micro-Credit in Bangladesh* (Dhaka: The University Press Limited, 2007); Karim, "Demystifying Microcredit"; Muhammad, "Monga, Micro Credit and the Nobel Prize."

78. Johanna Brenner, "Transnational Feminism and the Struggle for Global Justice," in *New Politics* 9, no. 2 (2003): 6.

79. Naila Kabeer, "Conflicts over Credit: Re-Evaluating the Empowerment Potential of Loans to Women in Rural Bangladesh," in *World Development* 29, no. 1 (2001).

80. Ibid., 66.

81. Ibid., 67.

82. See the following authors: Jael Silliman, "Expanding Civil Society: Shrinking Political Spaces—The Case of Women's Nongovernmental Organizations," in *Social Politics*, 1999, Vol. 6 (1): 23–53; Rahman, *Women and Microcredit in Rural Bangladesh;* Muhammad, "Monga, Micro Credit and the Nobel Prize"; Fernando, "Microcredit and the Empowerment of Women"; Katherine Rankin, "Social Capital: Microfinance, and the Politics of Development, in *Microfinance: Perils and Prospects*, ed. Jude Fernando (New York: Routledge), 2007, 89–111; Ahmad, *Socio-Economic and Indebtedness-Related Impact of Micro-Credit in Bangladesh;* Haque and Yamao, "Can Microcredit Alleviate Rural Poverty?"; Hotze Lontz and Otto Hospes (eds.), *Livelihood and Microfinance: Anthropological and Sociological Perspectives on Savings and Debt* (Delft, Netherlands: Eburon Academic Publishers, 2004); Thomas Dichter and Malcolm Harper (eds.), *What's Wrong with Microfinance?* (Warwickshire, UK: Practical Action Publishing, 2007); Bateman, *Why Doesn't Microfinance Work? The Destructive Rise of Local Neoliberalism* (London: Zed Books, 2010); Ananya Roy, *Poverty Capital: Microfinance and the Making of Development* (London: Routledge, 2010); Manzurul Mannan, "BRAC: Anatomy of a 'Poverty Enterprise,'" *Nonprofit Management and Leadership* 20 (2009), 219–33.

83. Rahman, *Women and Microcredit in Rural Bangladesh*, 121.

84. Ibid., 148.

85. Jude Fernando, "Microcredit and Empowerment: Visibility without Power," in *Micro-Finance: Perils and Prospects*, ed. Jude Fernando (New York: Routledge, 2007), 223.

86. Ibid., 227.

87. Muhammad, "Monga, Micro Credit and the Nobel Prize," 171. Anu Muhammad teaches economics at Jahangirnagar University. He conducted the research in 1995, 1999, and 2005. He did surveys in fifteen villages with his students.

The villages were selected from different districts of the country: Chittagong, Dhaka, Comilla, Tangail, Mymensingh, Jessore, Manikganj, and Faridpur.

88. Ahmad, *Socio-Economic and Indebtedness-Related Impact of Micro-Credit in Bangladesh*, 45.

89. Ibid., 44.

90. Kabeer, "Conflicts over Credit," 66.

91. Michael Herzfeld, *Anthropology: Theoretical Practice in Culture and Society* (Malden, Mass.: Blackwell Publishers, 2001), 154.

92. Anna Lowenhaupt Tsing, *Friction: An Ethnography of Global Connections* (Princeton, N.J.: Princeton University Press, 2005), 6.

1. The Structural Transformation of the NGO Sphere

1. Jude Fernando and Alan Heston, "NGOs between States, Markets and Civil Society," in *The Role of NGOs, Charity and Empowerment*, eds. Jude Fernando and Alan Heston, The Annals of the American Academy of Political and Social Science (London: Thousand Oaks, 1997), 10.

2. Varun Gauri and Julia Galef, "NGOs in Bangladesh: Activities, Resources and Governance," in *World Development* 33 (2005): 2045.

3. Michael Edwards and David Hulme, *Non-Governmental Organizations—Performance and Accountability* (London: Earthscan Publications, 1995), 5.

4. Gilles Nancy and Boriana Yontcheva, "Does NGO Aid Go to the Poor? Empirical Evidence from Europe," International Monetary Fund Working Paper, February 2006, 5.

5. William Fisher, "Doing Good? The Politics and Anti-Politics of NGO Practices," in *Annual Review of Anthropology* 26 (1997): 443.

6. Jael Silliman, "Expanding Civil Society: Shrinking Political Spaces—The Case of Women's Nongovernmental Organizations," in *Social Politics* 6 (1999): 25.

7. See Lauren Leve and Lamia Karim, "Privatizing the State: Ethnography of Development, Transnational Capital, and NGOs," in *Political and Legal Anthropology* 24, no. 1 (May 2001): 53–58.

8. World Bank, *Pursuing Common Goals* (Dhaka: World Bank Publications, 1996).

9. According to the Ministry of Social Welfare (2000). This number includes civic organizations that do not participate in development programs.

10. S. M. Rahman, "A Practitioner's View of Challenges Facing NGO-Based Microfinance in Bangladesh," in *What's Wrong with Microfinance?*, eds. Thomas Dichter and Malcolm Harper (Warkwickshire, UK: Practical Action Publishing, 2007), 193.

11. Ibid.

12. http://www.ngoab.gov.bd/Staticstics.html (accessed November 5, 2010).

13. Gono Shahajya Sangstha (GSS) is now defunct. Allegations of sexual harassment were brought against its leader, Mahmudul Hasan, who was a leader in the NGO-led civil society initiative in Bangladesh. In a private conversation, a donor

representative told me that the German donors did not like his political work and helped to bring him down.

14. World Bank, *Pursuing Common Goals*, 45.

15. Bangladesh Bank Report (2006). The Bangladesh Bank report did not name the specific MFIs. I would assume them to be Grameen Bank, BRAC, and ASA.

16. Kendall Stiles, *Civil Society by Design: Donors, NGOs and the Intermestic Development Circle in Bangladesh* (Westport, Conn.: Praeger Publishers, 2002), 127.

17. Rehman Sobhan, "The Political Economy of Micro-Credit," in *Who Needs Credit? Poverty and Finance in Bangladesh*, eds. Geoffrey Wood and Iffath Sharif (Dhaka: University Press Limited, 1997), 133.

18. Shahidur Khandker, "Microfinance and Poverty: Evidence Using Panel Data from Bangladesh," *The World Bank Economic Review* 19, no. 2 (2005): 265.

19. Anu Muhammad, "Integration, Polarization and Retreat: Some Observations on SAP, PAP and NGO Exercises in Bangladesh" (paper presented at the Center for Human Resources Development jointly sponsored by Jahangirnagar University and Morgan State University, Dhaka, Bangladesh, August 29, 1996), 4.

20. Ibid.

21. Hasan Zaheer, *The Separation of East Pakistan: The Rise and Realization of Bengali Muslim Nationalism* (Karachi, Pakistan: Oxford University Press, 1994), 21–27.

22. Bangladesh is a market for Indian goods. The Bangladeshi public see their daily lives under the shadow of Indian hegemony.

23. Talukder Maniruzzaman, "Bangladesh in 1975: The Fall of the Mujib Regime and Its Aftermath," *Asian Survey* 16 (1976): 119.

24. One such highly publicized assassination was that of Siraj Sikder, the leader of the East Bengal Communist Party, who was gunned down in January 1975 while in police custody. See Maniruzzaman (1976).

25. Craig Baxter and Syedur Rahman, "Bangladesh Military: Political Institutionalization and Economic Development," in *Journal of Asian and African Studies* 26 (1991): 49.

26. Ibid.

27. Ibid.

28. Ibid., 50.

29. Ibid., 53.

30. Stanley Kochanek, *Patron-Client Politics and Business in Bangladesh* (New Delhi: Thousand Oaks and Sage Publications, 1991), 317.

31. Shelley Feldman, "NGOs and Civil Society (Un)stated Contradictions," in *The Role of NGOs, Charity and Empowerment*, eds. Jude Fernando and Alan Heston (London: Thousand Oaks, 1997), 53.

32. Ibid.

33. Sara White, *Arguing with the Crocodile* (London: Zed Books, 1992), 15.

34. Much has been written about Islamization in Bangladesh. See Naila Kabeer, "The Quest for National Identity," in *Women, Islam and the State*, ed. Deniz Kandyoti

(Philadelphia: Temple University Press, 1991); Feldman, "NGOs and Civil Society (Un)stated Contradictions"; "Gender and Islam in Bangladesh: Metaphor and Myth," "in *Understanding Bengal Muslims*, ed. Rafiuddin Ahmed (New Delhi: Oxford University Press, 2001); and Lamia Karim, "Democratizing Bangladesh: State, NGOs and Militant Islam," in *Cultural Dynamics* 16 (2004), among others.

35. Shelley Feldman, "Gender and Islam in Bangladesh: Metaphor and Myth," 217.

36. Karim, "Democratizing Bangladesh," 296.

37. Kabeer, "The Quest for National Identity," 115–43.

38. Karim, "Democratizing Bangladesh," 295.

39. Kabeer, "The Quest for National Identity."

40. White, *Arguing with the Crocodile*, 14.

41. Kochanek, *Patron-Client Politics and Business in Bangladesh*, 335.

42. See Feldman, "NGOs and Civil Society (Un)stated Contradictions."

43. See Karim, "Democratizing Bangladesh."

44. At the time of my research, all newspapers in Bangladesh were owned either by political parties or by businesses affiliated with a major political party; hence, they were identified as pro-establishment or anti-establishment in public. Prior to the emergence of the Internet and satellite TV, the government controlled the printing presses by controlling their supply of paper, ink, etc. However, the Internet and cable TV have loosened the government's control over the media and has led toward democratization of news and information. In a face-to-face society, news is often exchanged by text messaging that bypasses state control, and it is a new democratic tool in the hands of people.

45. Faruqi Ziaul Hasan, *The Deoband School and the Demand for Pakistan* (London: Asia Publishing House, 1963). The Deoband School (northern India) teaches Muslims to remain vigilant against the corruption of Islam by foreign elements.

46. Bangladesh Bureau of Educational Information and Statistics, Madrassah Education, 2005, http://www.banbeis.gov.bd (accessed July 15, 2008).

47. Mary Tembon and Lucia Fort, *Girls' Education in the 21st Century: Gender Equality, Empowerment and Economic Growth* (Washington, D.C: The World Bank, 2008).

48. www.amwab.org. Many Islamic NGOs are not registered with AMWAB. According to a 2007 Transparency International report, there are 4,000 Islamic NGOs operating inside the country with little or no financial accountability.

49. Jude Fernando, "A Political Economy of Non-Governmental Organizations in Bangladesh and Sri Lanka" (PhD diss., University of Pennsylvania, 1998), 147.

50. Ibid.

51. Richard W. Timm, *Forty Years in Bangladesh: Memoirs of Father Timm* (Dhaka, Bangladesh: CARITAS, 1995), 260.

52. Ibid., 260–61.

53. Ibid.

54. Ibid.

55. ADAB is an umbrella organization of developmental NGOs in Bangladesh. In 1998, its membership stood at 922. Nineteen percent of its 1997–1998 budget went to democracy training and publicity. ADAB Annual Report 1997–1998.

56. Stiles, *Civil Society by Design*, 43.

57. Ibid.

58. Most villagers in Bangladesh now have access to tube-well water, although the latest reports show that 60 percent of the water is arsenic contaminated.

59. Highest-ranking colonial bureaucrat in undivided British India.

60. Timm, *Forty Years in Bangladesh*, 258.

61. Interview with the director of Nijera Kori, Khushi Kabir, February 1, 1999.

62. BRAC research publications reveal a shift from studies that advocated the need to change rural structures toward studies that emphasize neoliberal policies, women's rights, and microenterprises.

63. The issue over education has always been contentious between BRAC and the clerical establishment. During the 1993–1994 crisis, BRAC's textbooks were used as evidence of their so-called teachings against Islam. Those books have all been removed by BRAC. The current pedagogical focus in BRAC textbooks is on the rights of girls and women. At BRAC offices I saw posters that depicted social vices—for example, pictures of men beating their wives and pictures comparing food allocations between daughters and sons, with the sons always getting the best portions of servings. In my conversations with religious men in villages, they said, "BRAC is now teaching that Muslim men beat their wives. They are teaching our children that Muslim fathers are bad people." BRAC's approach is the inculcation of an ethic of social citizenship. Needless to say, this social citizenship comes in conflict with the goals of the clergy. See Stacey Pigg, "Inventing Social Categories through Place: Social Representations and Development in Nepal," in *Comparative Studies in Society and History* 34, no. 93 (1992): 493–513. She offers a nuanced analysis of the pedagogical aspects of development in Nepal.

64. Interview with Tanvir Mokammel, former leftist activist and filmmaker.

65. Interview with Professor Badruddin Umar, leftist political activist, April 19, 1998.

66. Syed Hashemi, "The NGO Non-Alternative in Bangladesh," (paper presented at the Department of Economics, Jahangirnagar University, Dhaka, 1989), 18. However, Hashemi failed to extend his critique to the Western donors, the World Bank, and structural adjustment programs (SAP) that played a vital role in restructuring the economy.

67. Interview with Zakir Hossain, leftist activist and the director of a human rights NGO, Nagorik Uddyog (Citizens' Initiatives).

68. Syed Hashemi, "NGOs and Popular Mobilization in Bangladesh: The Shift in Empowerment Paradigms" (paper presented at the Department of Economics, Jahangirnagar University, Dhaka, 1997a), 11–12.

69. Ibid., 12–13.

70. The companies included South Asia Oil and Gas (Australia), Total Exploration Production (France), Niko Resources Ltd. (Canada), Chevron (USA), Texaco (USA), Maersk Loie (Denmark), Union Texas Murphy (USA), Tullow Oil PLC (UK), Pangaea Energy LLC, Enron Oil and Gas (USA), Mobil Eastern (USA), Petronas Carigali (Malaysia), Cairn Energy (UK), Shell Hydrocarbon, Unocal (USA), PTI Oil Gar, Triton (USA), Hondo Oil and Gas, Asia Energy, Oakland International (USA) and South Asia Oil Co. Ltd.

71. Fida M. Kamal, *Legal Options for the Indigenization of Foreign NGO Projects* (Dhaka: CDL Publications, 1993). Despite the heavy presence of NGOs, Kamal notes that "There is no legal definition of the term NGO in any government statutes in force in Bangladesh. . . . NGOs which work for the welfare and development of the community, or a section in the society, may or may not be a juridical entity."

72. Tanvir Mokammel, *NGO: Samrajyobased Ponchom Bahini* [NGO: The Fifth Pillar of Imperialism] (Dhaka: Jatiya Shahitya Prokashoni, 1987), 38–39.

73. Kochanek, *Patron-Client Politics and Business in Bangladesh*, 294–315.

74. Babar Sobhan, "Partners or Contractors? Relationship between Official Agencies and NGOs: Bangladesh," INTRAC Occasional Paper Series, no. 14 (March 1997), 7.

75. H. A. Quashem, "New Laws for the NGOs," *Holiday*, July 28, 1989. Exchange rate is not given due to the fluctuations of the taka.

76. Sara White, "NGOs, Civil Society, and the State in Bangladesh: The Politics of Representing the Poor," in *Development and Change* 30 (1999): 309.

77. In 1996, I visited Bangladesh immediately following the general elections. Several women in the villages told me that NGO Apas (formal address for older sister) and Sirs had told them to vote for either AL or BNP. More socially aware NGO members contradicted those statements and said, "Why should our Sirs/Apas tell us how to vote?" NGO officers vigorously denied that they told their clients to vote for either/or party. However, they did admit that they discuss with their clients in their voter-training programs the importance of voting for pro-poor (read NGO-friendly) candidates.

78. My interview with Fazle Abed, April 5, 1999. His prediction was borne out. Proshika lost its political power when BNP came to power in 2000. Proshika was investigated and charges were brought against Qazi Faruque for financial irregularities. See Nazmul Ahasan, "What Proshika Is Doing in the Name of Poverty Alleviation," *Daily New Age*, March 27, 2004.

79. Letter written to Father Timm of CARITAS by Dr. Zafarullah on his expulsion from ADAB, dated April 19, 1991.

80. Nazmul Kalimullah and Saleem Samad, "The NGO contest." *Holiday*, December 5, 1997.

81. Staff Reporter, "16 NGOs Put Their Fingers in the Pie of Politics and Gave Statements Demanding That the Verdict of the Gono Adalat Be Implemented," *Dhaka Courier*, December 16, 1992.

82. Hashemi, "NGOs and Popular Mobilization in Bangladesh," 8.

83. Ishtiaq Jamil and Manzurul Mannan, "A Study of Government-NGO Relations in Bangladesh in the Period 1992 and 1993: Collaborations or Confrontations?" (Dhaka: Unpublished document, 1994), 10.

84. Ibid.

85. Ibid., 11.

86. Staff Reporter, "ADAB beyond Government Control?" *Dhaka Courier*, August 28, 1992.

87. Jamil and Mannan, "A Study of Government-NGO Relations in Bangladesh in the Period 1992 and 1993," 13.

88. Interview with NGOAB director, Salehuddin Ahmed.

89. In my conversation with the director of NGOAB, I mentioned that in the villages I never heard of his people coming to monitor projects. In a calm tone he said, "How will you know? When we go, we disguise our identity." His statement is not wholly true in the context of bureaucrats in Bangladesh. In my experience, higher-ranking government officials make ceremonial entrances into villages in their imported SUVs. They usually notify local authorities of their official visits. During my research, I asked local populations about government officials visiting rural areas for NGO appraisals, and I did not hear of any such report. I had the opportunity to make several trips to different parts of Bangladesh that included government, NGO, and Western aid officials. In each of these trips, our hosts had been notified of our visit ahead of time, and appropriate measures were taken to entertain the guests.

90. Proshika, *Towards a Poverty Free World: 1999–2004* (Dhaka: Proshika Human Development Publication, 1999).

91. Ali Riaz, *God Willing: The Politics of Islamism in Bangladesh* (Lanham: Rowman and Littlefield, 2004); Lamia Karim, "Transnational Politics of Reading and the (Un)Making of Taslima Nasrin," in *South Asian Feminisms: Contemporary Interventions*, eds. Ania Loomba and Ritty Lukose (Durham, NC: Duke University Press, forthcoming).

92. See also Taj-ul Hashmi, *Women and Islam in Bangladesh: Beyond Subjection and Tyranny* (New York: St. Martin's Press, 2000), 105–13; Elora Shehabuddin, "Beware the Bed of Fire: Gender, Democracy and the Jama'at-I-Islami in Bangladesh," in *Journal of Women's History* 10 (1999): 148–71.

93. This story has become part of the mythology of BRAC in villages.

94. Interview with Manzurul Mannan, who had researched the militant Islamic backlash against NGOs.

95. These numbers are concocted by the clergy.

96. Interview with a former BRAC manager in my research area.

97. Interview with Mannan.

98. Conversations with former BRAC employees.

99. Interview with Mannan.

100. Farhad Mazhar of UBINIG pointed out the dynamics of rural dispossession through BRAC's work in sericulture. Later I asked a former BRAC manager who also corroborated the story.

101. Professor Anu Muhammad first communicated this point to me. I later confirmed it with a former BRAC employee in my research area.

102. Since interviewee worked for an NGO, he requested anonymity.

103. BRAC Cyclone Sidr Emergency Relief and Rehabilitation One Year Anniversary Report (New York: BRAC USA, 2008).

104. Hasan Mahmud, "Unintended Consequences of Micro-Credit in Bangladesh: An Evaluation from Human Security Perspective," in *Asian Social Science* 4, no. 10 (2008): 1–5.

2. The Research Terrain

1. Michel Foucault, "Governmentality," in *Essential Works of Foucault: 1954–1984*, eds. Paul Rabinow and Nikolas Rose (New York: The New Press, 2003), 236.

2. Ibid., 243.

3. Ibid., 234.

4. George Marcus, "Ethnography in/of the World System: The Emergence of Multi-sited Ethnography," in *Ethnography through Thick and Thin*, ed. George Marcus (Princeton, N.J.: Princeton University Press, 1998), 91.

5. Ibid.

6. Ibid., 92.

7. Nancy Naples, "A Feminist Revisiting of the Insider/Outsider Debate: The Outsider Phenomenon in Rural Iowa," in *Qualitative Sociology* 19, no. 1 (1996): 83–106.

8. Ibid., 84.

9. Marcus, "Ethnography in/of the World System," 90.

10. Katherine Rankin, "Social Capital, Microfinance, and the Politics of Development," in *Micro-finance: Perils and Prospects*, ed. Jude Fernando (London: Routledge, 2007), 91.

11. Staff Reporter,"Proshika Reen Adaye Protarona Mamla O Police Barari Mormantik Poriniti" [Police Brutality in Proshika Loan Default Case Results in Tragedy], *Bhorer Kagoj*, August 2, 1997.

12. The rate of exchange in 1998–1999 fluctuated between 45–47 taka. I use the 46 Taka: 1 USD ratio as the exchange rate to determine dollar equivalents.

13. Staff Reporter, *Bhorer Kagoj*, August 2, 1997.

14. The position of Union Council chairman is a source of political and economic power in rural society. He is traditionally a member of the rural elite.

15. I found that NGOs did not distinguish between the rural poor and the middle class in front of Western observers who may not be aware of the subtle points of local class distinctions.

16. Human rights NGOs have attempted to democratize the concept of the shalish by organizing women and poor farmers into parallel shalishes. However, NGO-led shalishes are not socially binding on the community, and they are often treated as kangaroo courts by the local elites.

17. NGOs make a distinction between the official rate and the effective rate (the actual amount charged to the borrower.) According to NGO officials, a 15 percent simple rate would be a 30 percent effective rate of interest. There are many ways to calculate these interest rates. For an analysis of these interest rates, see Stuart Rutherford, *The Poor and Their Money* (New Delhi: Oxford University Press, 2000).

18. The question of overlapping—that is, how NGOs will maintain their territories and creditworthy clients—continues to be an issue that strains relations among the leading NGOs.

19. Mymensingh is a district next to Tangail.

20. I have a long-term relationship with the Garo community of Modhupur, Mymensingh, that dates back to 1995.

21. In Modhupur, a local teacher had told me that Proshika officials had shown forest wood lots to donors claiming that their NGO had planted these lots as part of their environmental protection program. He and the villagers who were present at the site corrected Proshika officials and told the donors that they had planted these saplings with help from the Forest Department.

22. Transparency International of Bangladesh, "Corruption Database Report: Summary of Findings," July 5, 2006.

23. Information provided by the Thana Office.

24. The names of Tareque, Anowara, and Rina are pseudonyms.

25. Aminur Rahman, *Women and Microfinance in Rural Bangladesh: An Anthropological Study of the Rhetoric and Realities of Grameen Bank Lending* (Boulder, Colo.: Westview Press, 1999), 30.

26. My father spoke in the dialect of Comilla with his relatives, but not with us.

27. Jude Fernando, "Microcredit and Empowerment of Women: Visibility Without Power," in *Micro-finance: Perils and Prospects,* ed. Jude Fernando (London: Routledge, 2007), 226.

28. Dipesh Chakraborty, "Adda, Calcutta: Dwelling in Modernity," in *Public Culture* 11 (1999): 109–45. He has written on Bengalis' penchant for adda.

29. The late professor Abdur Razzak (1914–1999) exemplifies this tradition of intellectual discourse. Although he attended the London School of Economics after World War II, he returned home without obtaining his PhD. During his lifetime, he did not author a single scholarly article. His role as a teacher/thinker was legendary. To this day, he is venerated as a "teacher of teachers."

30. James Scott, *Domination and the Arts of Resistance: Hidden Transcripts* (New Haven, Conn.: Yale University Press, 1990), 188.

31. NGOs' forced loan recovery from bereaved families received ample negative press coverage in the 1990s. After 2000, Grameen Bank instituted a policy that all debts would be forgiven if the member died prior to paying off the debt. To what extent this actually occurs on the ground requires independent research.

32. Rahman, *Women and Microcredit in Rural Bangladesh*, 56–59.

33. Deborah Balk, "Defying Gender Norms in Rural Bangladesh: A Social Demographic Analysis," in *Population Studies* 51, no. 2 (1997): 154.

34. Ibid.

35. See Jitka Kotalova, *Belonging to Others: Cultural Construction of Womanhood in a Village in Bangladesh* (Dhaka, Bangladesh: University Press Limited, 1996); Santi Rozario, *Purity and Community Boundaries* (London: Zed Books, 1992).

36. Balk, "Defying Gender Norms in Rural Bangladesh," 157.

37. Ibid.

38. I heard of this concept from the late poet Ahmed Sofa.

39. Manzurul Mannan, "Culture, Cash and Credit: The Morality of Money Circulation," paper presented at the European Network of Bangladesh Studies Workshop (University of Bath, UK, 1998), 3–4.

40. The five pillars of Islam for Sunni Muslims are: (a) shahada or monotheism and the acceptance of Muhammad as god's messenger; (b) salat or daily prayers; (c) zaqat or alms to the needy; (d) ritual fasting during the month of Ramadan; and (e) hajj or pilgrimage to Mecca for those who are able.

41. Mannan, Ibid.

42. The Quran commands the faithful to repay all debts prior to death.

3. The Everyday Mediations of Microfinance

1. These figures are from my follow-up research in 2007. They have been calculated at the exchange rate of 67 taka = 1 USD.

2. In 2007, BRAC offered loans in categories called Dabi, Unnoti, Progoti, Agriculture/Livestock, and Targeted Ultra Poor Programme. Grameen Bank loans consisted of Basic, Micro Enterprise, Housing, Education, and Beggar loans. ASA had loans in diverse categories such as Small, Small Business, Small Investor, Seasonal, Education, IT, Agriculture, Sanitation, and School Computer. Only Proshika had loans in two categories, Small and Agricultural/Livestock.

3. The following rates were in effect in 2007: 10 percent (GB), 10.5 percent (ASA), 12.5 percent BRAC, and 14 percent (Proshika). In all four organizations, a borrower had to pay 25 taka (10 cents) per every 1,000 taka ($14) borrowed every week. So, per week, a borrower paid 250 taka ($3.73) on a 10,000 taka ($149) loan. In addition, the borrower paid 20 taka (30 cents) per week into a savings account. Only ASA had a lower amount of savings, between 10 and 20 taka (15 to 30 cents). All of them charged members a one-time fee as a new member's fee and for a savings

book. In addition to these fees, there are hidden costs attached to these loans that vary according to the type of loan and organization.

4. See Qazi Kholiquzzaman Ahmad, *Socio-Economic and Indebtedness Related Impact of Micro-Credit in Bangladesh* (Dhaka: The University Press Limited, 2007). His study is of rural indebtedness among microfinance borrowers.

5. Muhammad Yunus, *Creating a World without Poverty: Social Business and the Future of Capitalism* (Philadelphia: Public Affairs Book, 2007), 223.

6. Ibid., 244.

7. "Grameen, Danone to Start Social Business Enterprise," November 15, 2006. http://www.domain-b.com/finance/banks/2006/20061115_start.html (accessed March 1, 2009).

8. Yunus, *Creating a World without Poverty*, 149–52.

9. Ibid., 152.

10. Jonathan Sterne and Carol Stabile, "Using Women as Middle Men: The Real Promise of ICTs," in *Feminist Media Studies* 3, no. 3 (2004): 364.

11. Arvind Singhal, Peter Svenkerud, Prashant Malavia, Everett Rogers, and Vijay Krishna, "Bridging Digital Divides: Lessons Learned from IT Initiatives of the Grameen Bank of Bangladesh," in *Media and Glocal Change: Rethinking Communication for Development*, eds. Oscar Hemer and Thomas Tufte (Goteberg, Sweden: Nordicom, 2005), 427.

12. Jean Camp and Brian Anderson, "Grameen Phone: Empowering the Poor through Connectivity," 1999. http://www.telecommons.com/villagephone/Camp_article12_99.htm, 7.

13. Sterne and Stabile, "Using Women as Middle Men," 365.

14. See Singhal et al., "Bridging Digital Divides," and Camp and Brian, "Grameen Phone."

15. Grameen Phone Annual Report 2007.

16. Yunus, *Creating a World without Poverty*, 242.

17. Singhal et al., "Bridging Digital Divides," 429.

18. Ibid.

19. Yunus, *Creating a World without Poverty*, 80.

20. British Broadcasting Service, "Jitters over Bangladesh IPO Delay," March 4, 2009. http://www.bbcnews.com (accessed March 10, 2009)

21. At the time of my research, the term microcredit was in use; hence, I use it in the ethnographic chapters 2, 3, 4, 5, and 6. In recent years, microcredit has been replaced by the new term microfinance, although these two terms refer to the same loan programs.

22. Muhammad Yunus with Alan Jolis, *Banker to the Poor* (Dhaka: University Press Limited, 1998).

23. Ibid., 147.

24. Ibid., 142.

25. All the NGOs I studied emulated this basic structure: group responsibility of individual loans; strict recovery through weekly (ASA and Grameen), biweekly meetings (BRAC), or monthly meetings (Proshika); and in some instances, product tie-ins with loans (e.g., hybrid seeds with agricultural loans or breeder chickens for BRAC loans).

26. The member rolls and groups have increased since 1999, but the basic structure of group accountability remained the same.

27. Aminur Rahman, *Women and Microcredit in Rural Bangladesh: An Anthropological Study of the Rhetoric and Realities of Grameen Bank Lending* (Boulder, Colo.: Westview Press, 1999), 149.

28. The Web site "Grameen Bank at a Glance" offers the bank's operating information. http://www.grameen-info.org.

29. Syed Hashemi and Lamiya Morshed, "Grameen Bank: A Case Study," in *Who Needs Credit? Poverty and Finance in Bangladesh,* eds. Iffath Sharif and Geoffrey Wood (Dhaka: University Press Limited, 1997), 218.

30. At the time of my research in 1998–1999, the Grameen Bank had decided to lower the payment schedule from fifty-two weeks to fifty weeks, which would mean a rise in the weekly installment (kisti) paid by the borrowers. For poor people, a weekly rise of a few takas posed a tremendous hardship.

31. He gave the aggregate breakdown of the Revolving Loan Fund, the recycling of revenues back into the NGO loan pool, as follows: 20 percent from member savings and 15 percent from service (interest) charges. Interview with author.

32. Jonathan Morduch, "The Microfinance Promise," in *Journal of Economic Literature* 37 (1999): 1585.

33. Ibid.

34. Morgen Brigg, "Disciplining the Developmental Subject: Neoliberal Power and the Governance through Micro-Credit," in *Micro-Finance: Perils and Prospects,* ed. Jude Fernando (New York: Routledge, 2007), 79.

35. Marilyn Carr, Martha Chen, and Renana Jhabvala, *Speaking Out: Women's Economic Empowerment in South Asia* (London: International Technology Publications, 1996), 5.

36. See also Rahman, *Women and Microcredit in Rural Bangladesh,* 136–37. He notes that two bank managers in his area defied upper-management instructions to increase loan disbursements, knowing that it would increase loan defaults later. They both had to pay a price: the Bank withheld their promotion for six months.

37. See Stephanie Charironenko and S. M. Rahman, *Commercialization of Microfinance: Bangladesh* (Manila: Asian Development Bank, 2002); Ahmad, *Socio-Economic and Indebtedness Related Impact of Micro-Credit in Bangladesh.*

38. Jude Fernando, "Microcredit and Empowerment: Visibility Without Power," in *Micro-Finance: Perils and Prospects,* ed. Jude Fernando (New York: Routledge, 2007), 223.

39. In my visit to Grameen Bank in Tangail, I watched this spectacle unfold. The women borrowers would often say, "My husband does X with the money." The assistant manager who processed the loans would change the loan type from an agricultural loan to a cow loan, for example, in order for them to access the amount of money that they wanted.

40. Jeffrey Pereira, "Those Who Think Microcredit Is the Only Key to Development Are Making a Huge Mistake" [Bengali], *Adhuna* (Jan–Mar 1998): 29–30.

41. Kim Wilson, "The Moneylender's Dilemma," in *What's Wrong with Microfinance?*, eds. Thomas Dichter and Malcolm Harper (Warwickshire, UK: Practical Action Publishing, 2007), 97–108.

42. Kendall Stiles, *Civil Society by Design: Donors, NGOs and the Intermestic Development Circle in Bangladesh* (Westport, Conn.: Praeger Publishers, 2002), 127.

43. Syed Hashemi, "NGO-State Relations in Bangladesh" (paper presented at the Conference on NGOs in Aid: A Reappraisal of 20 Years of NGO Assistance, Center for Development Studies, Bergen, Norway, 1997), 4.

44. In an interview, Fazle Abed of BRAC made the argument that it was necessary for women to drive a motorcycle or ride a bicycle at work. Otherwise, women employees cannot be as competitive as male employees since NGO workers have to travel long distances. This decision had positive and negative consequences for women. Rural men have grudgingly accepted this new image of women because they also receive benefits from NGOs. However, women who ride motorbikes and bicycles continue to face harassment and find it difficult to get married.

45. See Deborah Balk, "Defying Gender Norms in Bangladesh: A Social Demographic Analysis," in *Population Studies* 51 (1997): 156.

46. My study did not include the measurement of rural caloric intake. These comments are based on my observations of rural life.

47. In the 1995 BRAC Rural Development Report, it was noted that after joining BRAC, "women usually pay weekly savings from the sale of eggs, vegetables, or accumulated *mushti* rice. [It is common practice to save a handful of rice when cooking a meal, as a type of saving for unforeseen circumstances.] In these instances, the women were making savings decisions which could have important decisions for the subsistence for the family." Based on how one interprets the data, these strategies could mean different things: (1) women were increasing family wealth by selling chicken and eggs or (2) the daily caloric intake of the family was declining because resources were being redirected toward paying off the loans.

48. Fernando, "Microcredit and Empowerment: Visibility Without Power," 227.

49. Ibid., 223.

50. For a discussion of this point, see *Beacon of Hope: Main Findings of the RDP Impact Assessment Study* (Dhaka: BRAC Publication, 1995), 69.

51. See S. M. Haque and Masahiro Yamao, "Can Microcredit Alleviate Rural Poverty? A Case Study of Bangladesh," in *Proceedings of World Academy of Science, Engineering and Technology* 36 (2008).

52. Ahmad, *Socio-Economic and Indebtedness Related Impact of Micro-Credit in Bangladesh*, 44.

53. While some form of dowry was always practiced in rural Bangladesh, in pre-1971 days, dowry was usually a small sum of money or a gold ring for the groom. In the post-1971 environment, dowry demands run into thousands of takas, and they often include other consumer commodities, based on the groom's income potential.

54. Rahman, *Women and Microcredit in Rural Bangladesh*, 93.

55. Notions of honor and shame are not as strictly regulated in rural Bangladesh as in Arab countries. See the following for a discussion of the topic: Sarah White, *Arguing with the Crocodile* (Dhaka: University Press Limited, 1992); Jitka Kotalova, *Belonging to Others: Cultural Construction of Womenhood in a Village in Bangladesh* (Dhaka: University Press Limited, 1998); Santi Rozario, *Purity and Communal Boundaries: Women and Social Change in a Bangladeshi Village* (London: Zed, 1992).

56. See Anu Muhammad, "Monga, Micro Credit and the Nobel Prize," in *Micro Credit: Myth Manufactured*, ed. Farooque Chowdhury (Dhaka: Shrabon Prokashoni, 2007), 165–74. See also Rahman, *Women and Microcredit in Rural Bangladesh* (1999), and Fernando, *Microfinance: Perils and Prospects* (2007).

57. Researchers have found varying levels of loan control among women.

58. Syed Hashemi, Sidney Schuler, and Ruth Riley, "Rural Credit Programs and Women's Empowerment in Bangladesh," in *World Development* 24, no. 4 (1996): 635–53.

59. Gregory Massell, *The Surrogate Proletariat: Moslem Women and Revolutionary Strategies in Soviet Central Asia, 1919–1929* (Princeton, NJ: Princeton University Press, 1974).

60. Rahman, *Women and Microcredit in Rural Bangladesh*.

61. James Scott, *Weapons of the Weak: Everyday Forms of Peasant Resistance* (New Haven: Yale University Press, 1985).

62. Ibid., 184.

63. Hashemi and Morshed, "Grameen Bank: A Case Study," 218.

64. Hashemi et al., "Rural Credit Programs and Women's Empowerment in Bangladesh," 649.

65. Muhammad Mustafa Kamal, *Managing Microfinance in an Innovative Way* (Dhaka: ASA Publications, 2002), 94.

66. This was especially true for Grameen Bank employees.

67. Michel Foucault, "Governmentality," in *The Essential Foucault*, eds. Paul Rabinow and Nikolas Rose (New York: The New Press, 2003), 234.

68. Aiwah Ong, *Neoliberalism as Exception: Mutations in Citizenship and Sovereignty* (Durham, N.C.: Duke University Press, 2006).

4. The Social Life of Debt

1. The research was conducted in Tangail, a thriving commercial hub that is located sixty kilometers from Dhaka. Two assistants, one female and one male,

helped me with the research. This research was based on in-depth interviews with the women, and not on ethnography, which would have required long-term fieldwork with the community. Interviews were conducted with seven women, three from urban areas and four from peri-urban areas. All these women lived close to markets, and they had purchased their phones between 2001 and 2005. My research assistants had met with local Grameen Bank officials and were provided the names of these borrowers. Hence, there was a built-in bias in this study group. Grameen officials probably gave the contact information of their successful borrowers to my assistants.

2. *Microcredit Summit News* 2, no. 1 (June 2004).

3. Jean Camp and Brian Anderson, "Grameen Phone: Empowering the Poor through Connectivity," 1999, 3. http://www.telecommons.com/village-phone/Camp_article12_99.htm (accessed September 10, 2008).

4. The GPS purchase amounts varied between 5,000 to 10,000 taka for these women. These were long-term pension plans. They were told that their initial investment would double within ten years.

5. I could not verify the prices quoted because the figures spanned dates from 2001 to 2007. However, my research assistants who were cell phone users told me that these prices were much higher than the commercial rates available.

6. See Richard Shaffer, "Unplanned Obsolescence," December 19, 2007, 3. Shaffer writes about Taiyeb Ali, a cattle trader he met in Bangladesh. In the past, Ali spent a month near the border with India selecting cattle for purchase during the Muslim festival of Eid-ul-Adha (Festival of the Sacrifice). With the advent of the cell phone, he could monitor his cattle purchases from Dhaka. When demand rose, Ali purchased more expensive animals, and when it fell, he bought cheaper animals. The cell phone allowed him to manage his inventory and time more efficiently. However, as Shaffer points out, the real beneficiaries of cell phones have been male business people. http://www. fastcompany.com/magazine/118/unplanned-obsolescence. html (accessed August 20, 2008).

7. Jonathan Sterne and Carol Stabile, "Using Women as Middle Men: The Real Promise of ICTs," *Feminist Media Studies* 3, no. 3 (2004): 364.

8. Shaffer, "Unplanned Obsolescence."

9. The exchange rate is calculated at 46 taka for 1998–1999.

10. A boxlike musical instrument used in South Asia as an accompaniment to music.

11. Aminur Rahman, *Women and Microcredit in Bangladesh: An Anthropological Study of the Rhetoric and Realities of Grameen Bank Lending* (Boulder, Colo.: Westview Press, 1999). He noted that women from powerful lineage groups in the village became dominant within Grameen group meetings. NGO managers told me that groups of women often form networks and threaten to withhold payments unless their chosen clients were given loans.

12. I tried to meet with Qazi Faruque, the director of Proshika, but I could not get an interview with him. In 1998–1999, Faruque was the most important NGO leader, given his political links to Awami League (the party in power at that time) and the financial support from Canadian aid organization CIDA to Proshika.

13. My conversations with NGO researchers and managers.

14. Name changed to protect privacy.

15. The work of feminist organizations in Bangladesh has made it possible for rural women to report rapes and other gender crimes to the police, although the police are lax to take action against elites.

16. The BRAC chicken program expanded under the Income Generation for Vulnerable Group Development Program (IGVGDP), run by the World Food Program and the Bangladesh government with BRAC as the local distributor. VGD members were identified by BRAC and by the local Union Council chairman from each village, and they were given a government VGD card. Every month each cardholder would get 31.5 kilograms of wheat.

17. Women chick rearers, former BRAC managers, and several local researchers supplied this information.

18. Tareque, a former BRAC manager, shared this point with me. He said, "We would go to VGD members' homes and tell them that they had to raise the chickens. We would then select a place in the house for that purpose and help set it up accordingly."

19. There were many allegations of BRAC wheat theft. A former BRAC manager told me that BRAC managers would steal wheat from the VGD members. Instead of giving each member 31.5 kilograms of wheat as required by law, they gave only 27.5 kilograms. According to him, this happened in all BRAC offices, although the quantity siphoned off might vary. They sold the siphoned wheat on the open market, and the profits were shared among the members of the management team. In 1998, the price of 1 kilogram of wheat was 8 taka on the open market. So, in Pirpur Thana the BRAC office was unofficially getting 4 × 8 × 2040 (the number of VGD members) = 65,280 taka ($1,484) per month. If the office had a high rate of defaults that it could not effectively recover, management would replace that money with the sale of VGD wheat money. I verified this information of wheat theft from other sources—researchers, NGO borrowers, and local people.

20. Author's interview with Fazle Abed of BRAC, April 5, 1999.

21. Joseph Stiglizt, *Making Globalization Work* (New York: W.W. Norton, 2003), 51–53. Stiglitz writes that he visited a chicken-feed factory run by BRAC in 2003. He notes that facing high chicken mortality, BRAC workers set up "a program to take care of the baby chickens and pass them on to women when the chicks were old enough to survive. They found that high-quality chicken feed was necessary, so they opened an animal feed company and sold the feed to the women raising the chicks. Thus BRAC created wealth and jobs throughout the supply chain: from eggs to baby chicks, to processing nutritious feed for those chicks" (53). It appears from

Stiglitz's comments that he was provided with this information by BRAC officials. It is a retelling of the story from the official BRAC angle, and not from the women's perspective.

22. See Jahangir Alam, "Mora Murgi O Hashero Kisti Ditye Hoi [Dead Chickens and Ducks Have to Repay BRAC Loans]," in *Chinta* 7, no. 6: 39–40.

23. Farida Akhter of UBINIG shared her experiences with me regarding Dutch donor interest in introducing breeder chickens in Bangladesh. According to Akhter, several years ago she was asked by the Dutch Embassy to conduct research on chicken-rearing practices among rural women in Bangladesh. They supplied her with a questionnaire for the survey. The last question on the survey was the following: Would the women accept breeder (imported) chickens? Akhter found that the rural women surveyed said no because these chickens did not live in the humid conditions of rural Bangladesh without proper facilities that they could not provide. When Akhter discussed her findings with the Dutch Embassy, it became clear to her that their only interest in the research was in finding ways to sell breeder chickens to rural women. When she asked them if that was their intention, she was told that they wanted to investigate the introduction of roosters that would be crossbred with the local hen population to get high-yield varieties of breeder chickens. Upon hearing this, Akhter said she returned the research money to the Dutch Embassy.

24. Amartya Sen, *Development as Freedom* (New York: Anchor Press, 2000), 202.

5. NGOs, Clergy, and Contested "Democracy"

1. One of the largest human rights organizations in Bangladesh is the Manusher Jonno Foundation (MJF). http://www.manusher.org.

2. Anwar Ali, "Jama'atul Tentacles Spread in Five Years. Law Enforcers' Laid-Back Approach Made It Possible," *Daily Star,* August 19, 2005. The Ja'maat-e-Islami is the oldest Islamic party in the country. It seeks to establish Islamic rule through democratic means. Islamic Oikye Jote (IOJ) consists of seven smaller Islamic political parties, some of them with radical links. In 2001, the BNP government asked IOJ to enter into a coalition with them to win the parliamentary elections. Other smaller Islamic radical groups include Al Mujahideen, Jama'atul Jihad, Jama'atul Muhajideen Bangladesh (JMB [banned]), Ahle Hadith Andolan Bangladesh (AHAB), Jagroto Muslim Janata Bangladesh (JMJB [banned]), Har-ka-tul Jihad Islami (HUJI [banned]), Hizbut Tawhid, Tawhidi Janata, Islami Jubo Sangha, Islami Sangha, Al Falah A'am Unnayan Shanstha, and Shahadat-e al Hiqma.

3. Supriya Singh, *Jama'atul Mujahideen Bangladesh (JMB) A Profile,* IPCS Special Report 11 (New Delhi, India: Institute of Peace and Conflict Studies, 2006).

4. Fatwa is an edict offered by a mufti in Islamic jurisprudence. Fatwa rulings can range from the sighting of the moon for the celebration of the Muslim holiday Eid, to decisions regarding birth, death, marriage, adultery, and divorce, for example. Thus, by making all fatwas illegal and extrajudicial, the ruling effectively rendered the clergy's primary role as the custodians of morality irrelevant.

5. Ahmadiyya Muslim Jamaat follows the nineteenth-century leader Ghulam Mirza Ahmad of Punjab (India) as a prophet of Islam. According to Sunnis, Muhammad was the final prophet, and to accept a prophet after him is akin to heresy. Ahmadiyyas have been declared non-Muslims by the Pakistani government. The Ahmadiyya community in Bangladesh has around 100,000 people, and they have lived in relative anonymity. The attacks against them began in the late 1990s, but resurfaced with more organizational vigor in 2003.

6. Police investigation revealed that the Islamic parties behind these bombings were the banned Jama'atul Muhajideen Bangladesh (JMB) and Jagroto Muslim Janata Bangladesh (JMJB). Western donors had forced the BNP government to ban these two groups in early 2005 because of their suspected ties to Al Qaeda, and because of their alleged bombings of BRAC and Grameen offices. While these groups have been prohibited and some of their leaders executed for the bombings, multiple Islamic fringe groups with links to Middle Eastern radicals remain active underground.

7. Awami League candidate A. K. Khondokar won the elections.

8. These types of accusations are commonplace between the two national parties.

9. *Proshika Activity Report 1997–98* (Dhaka: Proshika Publications, 1998), 61–62.

10. Staff. "Grass-Roots Democracy" [Bengali], *Adhuna* (Dhaka: ADAB Publications, 1998).

11. "Considerations of Reports Submitted by States Parties under Article 18 of the Convention of the Elimination of All Forms of Discrimination against Women." Third and fourth periodic reports of States parties: Bangladesh, p. 26. http://www.un.org/esa/gopher-data/ga/cedaw/17/country/Bangladesh/C-BGD3-4-EN.

12. Lamia Karim, "Democratizing Bangladesh: State, NGOs and Militant Islam," in *Cultural Dynamics* 16, nos. 2 and 3 (2004): 291–318.

13. Bangladesh signed CEDAW on November 6, 1984, with two reservations: Article 2 and Article 16c. For details, see Sarah Altschuller, "Rights and Challenges for Women," in *Human Rights in Bangladesh*, ed. Hameeda Hossain (Ain o Salish Kendra: Dhaka, 2003), 196–97. For signatory information, see http://www.un.org/womenwatch/daw/cedaw/cedaw.htm.

14. Bangladeshi Sunni Muslims follow the Hanafi School of Islamic law. For Muslims, UCC would mean the following: daughters would receive equal share of parental property (under Muslim personal law daughters receive half of what sons receive); verbal divorce would be made illegal; marriages would have to be registered in local courts; gender discrimination would not be allowed in legal testimony (under sharia laws, testimonies from two women are equal to the testimony of one man); women would not be required to provide four adult witnesses to a rape; and child support and alimony would be decided by courts, and not the clergy.

15. Altschuller, "Rights and Challenges for Women," 197.

16. Ibid., 203.

17. Ibid., 204.

18. Newspapers reported the following figures for fatwas between the years 1997 and 2001: thirty-four in 2001; thirty-one in 2000; twenty-six in 1999; twenty-eight in 1998; and twenty-eight in 1997. From Altschuller, "Rights and Challenges for Women."

19. Middle-class families will employ a graduate of the madrassah to teach their children in Islamic religious instruction.

20. Delwar Hossain Saidi, "Islam o Narir Odhikar [Islam and Women's Rights]." My translation of the audiotape (Dhaka: Spondon Audio Visual Center).

21. Staff Reporter, "NGO Kormira Polatok [NGO Workers in Hiding]," *Prothom Alo,* December 11, 1998.

22. Staff Reporter, "Brahmanbariay Teen Deener Nepothey [Behind Three Days in Brahmanbaria]," *Bhorer Kajog,* December 16, 1998.

23. *Samaj Chetona* (a socialist monthly) gives the figure between 4,000 and 5,000. Aksir Chowdhury's Human Rights Report listed the figure between 8,000 and 10,000. I would go with the lower figure.

24. Other members included Aroma Goon, deputy chair of ADAB; Ayesha Khanom of Mahila Parishad (Women's Group); Maleka Begum (GSS); barrister Tanya Amir Doha; Laila Arjumand Banu (ADAB); Shireen Banu Mitil; Rokeya Kabir; Shahana Farook; and Fawzia Khondokar. All of these women are active in the NGO community and women's issues. Maleka Begum, "Brahmanbaria Muktijuddher Utshabe Shantrashi Hamla: Protokhodorshir Diary [Attack on Brahmanbaria Freedom Celebration: An Eyewitness Account]," *Prothom Alo,* December 11, 1998.

25. The symbolism of throwing stones at "trespassing" women was not lost on anyone.

26. Staff Reporter, "Brahmanbariar NGO Shanggotito Ghar-Bari Loot Hoyeche [Houses of NGO Members Looted in Brahmanbaria]," *Prothom Alo,* December 12, 1998.

27. Islamic State of Brahmanbaria is an ironic name. Brahmanbaria literally translates as "the home of Brahmins." In undivided Bengal, a high number of Brahmins lived in this town, hence its name. In recent years, the Yunusia Madrassah tried to change the name of the town to Islambari, but the change was strongly opposed by the local people.

28. Brahmanbaria is on the smuggling route between India and Bangladesh. Drugs, gold, alcohol, and women, among other things, are transported through this area. It has also developed a notorious reputation as a crime syndicate. A few powerful local crime families control local moneylending. The scale of this commercial moneylending in this town is enormous, and it cannot be compared to the scale of moneylending practiced in the villages. The claims of some people and NGOs that this incident was instigated by local moneylenders angry with NGOs for taking away their clients is not credible.

29. The day commemorates the work and life of Bengali Muslim feminist writer and activist Begum Rokeya Sakhwat Hossain, who pioneered the education of Muslim girls in undivided Bengal. She died in 1930. Her most famous article written in English is "Sultana's Dream."

30. Name changed to protect privacy.

31. Liquor consumption is banned for Bangladeshi citizens. Observant Muslims do not consume liquor.

32. Staff Reporter, "Brahmanbariay Shohingshutar Pechone Sharther Khela [The Play of Personal Politics behind the Brahmanbaria Melee]," *Prothom Alo*, December 13, 1998. Also based on my interviews with local people.

33. He wanted to remain anonymous.

34. When I interviewed the clergy, they could not produce these texts, nor did they think it necessary to have these texts. Their word was sacrosanct. Journalists and political leaders who were present at the briefing told me that the clergy had some old and torn books that they held up as examples.

35. For the tradition of Satya Pir in Bengali, see Richard Eaton, *The Rise of Islam and the Bengal Frontier: 1204–1760* (Berkeley: University of California Press, 1993), 279–81. Eaton writes, "The idea of Islam as a closed system with definite and rigid boundaries is a product of nineteenth and twentieth century reform movements, whereas for rural Bengalis of the premodern period, the lines separating the 'non-Islam' from 'Islam' appear to have been porous, tenuous and shifting" (273). While his comments refer to medieval Islam in Bengal, they hold true for the religious practices among contemporary rural Bangladeshis, despite their increased exposure to Islam from the Middle East.

36. The actual slogans are (1) "I will not live in a broken house, I will not leave Grameen Bank;" and (2) "I will cast my vote for whomever I choose." The clergy routinely distort these slogans to suit their agendas.

37. His comment is in reference to the Muslim Family Laws Ordinance of 1961, which made verbal divorce (talaq) illegal in Pakistan. This law remains in effect in Bangladesh. Prior to the conflicts with the clergy in 1993, BRAC books contained this information to educate rural people about their legal marital rights. Following the events of 1994, BRAC has removed these old textbooks from circulation.

38. The Muslim clergy bring up this allegation all the time. This point has been discussed in chapter 1.

39. In 1998 and 1999 two such incidents occurred that received wide news coverage. There was a bomb attack on a cultural troupe in northern Bangladesh that killed several people. Another attack that created wide controversy was on national poet Shamsur Rahman by a radical Islamic group called Hirkatul Jihad. Public opinion on this attack was divided; some believed in the genuineness of the attack, while others claimed that it was staged for political purposes.

40. This refers to the time of the Four Caliphs of Islam following the death of Prophet Muhammad.

41. Kendall Stiles, *Civil Society by Design: Donors, NGOs and the Intermestic Development Circle in Bangladesh* (Westport, Conn.: Praeger Publishers, 2002).

42. Granting agencies often have training sessions with "violentologists" on how to forecast and manage violence.

43. Gregory Massell, *The Surrogate Proletariat: Moslem Women and Revolutionary Strategies in Soviet Central Asia, 1919–1929* (Princeton, N.J.: Princeton University Press, 1974). Proshika's instrumentalization of rural women as democratic agents is analogous to Massell's notion of the invention of Muslim women in Soviet Central Asia as the proletariat by the Communist Party.

44. Anu Muhammad, "NGO Kormi and Project Sangskriti [NGO Worker and Project Culture]," in *Rashtra and Rajniti: Bangladesher Dui Doshok* (Dhaka: Sandesh Publishers, 2000), 318–23.

45. See "Brahmanbariay Moulobadi Hamlar Protibade Koroniyo Nirdhrarone Mothbinimoi Shabha Agamikaal [Open Discussion on the Fundamentalist Attacks in Brahmambaria and an Action Plan]," *Prothom Alo,* December 11, 1998, "Brahmanbariar Moulobadi Goshtir Birudhe Grina Janate Shara Deshe Nagorik Samabesher Siddhanto [Citizens' Protest Meetings against Fundamentalism Planned All Over Bangladesh]," *Prothom Alo,* December 13, 1998, and "Brahmanbariar Ghotona Todonte Committee Gothon Kora Hobe [Committee to Be Formed to Investigate the Brahmanbaria Incident]," *Prothom Alo,* December 14, 1998.

6. Power/Knowledge in Microfinance

1. Arturo Escobar, *Encountering Development: The Making and Unmaking of the Third World* (Princeton, N.J.: Princeton University Press, 1995), 23.

2. Barbara Cruikshank, *The Will to Empower: Democratic Citizens and Other Subjects* (Ithaca: Cornell University Press, 1999), 76.

3. Sarah White, "NGOs, Civil Society, and the State in Bangladesh: The Politics of Representing the Poor," in *Development and Change* 30 (1999): 307–26.

4. Escobar, *Encountering Development,* 5.

5. Cruikshank, *The Will to Empower,* 4.

6. Vijay Prashad, "NGO Anthropology," *Left Curve* 23 (1999): 72–81.

7. Jude Fernando, "Microcredit and the Empowerment of Women: Blurring the Boundaries between Development and Capitalism," in *Micro-Finance: Perils and Prospects,* ed. Jude Fernando (London: Routledge, 2007), 4.

8. I have selected BRAC and Grameen Bank over Proshika and ASA because they have more established research organizations.

9. Aminur Rahman, *Women and Microcredit in Rural Bangladesh: An Anthropological Study of the Rhetoric and Realities of Grameen Bank Lending* (Boulder, Colo.: Westview Press, 1999), 11.

10. See Syed Hashemi, Sidney Schuler, and Anne Riley, "Rural Credit Programs and Women's Empowerment in Bangladesh," *World Development* 24, no. 4 (1996): 635–53.

11. Marilyn Carr, Martha Chen, and Renana Jhabvala, *Speaking Out: Women's Economic Empowerment in South Asia* (London: International Technology Publications, 1996), 8.

12. Both BRAC and Proshika had their own printing presses. Proshika also owned a state-of-the-art audiovisual unit.

13. H. I. Latifee, *Introduction to Grameen Trust* (Dhaka: Grameen Trust Publications, 1997). I could not access the budget for Grameen Poverty Research, but by Bangladeshi standards it is very substantial.

14. *Doriddo Gobeshona Sharangsho* [Poverty Research Summary] (Dhaka: Grameen Trust, Vol. 4, December, 1998), 91–98.

15. *BRAC Research 1998* (Dhaka: BRAC Publications), 7. The annual reports of BRAC, Grameen Bank, and Proshika did not provide budget allocations for their research programs.

16. Margaret Keck and Kathryn Sikkink, *Activists beyond Borders: Advocacy Networks in International Politics* (Ithaca: Cornell University Press, 1998).

17. Cruikshank, *The Will to Empower*, 68–69.

18. Arjun Appadurai, *Modernity At Large: Cultural Dimensions of Globalization* (Minneapolis: University of Minnesota Press, 1996), 34–35.

19. I contacted Mr. X and interviewed him extensively on the 1993–1994 attacks on BRAC. I did show him the document provided by BRAC, but he said that it was an edited version of the original report. Given his contractual obligations to BRAC, he was unable to provide me with those details that were critical of BRAC's operations.

20. Mokbul Ahmad, *NGO Fieldworkers in Bangladesh* (Burlington, Vt.: Ashgate Publishing Company, 2002), 11.

21. *The Net: Power Structure in Ten Villages* (93 pages); *Who Gets What and Why: Resource Allocation in a Bangladeshi Village* (197 pages); *Ashram Village: An Analysis of Resource Flows* (125 pages); *Peasant Perceptions: Credit Needs, Famine, Sanitation* (91 pages). These are all research publications in the early 1980s by BRAC (Dhaka: BRAC Publications).

22. Muhammad Yunus, "Microcredit: Most Powerful Weapon to Fight Poverty," Grameen Dialogue, no. 36, October, 1998.

23. Muhammad Yunus, *Creating a World without Poverty: Social Business and the Future of Capitalism* (Philadelphia: Public Affairs Book, 2007), 240.

24. I was provided the poverty index questionnaire.
(Questions 1–5 refer to personal information of borrower (name, group affiliation, etc.)
Question 6. Do you possess the ability to eat three meals a day?
Question 7. Do all members of the family have winter clothes?
Question 8. Do you possess a tin-roofed house valued at 25,000 taka?
Question 9. Do all family members sleep on a cot or bed?
Question 10. Do all members use a mosquito net?
Question 11. Do all children above age six attend school?

Question 12. Do you pay your installment from income?

Question 13. Do you have additional sources of income?

Question 14. Is your lowest monthly installment 300 taka?

Question 15. Do you use a pit or sanitary latrine?

25. See BRAC Research, 1998; Grameen Poverty Research Newsletters, and Grameen Poverty Research, 1998.

26. Staff Reporter, "Dhaka University Takes Initiative to Halt Consultancy Business and Part-Time Job of Teachers," *Bhorer Kajog*, April 12, 1999.

27. While I was conducting my fieldwork, I had occasion to witness how such grants were given, and I heard of many such perks being distributed by NGO officers to their friends and relatives.

28. I was told the following anecdote by a local consultant. At a diplomatic function, the consultant was speaking with the Dutch ambassador. The consultant asked the Dutch ambassador why his country supported aid programs when there was so much evidence that these programs were not benefiting the poor but rather the middle farmers and the rural middle class. The ambassador finally confessed that the real reason for aid to Bangladesh was a large pool of unemployed Dutch youth that could work in the development industry. I have been told in private communication by several Western consultants that the real reason for the existence of aid programs is to "benefit the aid-giving country." On another occasion, I had dinner at a CIDA official's house, where a Canadian consultant (an anthropologist by training) confessed to me, "The poverty industry is really for the nationals of the aid-giving nation. I tried to find a job as a university professor in Canada but that did not come through. So, here I am, working as a consultant evaluating CIDA-funded programs."

29. After the independence in 1971, in keeping with the demands of Bengali nationalists, Bengali was made the national language of the country and the medium of language instruction was changed to Bengali.

30. Given the dire economic situation facing the middle class as well, most people have a second source of income in Bangladesh.

31. A good example of this debate was carried in *Dhaka Courier* in its August through October 1989 issues.

32. Staff Reporter, "TIB Terms NGOs Mid-Level Corrupt," *BangladeshNews.com.bd*, October 5, 2007.

33. Proshika uses the word *eradication*, which is used to differentiate its credit model from the dominant Grameen model, although as I have indicated earlier, the Proshika model is a mere reworking of the Grameen model.

34. Interview with author on April 15, 1999.

35. Interview with BIDS researcher on February 27, 1999. Name withheld.

36. This source wished to remain anonymous.

37. Geoffrey Wood and Iffath Sharif, *Who Needs Credit? Poverty and Finance in Bangladesh* (Dhaka: University Press Limited, 1997). The "Introduction" gives a clear

account of the close links between UK-based researchers, overseas aid organizations, and NGOs.

38. Manzurul Mannan, "Engaging Deshi Anthropologist in Development: A Reflection on Current Practices," in *Contemporary Anthropology*, ed. Nurul Alam (Dhaka: Jahangirnagar University Press, 2000), 51.

39. There is research that is critical of NGO practices; however, within NGO-dominated research spaces, these researchers are not cited or engaged with seriously.

40. Arturo Escobar, "Imagining a Post-Development Era," in *The Anthropology of Development and Globalization: From Classical Political Economy to Contemporary Neoliberalism*, eds. Marc Edelman and Angelique Haugerud (Malden, Oxford: Wiley-Blackwell, 2005), 343.

41. Nowadays conferences are held at the Radisson Hotel, which is next to the Zia International Airport. Visiting dignitaries can attend poverty conferences and depart from the country quickly.

42. Mahfuzur Rahman, "Professor Yunus and Economics," *Daily Star,* April 17, 1998; Kabir U. Ahmad, "Professor Yunus on Economics," *Daily Star,* April 19, 1998.

43. Syed Hashemi, "Yunus Versus Neoclassical Theology," *Daily Star,* August 23, 1998.

44. Jonathan Crush, *The Power of Development* (London: Routledge, 1995), 5.

45. As these institutions have become more powerful in recent years, their gate-keeping of information has also hardened. For example, when an article written by Manzurul Mannan entitled "BRAC: Anatomy of a 'Poverty Enterprise'" was published in 2009, I had forwarded it to a colleague at BRAC University. My e-mail bounced back with the following message:

> Our e-mail content detector has just been triggered by a message you sent:
>
> To: XX@bracu.ac.bd
>
> Subject: Re: Hello!
>
> Date: Mon Dec 28 12:04:50 2009
>
> One or more of the attachments (Poverty Enterprise.BRAC.pdf) are on the list of unacceptable attachments for this site and will not have been delivered. Consider renaming the files to avoid this constraint.

It should be noted that censorship of the article led to an increased interest among BRAC employees, resulting in the article being widely circulated through an informal network. Several employees also wrote to the author and thanked him for his critical assessment of their organization.

Conclusion

1. Muhammad Yunus, *Jorimon and Others: Faces of Poverty* (Dhaka, Bangladesh: Grameen Bank Publication, 1991), xiv.

2. Muhammad Yuus and Jolis, *Banker to the Poor* (Dhaka, Bangladesh: University Press Limited, 1998), 9.

3. Her mother's story is under Tara Bewa in *Jorimon and Others: Faces of Poverty*, 216–31.

4. According to Khushi Kabir of Nijera Kori, she had taken up the family's cause with the Grameen Bank, but Professor Yunus refused to write off the debt because it would set a "poor precedent."

5. Michael Edwards and David Hulme, *Non-Governmental Organizations— Performance and Accountability* (London: Earthscan Publications, 1995), 5.

6. David Hulme and Thankom Arun, Introduction in *Microfinance: A Reader* (New York: Routledge, 2009), 1.

7. Qazi Kholiquzzaman Ahmad, *Socio-Economic and Indebtedness-Related Impact of Micro-Credit in Bangladesh* (Dhaka, Bangladesh: University Press Limited, 2007), xviii.

8. Jael Silliman, "Expanding Civil Society: Shrinking Political Spaces—The Case of Women's Nongovernmental Organizations," *in Social Politics* (1999): 46.

9. Shelley Feldman, "NGOs and Civil Society (Un)stated Contradictions," in *The Role of NGOs, Charity and Empowerment*, eds. Jude Fernando and Alan Heston, The Annals of the American Academy of Political Science (Calif.: Thousand Oaks, 1997), 60.

Index

Note: An *f* indicates a figure; *t*, a table.

Abed, Fazle, 14, 21, 78, 125, 178, 229n44

abuse: physical, 152; of power, 203; spousal, 75, 86, 87; verbal, 85, 142, 152; of women, 90

ADAB. *See* Agricultural Development Agencies in Bangladesh (ADAB); Association of Development Agencies in Bangladesh (ADAB); Agricultural Development Agencies in Bangladesh (ADAB)

adda, 53, 57, 146

Agricultural Development Agencies in Bangladesh (ADAB), 13–14

Ahmed, Qazi, xxx

Ain-o-Salish Kendro (ASK), 134

Alia Moderesin Madrassah, 12

"Allah or Apa," 27

Al Qaeda, 234n6

AMWAB. *See* Association of Muslim Welfare Agencies in Bangladesh (AMWAB)

Anti-Dowry Law (1983), 137

Appadurai, Arjun, xxiii, 171

ASA. *See* Association for Social Advancement (ASA)

Asian Development Bank, 24; and People's Tribunal, 205

ASK. *See* Ain-o-Salish Kendro (ASK)

assets: xvi, xxviii, 37, 45, 81,83, 87, 90, 117, 148, 149

Association for Social Advancement (ASA), xv, xx, 5, 14, 118; arrests, 120; and Bazaar Samity, 102; fiscal discipline, 120; pressure, 121

Association of Development Agencies in Bangladesh (ADAB), 13, 14, 21, 160

Association of Muslim Welfare Agencies in Bangladesh (AMWAB), 13

Association of Voluntary Agencies in Bangladesh (AVAB), 13

AVAB. *See* Association of Voluntary Agencies in Bangladesh (AVAB)

Awami League government, 9

Awami League party, 6, 10, 19, 21, 93, 135, 142, 145, 157, 160, 232n12

Ayesha Abed Library, 171

Ayodhya riots, 26

Azam, Golam, 9, 22

Babri Masjid, 26

Badal Shah case, 43–45, 74

BancoSol, xxvi

Bangladesh: civilian rule, 6; clergy, 25–30; clientelist culture, 153; corruption, 179; cultural shifts since 1980, 136–37; education, 12; extended family, role of, 200; as failed state, 1, 179; famine, 7;

LAMIA KARIM is associate professor of cultural anthropology at the University of Oregon, Eugene.